HELL ON TRIAL

THE CASE FOR
ETERNAL PUNISHMENT

HELL ON TRIAL

THE CASE FOR ETERNAL PUNISHMENT

ROBERT A. PETERSON

Robert A. Peterson

P&R

P U B L I S H I N G

P.O. BOX 817 • PHILLIPSBURG • NEW JERSEY 08865-0817

To the person
who first taught me to think theologically,
Professor Robert J. Dunzweiler,
Biblical Theological Seminary

Library of Congress Cataloging-in-Publication Data

Peterson, Robert A., 1948–
    Hell on trial : the case for eternal punishment / Robert A. Peterson.
       p.   cm.
    Includes bibliographical references and index.
    ISBN 0-87552-372-2
    1. Hell—Christianity—History of doctrines.   2. Hell—Biblical teaching.
I. Title.
BT836.2.P48 1995
236'.25—dc20   95-11676

Contents

Foreword

We cannot magnify God's love by minimizing his holy wrath against sin. Some of the most tender pleadings in Scripture are Jesus' warnings to unrepentant unbelievers in danger of being caught up in the eternal wrath of God. It is only in this context that the real wonder of God's love can be understood and appreciated.

Hell on Trial: The Case for Eternal Punishment shines the clear light of Scripture on a truth too often made murky by critics and so-called scholars who find ways to manipulate the text rather than letting the Bible speak plainly for itself. Dr. Robert A. Peterson *does* let God's Word speak for itself—and that is what makes his case so convincing.

I am very grateful for this excellent work. It provides a sound and effective antidote to a subtle trend currently poisoning evangelicalism with unbelief. With clarity yet superb scholarship Dr. Peterson responds to the frightening corruption of divinely revealed truth. My prayer is that this much-needed corrective will receive the wide hearing it deserves.

JOHN F. MACARTHUR, JR.

Foreword

It is always important for us to discern why, at a particular time, certain issues come to the fore and engage the church's attention. Usually, the reason for this resolves itself into a choice between two options. Either the issue arises from within the church, as heretical deviations make their way through its life, leaving trouble and confusion in their wake, or the issue arises from without, as the surrounding culture intrudes worldly expectations and appetites upon the church, robbing it of its vision and conviction. And there is little doubt in my mind that in the case before us, the uniqueness of Christian faith and the reality of God's abiding judgment upon unbelief, it is our modernized and secularized culture that is principally unsettling the church. I am most grateful for Robert Peterson's solid, careful, and workmanlike exposition of biblical truth in response to this.

Our contemporary culture works to unsettle this biblical teaching in two main ways. First, insofar as our culture is secularized, it pressures all of those who live within it to marginalize God, to push the reality of his character and the truth of his Word to the periphery of life. A faith that is secularized in these ways does not necessarily deny the truth of God's ways; it simply makes that truth seem inconsequential. A secularized faith is therefore not one marked by outright unbelief but rather one in which that belief has become tame and harmless. Second, our secularized culture has spawned a deep-seated relativism, which reduces truth to personal preference. In America, no objection is made to anyone's holding any private belief, even the private belief in hell, because the right to hold such views is secured by the Constitution. The objection arises only when anyone imagines that that belief is true, true not only for oneself but for all others as well. Since 70 percent of Americans do not believe in such truth, those who do have become a minority and are expected to behave as such. For them to think that God has, indeed, given us his truth is to appear arrogant and intolerant. What is worse, it is uncivil in a culture that tolerates many moral vices but will not tolerate what is religiously uncivil.

It is, admittedly, difficult to show beyond a shadow of a doubt that the blurring of the edges of faith that is happening within the church today is being fed by these cultural attitudes. But the awkward fact is that the church, for nineteen hundred years, has believed in the uniqueness of Christ, the truth of his Word, and the necessity of God's judgment of the impenitent; and we have to ask why, in the late twentieth century, some or all of these beliefs now seem to have become so unbelievable. Is it that new exegetical discoveries now cast doubt upon what the church has always believed? Are there new archeological finds? Is it that the church has simply misread the Bible and done so consistently over so long a period of time? No, these truths today have become awkward and disconcerting to hold not because of new light from the Bible but because of new darkness from the culture.

It may seem, on the face of it, that little is lost and much is gained if the embarrassing truth about hell is allowed to suffer from a little benign neglect in the church. The church, it might be thought, has said enough on this subject in past ages. Today, such talk has a strange and unfriendly ring to it and one quite incompatible with the program of marketing the faith. What is not always understood, however, is that whatever appeal this kind of polite and civil Christianity may have, it is an appeal that is passing and empty. A God who is without wrath is a God whose Christ has no cross, and if he has no cross, it can only be because we are thought to have no need of his cross. While there have always been those in the church eager to believe such happy propositions, in the end what remains is a faith remade in the likeness of fallen human life, which, in consequence, has lost truth and reality. No only so, but it will also have lost its hope entirely. For Christian hope rests upon the fact not that evil can be ignored, or that it will simply fade away, but that it has been judged at the cross. There is a day coming, therefore, when truth is going to be put forever upon the throne and error forever on the scaffold.

May God, in his grace, hasten that day! And until that day when his purposes are finally consummated, may he strengthen his people to believe his Word, to give gracious and wise witness to its truth in our world, and to seek his glory in all things!

David F. Wells

Acknowledgments

I express my appreciation to the following people who contributed to the writing of this book:

My wife Mary Pat, and our sons Robby, Matt, Curtis, and David, for their love, prayers, and encouragement.

Friends for reading the manuscript and making suggestions: Greg Huffman, Debbie Larson, James Pakala, Diane Preston, Tom Russell, Floyd Simmons, Larry Steinbrueck, and Ralph Warren.

My student Jimmy Agan, for valuable editorial assistance.

Fellow professors for taking time from busy schedules to offer comments: David Calhoun, Nigel Cameron, Larry Dixon, Daniel Doriani, Millard Erickson, John Franke, V. Philips Long, John MacArthur, Leon Morris, Roger Nicole, J. I. Packer, J. Robert Vannoy, Robert Vasholz, David Wells, and Robert Yarbrough.

William Klousia and Thomas McCort, for giving me the privilege of directing their Th.M. theses on the doctrine of hell in the Synoptic Gospels and the book of Revelation, respectively.

My student-assistant Tom Coleman, for proofreading and compiling the indices. My students David Owen Filson and Stuart Latimer, Jr., for proofreading.

Editor Thom Notaro, for cordial help and wise counsel.

The Lord Jesus Christ, the Savior of the world, for saving me and my household.

1

Hell on Trial

The date is 1 September 1983. Put yourself in the place of three different people on this fateful day. First, imagine you are the pilot of Korean Air Lines Flight 007 traveling from Anchorage to Seoul. This flight begins just as the thousands of others you have flown. You follow procedures to the letter, but something goes wrong. Your instruments malfunction, though you don't become aware of it until it is too late. In your hands rest the lives of your crew and 269 passengers.

Second, picture yourself as a passenger on this flight. You board the aircraft eager to return to your family in Seoul; you have been away on business for a week and really miss them. You can hardly wait to hold your wife in your arms and to see the shining faces of your children. You can almost hear the squeals of your little girls, who are always so happy to see you. How good it will be to share a meal together and catch up on what has been going on in their lives! You gaze out the window, as is your custom, until you fall asleep, never suspecting the horror to which you will awaken.

Third, imagine you are the wife of the businessman just mentioned. You rose early this morning to make sure everything would be perfect for your husband's return. You bathed the girls and dressed them nicely and spent extra time preparing to look your best. You have cooked his favorite meal and are anxiously awaiting your family's reunion. "Girls," you call out, "it's time to go to the airport to get Daddy!" How will you ever console them when they learn their father is not coming home? Who will fill the void in your own life?

Little did the pilot and passengers of the Korean Air Lines 747 or their relatives realize what the day would bring when they awoke on 1 September 1983. All envisioned an uneventful flight from Anchorage to Seoul. KAL 007 would stray far off its intended course, however, and be shot down by a Soviet SU–15 interceptor missile, killing the pilot, crew, and all 269 passengers.

No one could foresee the immeasurable consequences of taking that flight. Trusting the faulty information his instruments provided, the pilot steered his plane to disaster. With complete confidence in the pilot and crew to return him to his family, the businessman slept peacefully. His wife and children thought of one thing only on their way to the airport: a joyful reunion.

There is a day of even greater unforeseen catastrophe in store for men and women who die without Christ. Little do they imagine the horror that awaits them. Though the church has traditionally taught that the fate of the lost is eternal punishment, fewer and fewer people are willing to think seriously about that dreadful prospect. Can the future of unbelievers really be that bad? Today a growing number of scholars are answering no.

As theories of the afterlife multiply, so does confusion among pastors on this most important topic. Like misguided pilots, many pastors are leading their flocks to untold destruction. Their parishioners, like trusting passengers, rest in a false assurance that their souls are being guided safely around all spiritual harm. Neither they nor their loved ones realize how far off course they have drifted, and that what lies ahead is a fate worse than physical death.

Confusion about the afterlife—is there anything more tragic? What are the competing views about the destiny of the wicked, and how do they measure up to Scripture? As scholars challenge historic teachings on hell, how solid is the biblical evidence for eternal punishment? And what difference should that biblical teaching make in our lives? Those are the concerns of this book.

In order to understand and then respond to the current confusion over the fate of the unsaved, we need first to set forth clearly the leading views in the debate today:

- Life After Death Is Unlikely.
- Everyone Goes to Heaven.
- Unbelievers Get a Chance After Death.
- Unbelievers are Ultimately Destroyed.
- Unbelievers Suffer Eternally in Hell.

Let us examine each of these views in turn.

Life After Death Is Unlikely

British philosopher, mathematician, and social reformer Bertrand Russell (1872–1970) was an agnostic. Although he regarded it as impossible to know for certain what happens after death, he thought it likely that death was the end of our existence. Belief in immortality, he thought, is rooted in fear.

> Immortality removes the terror from death. People who believe that when they die they will inherit eternal bliss may be expected to view death without horror, . . . I believe that when I die I shall rot, and nothing of my ego will survive. I am not young, and I love life. But I should scorn to shiver with terror at the thought of annihilation. Happiness is none the less true happiness because it must come to an end, nor do thought and love lose their value because they are not everlasting.[1]

According to Russell one of the gains of modern science is the dispelling of religious myths, such as heaven and hell. The realm of life after death was described best, he thought, by Samuel Butler's imaginary utopia Erehwon—which is *nowhere* spelled backward. Better to reject the myths, face the facts, and make the most of this life, for it is all there is.[2]

Russell remained unconvinced by Anglican Bishop Barnes's arguments for immortality. The bishop contended for immortality based on an admiration for the excellence of the human mind, which alone is capable of feats such as designing Westminster Abbey, making airplanes, and calculating the distance to the sun. On this basis, Russell countered, one could argue for the immortality of other creatures, since they too perform clever feats; it all depends on one's perspective. Russell chided the bishop with characteristic wit.

> Man, says Dr. Barnes, is a fine fellow because he can make aeroplanes. A little while ago there was a popular song about the cleverness of flies in walking upside down on the ceiling with the chorus: "Could Lloyd George do it? Could Mr. Baldwin do it? Could Ramsay Mac do it? Why, NO." On this basis a very telling argument could be constructed by a theologically-minded fly, which no doubt the other flies would find most convincing.[3]

Russell saved his strongest words for the biblical doctrine of hell. He faulted Jesus for teaching this doctrine and blamed him for the untold cruelty it has caused in history.

> There is one very serious defect to my mind in Christ's moral character, and that is that He believed in hell. I do not myself feel that any person who is really profoundly humane can believe in everlasting punishment. Christ certainly as depicted in the Gospels did believe in everlasting punishment, and one does find repeatedly a vindictive fury against those people who would not listen to His preaching—an attitude which is not uncommon with preachers, but which does somewhat detract from superlative excellence. . . . I really do not think that a person with a proper degree of kindliness in his nature would have put fears and terrors of that sort into the world. . . . I must say that I think all this doctrine, that hell-fire is a punishment for sin, is a

doctrine of cruelty. It is a doctrine that put cruelty into the world and gave the world generations of cruel torture; and the Christ of the Gospels, if you take Him as His chroniclers represent Him, would certainly have to be considered partly responsible for that.[4]

Bertrand Russell cannot be accused of mincing words. He didn't believe in life after death, and he condemned Jesus' doctrine of hell as morally repugnant. While few people today would be as blunt as Russell, many agree with his basic conclusions. Let's consider a more optimistic assessment of the fate of human beings.

Everyone Goes to Heaven: Universalism

John Hick (1922–) is a world-famous British philosopher of religion. He recounts his spiritual pilgrimage in the introduction to his book *God Has Many Names*. He tells how as a young man studying law in Great Britain at the University College, Hull, he experienced a religious conversion to evangelical Christianity.

> I underwent a spiritual conversion in which the whole world of Christian belief and experience came vividly to life, and I became a Christian of a strongly evangelical and indeed fundamentalist kind. . . . I entered with great joy into the world of Christian faith. At this stage I accepted as a whole and without question the entire evangelical package of theology—the verbal inspiration of the Bible; creation and fall; Jesus as God the Son incarnate, born of a virgin, conscious of his divine nature and performing miracles of divine power; redemption by his blood from sin and guilt; his bodily resurrection and ascension and future return in glory; heaven and hell.[5]

Today, however, John Hick rejects the evangelical theology he once accepted, and shows particular contempt for the traditional doctrine of hell. Indeed, he labels the idea that God inflicts sinners with unending torment a "grim fantasy," and "a serious perversion of the Christian Gospel."[6] Furthermore, he finds eternal punishment "morally revolting" because it attributes "to God an unappeasable vindictiveness and insatiable cruelty."[7]

What caused Hick to abandon the faith he once embraced? Two forces combined to lead him away from his former evangelical convictions: the study of philosophy, and involvement with people of other faiths.

In the years following the publication of his first book, *Faith and Knowledge,* Hick pondered the difficult questions of theodicy, the defense of God's goodness in a world filled with evil and suffering. As a result, he penned *Evil and the God of Love* (1966), in which he argued that God ordered a world that contains real evil as a means of achieving his ultimate goal. This goal was "the creation of the infinite good of a Kingdom of Heaven within which His creatures will have come as perfected persons to love and serve Him." Moreover, God would lead *all people* to this ultimate perfection through a process involving their free response.[8]

By 1966, therefore, Hick espoused universalism, the belief that in the end all human beings will be saved. Of course, in so doing he rejected the historic Christian doctrine of hell. He concluded that holding to eternal condemnation only compounds the problem of evil: "Misery which is eternal and therefore infinite would constitute the largest part of the problem of evil."[9] Furthermore, endless punishment is incompatible with Jesus' message of love. "If we see as the heart of his [Jesus'] teaching the message of the active and sovereign divine love, we shall find incredible and even blasphemous the idea that God plans to inflict perpetual torture upon any of His children." In addition, if the traditional view of hell is accepted, it makes the eternal sufferings of the damned in hell pointless, because these sufferings are not constructive.[10]

In recent years Hick has turned his attention to the world's religions. He has contemplated the claims of these various religions to be based upon revelations from God and asked, "If what Christianity says is true, must not what all the other world religions say be in varying degrees false?" Moreover, this would mean that the majority of the human race is lost, since they don't believe in Jesus. Such a conclusion is unthinkable for Hick, since he already has decided that God will ultimately save everyone.[11]

This brings us to the second force that led Hick to abandon the evangelical faith: his contact with persons of other faiths. While Hick was pondering the claims of the world's religions, he moved to Birmingham, England, and was confronted with large communities of Muslims, Sikhs, Hindus, and Jews. Hick's experience with the diversity of faiths in Birmingham profoundly affected his life.

> Occasionally attending worship in mosque and synagogue, temple and gurdwara, it was evident that essentially the same kind of thing is taking place in them as in a Christian church—namely, human beings opening their minds to a higher divine Reality, known as personal and good and as demanding righteousness and love between man and man.[12]

As a result of these and many other contacts over the years, Hick has become one of the prime exponents of religious pluralism, the view that all religions lead to God. Indeed, Hick insists that God is one, although he is called by many names. He "translates" an ancient Indian religious poem in terms of modern religions.

> They call it Jahweh, Allah, Krishna, Param Atma,
> And also holy, blessed Trinity:
> The real is one, though sages name it variously.[13]

With evangelistic zeal Hick calls for what he terms a Copernican revolution in theology. This involves a "shift from a Christianity-centered or Jesus-centered to a God-centered model of the universe of faiths." Hick insists that we no longer view the world's religions as combatants, but as fellow pilgrims heading toward the same God.[14]

Hick does not sidestep the implications of his pluralism for the doctrine of Christ. He candidly admits, "If Jesus was literally God incarnate, the Second Person of the Trinity living a human life, so that the Christian religion was founded by God-on-earth in person, it is then very hard to escape from the traditional view that all mankind must be converted to the Christian faith."[15] Hick, however, rejects the

orthodox Christian faith, and concludes, "The idea that Jesus proclaimed himself as God incarnate, and as the sole point of saving
contact between God and man, is without adequate historical foundation and represents a doctrine developed by the church."[16] Put bluntly,
"That Jesus was God the Son incarnate is not literally true."[17]

Many evangelicals are surprised to learn that the majority of
Christendom's clergy today are hopeful universalists. These pastors do
not dogmatically assert universalism, as Hick does, but are nevertheless hopeful that all will be saved. I will evaluate Hick's universalism
in chapter 8. Here we turn our attention to a third opinion on the
destiny of the lost, which extends the time of decision beyond this life.

Unbelievers Get a Chance After Death: Postmortem Evangelism

Clark Pinnock (1937–) is a leading evangelical theologian who teaches
theology at McMaster Divinity College in Hamilton, Ontario, and
writes profusely. Known for shifting his views, by 1987 he had rejected
the traditional view of hell.

> . . . the semiofficial position of the church since approxi-
> mately the sixth century has been that hell lasts forever and
> that human beings thrown into it are tormented endlessly.
> To some, this has conveyed the picture of unceasing physi-
> cal burning, while to others in recent times the torment has
> been re-imaged in terms of mental and psychological suffer-
> ing. Whatever the image, the traditional understanding of
> hell is unspeakably horrible. How can one imagine for a
> moment that the God who gave his Son to die for sinners
> because of his great love for them would install a torture
> chamber somewhere in the new creation in order to subject
> those who reject him to everlasting pain?[18]

In its place Pinnock put the doctrine of the annihilation of the wicked.
"The 'fire' of God's judgment consumes the lost. According to this
understanding, God does not raise the wicked in order to torture them

consciously forever, but rather to declare his judgment upon the wicked and to condemn them to extinction, which is the second death (Rev. 20:11–15)."[19]

Recently Pinnock has come out in favor of what he calls "post-mortem encounter." This is a corollary of his view that God desires to save every person, which in turn is the foundation of his theology of world religions. He presents this theology in his recent book whose title he explains as follows:

> A *fundamental point* in this theology of religions is the conviction that God's redemptive work in Jesus Christ was intended to benefit the whole world. Hence the title—*A Wideness in God's Mercy*. The dimensions are deep and wide. God's grace is not niggardly or partial. To use a phrase of political columnist Ben Wattenberg's: "The good news is that the bad news is not true." For according to the Gospel of Christ, the outcome of salvation will be large and generous.[20]

Pinnock blames Reformed theology for publishing this "bad news." Calvinism obscures God's love, thereby creating a pessimism with regard to the salvation of all people.

> There is also a theological reason why we have felt uncomfortable with people of other faiths—a lack of confidence in God's generosity toward them. Dark thoughts have clouded our minds. For centuries, thanks largely to the Augustinian tradition that has so influenced evangelicals, we have been taught that God chooses a few who will be saved and has decided not to save the vast majority of mankind. God is planning (in his sovereign freedom) to send most of those outside the church to hell, and he is perfectly in his rights to do so. If as a result large numbers perish, theologians have assured us that God would feel no remorse and certainly deserve no blame. The result of such instruction is that many read the Bible with a pessimistic control belief and find it hard to relate humanly to other people. This is hardly

surprising. We have to answer the question, Does God love sinners at large or not?[21]

Pinnock believes that Reformed theology answers this question in the negative. He claims to have found a better answer.

> The first move theologically is to establish an optimism of salvation, to make it perfectly clear that God is committed to a full racial salvation. . . . I want evangelicals to move away from the attitude of pessimism based upon bad news to the attitude of hopefulness based upon Good News, from restrictivism to openness, from exclusivism to generosity. If we could but recover the scope of God's love, our lives and not just our theology of religions could be transformed.[22]

Pinnock finds this logic compelling: Since God loves and has provided salvation for every human being, he must, therefore, give each the opportunity to believe the gospel.

> The logic behind a postmortem encounter with Christ is simple enough. It rests on the insight that God, since he loves humanity, would not send anyone to hell without first ascertaining what their response would have been to his grace. Since everyone eventually dies and comes face to face with the risen Lord, that would seem to be the obvious time to discover their answer to God's call.[23]

Pinnock has a ready answer for those who suggest that unbelievers' encounter with God after death may be unpleasant: "God does not cease to be gracious to sinners just because they are no longer living." On this basis he concludes that there will be grace after death for the unevangelized. "Therefore, when humanity [after death] stands before God, they stand before a God of mercy and love."[24]

Pinnock is not espousing universalism; some may not get a chance after death. "The fate of some may be sealed at death; those, for example, who heard the gospel and declined the offer of salvation." Others may get a chance and not avail themselves of it. "The *oppor-*

tunity would be there for all to repent after death, but not necessarily the *desire*."[25]

I will critique Clark Pinnock's ideas in chapter 8. For now let me summarize his position: the church has erred in teaching that death is a cutoff point for grace and that everlasting punishment is the destiny of the unrepentant. On the contrary, Pinnock assures us, "If God really loves the whole world and desires everyone to be saved, it follows logically that everyone must have access to salvation."[26] Those who do not have sufficient access in this life will have it in the next. And if they then reject God's grace, their fate is extermination, not eternal condemnation.

So far, the idea of God's giving people a chance after death has not become popular in evangelical circles. The next view of the fate of the wicked, however, is rapidly gaining popularity, especially in Great Britain.

Unbelievers Are Ultimately Destroyed: Annihilationism

John Stott (1921–), former rector of All Souls Church in London, is recognized as a champion of evangelical Christianity. His preaching, teaching, evangelism, and writing for the cause of Christ have received deserved acclaim. Stott stunned the evangelical world when he tentatively defended the doctrine of the annihilation of the wicked.

The occasion for Stott's remarks was a dialogue with liberal theologian David L. Edwards in the book *Evangelical Essentials*. Stott and Edwards politely yet forthrightly debated scriptural authority, the significance of the cross, Christ's miracles, the place of the Bible in Christian ethics, and the church's message to the world.[27]

On this last topic, in response to Edwards's hope that universalism is true, Stott, "with great reluctance and with a heavy heart," addressed the subject of the fate of the wicked; he had not previously declared publicly whether he thinks the final destiny of the impenitent involves everlasting suffering or "a total annihilation of their being." Conceding that the former is the traditional view of the Christian church and that most evangelical leaders hold it today, he laments, "Emotionally, I find the concept intolerable." Yet, because

Scripture and not emotion must be Stott's supreme authority, he adduces four biblical arguments in favor of annihilationism.[28]

"First, language. The vocabulary of 'destruction' is often used in relation to the final state of perdition." Jesus warned, "Do not be afraid of those who kill the body but cannot kill the soul. Rather, be afraid of the One who can destroy both soul and body in hell" (Matt. 10:28). Commenting on this passage, Stott says, "If to kill is to deprive the body of life, hell would seem to be the deprivation of both physical and spiritual life, that is, an extinction of being."[29]

Scripture frequently speaks of unbelievers as "perishing." For example, John 3:16 promises, "For God so loved the world that he gave his one and only Son, that whoever believes in him shall not perish but have eternal life." Here eternal life is contrasted with "perishing." Stott insists that we take the biblical language of destruction and perishing at face value. "It would seem strange, therefore, if people who are said to suffer destruction are in fact not destroyed."[30]

Stott's second argument for annihilationism concerns the scriptural imagery depicting hell, especially that of fire. "Jesus spoke of 'the fire of hell' (Matt. 5:22; 18:9) and of 'eternal fire' (Matt. 18:8; 25:41), and in the Revelation we read about 'the lake of fire' (20:14–15)." We associate fire with torment because we have all felt the pain of being burned. Unfortunately, this has caused us to misread the Bible.

> The main function of fire is not to cause pain, but to secure destruction, as all the world's incinerators bear witness. Hence the biblical expression "a consuming fire" and John the Baptist's picture of the Judge "burning up the chaff with unquenchable fire" (Matt. 3:12, cf. Luke 3:17). The fire itself is termed "eternal" and "unquenchable", but it would be very odd if what is thrown into it proves indestructible. Our expectation would be the opposite: it would be consumed for ever, not tormented for ever. Hence it is the smoke (evidence that the fire has done its work) which "rises for ever and ever" (Rev. 14:11; cf. 19:3).[31]

The third argument for annihilation concerns the biblical concept of justice. Scripture declares that God will judge people according to their deeds, "which implies that the penalty inflicted will be commensurate with the evil done." To Stott's thinking, everlasting condemnation does not square with this principle.

> Would there not, then, be a serious disproportion between sins consciously committed in time and torment consciously experienced throughout eternity? ... I question whether "eternal conscious torment" is compatible with the biblical revelation of divine justice, unless perhaps (as has been argued) the impenitence of the lost also continues throughout eternity.[32]

Stott's fourth argument is based on biblical passages that purportedly teach universalism. Though he is not a universalist, he nevertheless finds it difficult to reconcile eternal torment with "the promises of God's final victory over evil" or with passages speaking of "God uniting all things under Christ's headship (Eph. 1:10)," and "reconciling all things to himself through Christ (Col. 1:20) so that in the end God will be 'all in all' or 'everything to everybody' (1 Cor. 15:28)."[33] While Stott is not persuaded of universalism by these and similar passages, they do raise questions in his mind about the final state of the wicked.

> These texts do not lead me to universalism, because of the many others which speak of the terrible and eternal reality of hell. But they do lead me to ask how God can in any meaningful sense be called "everything to everybody" while an unspecified number of people still continue in rebellion against him and under his judgment. It would be easier to hold together the awful reality of hell and the universal reign of God if hell means destruction and the impenitent are no more.[34]

In fairness to Stott it must be said that he does not dogmatize about annihilationism; he holds the position tentatively. Furthermore, he pleads for "frank dialogue among Evangelicals on the basis of Scripture." Nevertheless, he contends that "the ultimate annihilation of the wicked should at least be accepted as a legitimate, biblically founded alternative to their eternal conscious torment."[35] Some will be shocked to learn that other evangelical Christians are stronger than Stott in their affirmation of annihilationism. Among them are Philip E. Hughes, John W. Wenham, Stephen Travis, and Edward Fudge.[36]

How are we to respond to John Stott's case for the extinction of the wicked? Where will the frank dialogue he desires lead us? I plan to address these questions in chapter 9. We now will turn our attention to the traditional view of the final destiny of the unsaved.

Unbelievers Suffer Eternally in Hell: Orthodoxy

The four views we have introduced thus far have one thing in common—they all are alternatives to traditional orthodoxy. Their proponents reject the historical view of the church as being too harsh. Not all evangelicals do so, however. One who is knowledgeable of the previous views but nevertheless finds their arguments unconvincing is J. I. Packer. Packer (1926–), a British theologian who teaches at Regent College in Vancouver, is the author of the well-known book *Knowing God* and numerous other books and articles.

Packer is upset about these proposed modifications of the traditional view of hell. To him they are fighting words, as he explains using an illustration from the game of cricket.

> Half-way through the afternoon of Monday, July 20, 1981, in Leeds, Yorkshire, England was in trouble. It was the fourth day of the third of six five-day test matches against Australia. The first had been lost, the second drawn, and this, the third, now seemed doomed. The seventh player in England's second inning had just been dismissed with the score at 135; this was still 92 runs behind Australia's first inning total of 401, and only three more Englishmen remained to bat, while Australia had an entire second inning still to come. In cricket the batsmen (whom you may call strikers if you prefer) operate in pairs, and as the new man walked to the wicket, his partner, Ian Botham, who had so far scored 23, went to meet him. The following dialogue

then took place, in the idiom that you might call sportsman's swagger. Botham: "You don't fancy hanging around on this wicket for a day and a half, do you?" New batsman: "No way." Botham: "Right; come on, let's give it some humpty." Which they did, hitting the ball all over the field to such good effect that incredibly, England's score rose to 356, with Botham making 149, before the last man was out. Australia was then dismissed for less than the 129 runs needed to win, and an apparently inevitable defeat had been turned into a famous victory, vividly illustrating the truth that attack is the best form of defence.[37]

Packer then applies the illustration.

I tell you that story so as to tune you in to the fact that, as I see it, the subject area . . . requires that, like Botham, I too give it a bit of humpty, and attack. Truths that seem to me vital are threatened, and to reaffirm them effectively I shall have to hit out—not only at non-evangelicals, but at some of my evangelical brothers too. I have no wish to hurt anyone's feelings, but I must take a risk on that, for my judgment is that on matters so grave only forthright statement can be appropriate or adequate.[38]

Although he admits a certain attraction to universalism, Packer rejects it as "wishful thinking" and instead accepts the Bible's teaching that not all of mankind will be saved.

No evangelical, I think, need hesitate to admit that in his heart of hearts he would like universalism to be true. Who can take pleasure in the thought of people being eternally lost? If you want to see folk damned, there is something wrong with you! Universalism is thus a comfortable doctrine in a way that alternatives are not. But wishful thinking, based on a craving for comfort and a reluctance to believe that some of God's truth might be tragic, is no sure index of reality.[39]

Packer sees no escape from the fact that it is Jesus, the Savior of the world, who is chiefly responsible for the doctrine of eternal condemnation.

> Jesus himself is strong on the horrific consequences of rejecting him: as W. G. T. Shedd said a century ago, "Jesus Christ is the person who is responsible for the doctrine of eternal perdition." Granted that Jesus' references to weeping and gnashing of teeth, outer darkness, worm and fire, gehenna, and the great gulf fixed, are imagery, the imagery clearly stands for a terrible retribution.[40]

Packer believes that theologians who offer the unsaved a chance after death "through some kind of post-mortem encounter with Christ and his offer of mercy" engage in "speculation" that lacks "biblical warrant."[41]

Advocates of annihilationism (also called conditionalism) fare no better. Packer rejects John Stott's plea that annihilationism be accepted as an alternative to the traditional view.

> Respectfully, I disagree, for the biblical arguments are to my mind flimsy special pleading and the feelings that make people want conditionalism to be true seem to me to reflect, not superior sensitivity, but secular sentimentalism which assumes that in heaven our feelings about others will be as at present, and our joy in the manifesting of God's justice will be no greater than it is now. It is certainly agonizing now to live with the thought of people going to an eternal hell, but it is not right to reduce the agony by evading the facts; and in heaven, we may be sure, the agony will be a thing of the past.[42]

Where Do We Go from Here?

Five distinguished scholars and five conflicting views of the destiny of the wicked—as never before, hell is on trial. Testifying against eternal punishment are four "expert witnesses" who have set forth their views with passion and eloquence. They have made a strong impression on the public, resulting in confusion even among pastors over what to believe and proclaim concerning the afterlife.

The preaching dictum is ever so true: a fog in the pulpit is a mist in the pew. Misguided preachers breed confusion in the minds of their listeners. And many people today are confused about hell.

Being misinformed about hell can be disastrous. And so we must clear the air. We have heard the arguments of the four alternative views. Now it is time to hear the case for eternal punishment and to cross-examine its main adversaries. How will it fare against the other views? I am convinced with J. I. Packer that the historic doctrine of hell is supported by overwhelming evidence and is therefore true. It is a truth that people desperately need to understand with mind and heart and soul in order that they, and their loved ones, may avoid the greatest disaster—eternal condemnation at the hands of almighty God.

I respect my brothers in Christ with whom I differ in this book; I have learned from each of them. But for the sake of God's glory, the truth of his Word, the cross of Christ, and the mission of the church, I am burdened to defend the orthodox doctrine of hell.

The scheme of this book will be as follows: Chapters 2 through 5 explore the Bible's teaching on hell (as given by the Old Testament, Jesus, and the apostles). Chapters 6 and 7 survey the views of important figures throughout church history. There follows in chapters 8 and 9 a critique of approaches that reject the traditional doctrine (universalism, postmortem evangelism, and annihilationism). Chapter 10 offers a topical summary of the biblical teaching on hell, while chapter 11 connects eternal punishment with other important beliefs (God, sin, punishment, Christ's saving work, and heaven). Finally, chapter 12 tackles three difficult questions (What about purgatory? What is the fate of those who have never heard? What happens to babies who die?) and applies the doctrine of hell to both sinners and saints.

NOTES

1. Bertrand Russell, *Why I Am Not a Christian* (London: Unwin Books, 1967), 47. I credit Vernon Grounds, "The Final State of the Wicked," *Journal of the*

Evangelical Theological Society 24.3 (1981): 210, for pointing me to the Russell
quotations.

2. Russell, *Why I Am Not a Christian*, 24.
3. Ibid., 73.
4. Ibid., 22–23.
5. John Hick, *God Has Many Names* (London: Macmillan, 1980), 2.
6. John Hick, *Evil and the God of Love* (London: Macmillan, 1966), 385.
7. John Hick, *Death and Eternal Life* (New York: Harper & Row, 1976), 199–200.
8. Hick, *Evil and the God of Love*, 398–99.
9. Ibid., 377.
10. Ibid., 382.
11. Hick, *God Has Many Names*, 4.
12. Ibid., 5.
13. John Hick, *God and the Universe of Faiths* (London: Macmillan, 1973), 140.
14. Hick, *God Has Many Names*, 5–6.
15. Ibid., 6.
16. Hick, *God and the Universe of Faiths*, 145.
17. Hick, *God Has Many Names*, 72.
18. Clark Pinnock, "Fire, Then Nothing," *Christianity Today*, 20 March 1987, 40.
19. Ibid.
20. Clark Pinnock, *A Wideness in God's Mercy: The Finality of Jesus Christ in a
    World of Religions* (Grand Rapids: Zondervan, 1992), 17.
21. Ibid., 19.
22. Ibid., 19–20.
23. Ibid., 168–69.
24. Ibid., 170.
25. Ibid., 170–71.
26. Ibid., 157.
27. David L. Edwards and John Stott, *Evangelical Essentials: A Liberal-Evangelical
    Dialogue* (Downers Grove, Ill.: InterVarsity, 1988).
28. Ibid., 312–15.
29. Ibid., 315.
30. Ibid., 316.
31. Ibid., 316–18.
32. Ibid., 318–19.
33. Ibid., 319.
34. Ibid.
35. Ibid., 320.
36. Philip E. Hughes, *The True Image* (Grand Rapids: Eerdmans, 1989), 398–407;
    John W. Wenham, "The Case for Conditional Immortality," in *Universalism
    and the Doctrine of Hell*, ed. Nigel M. de S. Cameron (Grand Rapids: Baker,
    1992), 161–91; Stephen Travis, *I Believe in the Second Coming of Jesus* (Grand
    Rapids: Eerdmans, 1982), 196–99; Edward W. Fudge, *The Fire That Consumes*
    (Houston: Providential Press, 1982).

37. Kenneth S. Kantzer and Carl F. H. Henry, eds., *Evangelical Affirmations* (Grand Rapids: Zondervan, 1990), 107–8.
38. Ibid., 108.
39. Ibid., 117.
40. Ibid., 118.
41. Ibid., 119.
42. Ibid., 126.

2

The Witness of the Old Testament

This grace was given us in Christ Jesus before the beginning of time, but it has now been revealed through the appearing of our Savior, Christ Jesus, who has destroyed death and has brought life and immortality to light through the gospel. (2 Tim. 1:9–10)

God the Father planned to grant grace to his people before Creation. At his appointed time he disclosed that grace by sending his Son into the world to be its Savior. The Son's mission centered on the cross and the empty tomb; in the language of the apostle Paul quoted above, he "destroyed death." His mission also involved teaching. In fact, he taught as no teacher ever had before. This is what Paul meant when he said that "Christ Jesus . . . brought life and immortality to light through the gospel." Jesus spoke directly and plainly about eternal life. In addition, he brought clearer teaching on the fate of the wicked than that found in the Old Testament. We might say, therefore, that Christ Jesus also brought death and hell to light through the gospel.

In this chapter we will survey the Old Testament antecedents to Jesus' teaching. I find at least three perspectives helpful in summarizing the Old Testament's view of the fate of the ungodly:

- Primary Judgment Passages
- Passages Concerning Sheol
- Passages Suggesting Eternal Punishment

Primary Judgment Passages

Of all the peoples of the ancient Near East, Old Testament believers alone enjoyed the blessings of covenant relationship with Israel's God. Furthermore, he who promised "to be your God" to Abraham and his descendants (Gen. 17:7) primarily oriented the Israelites toward this world. Their preoccupation was not with life after death; it was with loving and obeying the Lord in this life. Their ideal was to walk with God all their days and then to die at a ripe old age with their children and grandchildren gathered around them. This earthly orientation is reflected in the promise attached to the fifth commandment: "Honor your father and your mother, as the LORD your God has commanded you, so that you may live long and that it may go well with you in the land the Lord your God is giving you" (Deut. 5:16).

That is not to say that the Old Testament is only concerned with this life, for it also speaks of the life to come. The point at present, however, is that the Israelites' chief interest is with life this side of the grave—particularly with national life.[1]

This earthly outlook is evident in the Old Testament passages depicting the major judgments of God on rebellious people. We see this already in the Garden of Eden, when God warned Adam that if he disobeyed God's command, it would result in certain death (Gen. 2:17). In spite of their Creator's warning, Adam and Eve disobeyed and died spiritually as a result, which was evidenced by their hiding from God and later dying physically (Gen. 3:8; 5:5). The text does not speak of life after death. Nor do the other Old Testament judgments, among the most important of which are the Flood, the destruction of Sodom and Gomorrah, the Egyptian plagues and the crossing of the Red Sea, and the captivities of Israel.

The Flood

Some of the saddest words in Holy Scripture are found in Genesis 6:5–6: "The LORD saw how great man's wickedness on the earth had become, and that every inclination of the thoughts of his heart was only evil all the time. The LORD was grieved that he had made man on the earth, and his heart was filled with pain."

God's response, of course, was to punish the evil by bringing floodwaters on the earth. Notice God's purposes for sending the Flood. He announced to Noah his intentions to "put an end to all people. . . . to destroy both them and the earth. . . . Everything on earth will perish" (6:13, 17). And God fulfilled his purposes. "Everything on dry land that had the breath of life in its nostrils died. Every living thing on the face of the earth was wiped out" (7:22–23). Later God made a covenant with Noah and promised never to destroy the earth again by a flood (9:11).

Three things stand out in the Flood account. First, we see that God is holy and he punishes sin. He responded to human wickedness by pouring out his wrath on the earth. Second, the punishment consisted of sudden physical death; there is no mention of life after death. Third, the Flood narrative exhibits a wide variety of vocabulary. The wicked "perish, die," are "put to an end, destroyed, wiped out, cut off"—all of which signifies a temporal, earthly judgment.

The Destruction of Sodom and Gomorrah

Genesis 19:24 records that "the LORD rained down burning sulfur on Sodom and Gomorrah." Why? Because "the outcry [to the LORD] against Sodom and Gomorrah is so great and their sin so grievous" (Gen. 18:20). The aftermath is stated plainly: "Thus he overthrew . . . all those living in the cities. . . . God destroyed the cities of the plain" (19:25, 29). In fact, the destruction was so devastating that when Abraham looked toward Sodom and Gomorrah the next morning, all he saw was "dense smoke rising from the land, like smoke from a furnace" (19:28).

The same observations made about the Flood apply here: God in his justice punishes sin, and the punishment of Sodom and Gomorrah was the cataclysmic loss of human life.

The Plagues of Egypt and the Crossing of the Red Sea

Although God spared believing Israelites by "passing over" their houses, in the final plague he "struck down all the firstborn in Egypt. . . . and there was loud wailing in Egypt, for there was not a house without someone dead" (Ex. 12:29–30). Finally, Pharaoh let the Israelites go. Upon hearing that they had left Egypt, however, he changed his mind and set out in hot pursuit with six hundred of his best chariots and officers (14:5–7).

The repercussions are well known. The LORD sent a powerful east wind and turned the sea into dry land. The waters were divided, and the Israelites went through the sea on dry ground, with a wall of water on either side (14:21–22). Pharaoh and his army chased them into the sea. At God's command "the sea went back to its place. . . . The LORD swept them into the sea. . . . Not one of them survived" (14:27–28).

God's temporal punishment of Egypt in the final plague and in the Red Sea similarly proclaims his holiness, his anger against sinners, and his power and majesty. The form that this punishment takes is the immediate loss of the Egyptians' lives at God's hand. Again, the text says nothing about life after death. The Song of Moses in response to God's action rehearses the themes of the revelation of God's character in his devastation of his enemies.

> I will sing to the LORD , for he is highly exalted. The horse and its rider he has hurled into the sea. . . . The LORD is a warrior; the LORD is his name. . . . The best of Pharaoh's officers are drowned in the Red Sea. . . . Your right hand, O LORD, was majestic in power. Your right hand, O LORD, shattered the enemy. In the greatness of your majesty you threw down those who opposed you. You unleashed your burning anger; it consumed them like stubble. . . . Who among the gods is like you, O LORD? Who is like you— majestic in holiness, awesome in glory, working wonders?

You stretched out your right hand and the earth swallowed
them. (Ex. 15:1, 3–4, 6–7, 11–12)

The Assyrian and Babylonian Captivities of Israel

The same themes resonate in the biblical accounts of both the Assyrian
conquest and captivity of Israel, and the Babylonian defeat and captivity of Judah. In the former the king of Assyria captured Samaria and
deported the Israelites to Assyria. Why did the Lord deliver his people
into the king of Assyria's hand? "All this took place because the
Israelites had sinned against the LORD their God. . . . They did wicked
things that provoked the LORD to anger." They failed to heed the
prophets and worshiped idols instead of God; in sum, they "violated
his covenant" (2 Kings 17:7, 11–12; 18:12).

We see more of the same in the account of the Babylonian
captivity. Nebuchadnezzar captured Jerusalem and burned down "every important building," including the temple and palace, and "Judah
went into captivity, away from her land" (Jer. 52:4, 13, 27). God
brought this judgment on Judah because the Israelites "did not keep
the commands of the LORD their God" (2 Kings 17:19). Indeed,
because of their unfaithfulness "he thrust them from his presence"
(v. 20).

The thrust of this fourth major judgment is the same as that of
the first three: God in his righteousness punished his people's sins with
physical death. It is true that this time not all of the Israelites died
immediately; thousands were taken into captivity. Nevertheless, few
of them returned from captivity. Instead, the vast majority died in
exile as punishment for their sins.

Conclusion

This probe of some of the primary Old Testament judgment passages yields valuable clues to God's disposition toward the wicked.
First, it confronts us with a biblical picture of God that seems out-
of-step with our contemporary world—God is not only loving and
kind, but also holy and just. After warning sinners of the consequences of despising his love, he punishes them if they continue to

rebel against him. God punishes sinners! How strange this sounds to modern ears! Yet, regardless of how strange it sounds, it is God's truth.

Because we are incapable of finding God on our own, we must listen to him speaking in his Word if we would know him. And God does not speak out of both sides of his mouth; the Bible paints a consistent portrait of his character. We will see that the Savior and his apostles share this view of God with the Old Testament writers. The Old and New Testaments summon us to "consider the kindness and sternness of God" (Rom. 11:22). As a result the Bible smashes modern idolatrous images of God even as it did idols of old. If our view of God differs from that given in holy Scripture, we must repent and bring our thoughts into conformity with God's.

Our review of the Old Testament judgment texts bears a second dividend. We find that the punishments described in them are consistently earthly and temporal, resulting in physical death. These passages do not speak of life after death or eternal destinies. This is significant in light of annihilationists' claims that the Old Testament supports their view of the extinction of the wicked.[2] Annihilationists correctly assert that the judgment passages use the "vocabulary of destruction." When God punishes the ungodly in the Flood, Sodom and Gomorrah, the plagues and Red Sea, and the captivities, Scripture speaks of him wiping them out, cutting them off, putting them to an end, overthrowing them. As a result the wicked are said to perish, die, and be consumed, shattered, and destroyed.

Annihilationists err, however, when they claim that these texts therefore teach the annihilation of the wicked. If that were the case, then these judgment passages would teach too much, for the "annihilation" depicted does not follow the resurrection and punishment of the wicked. Instead, it would entail cessation of existence at death—and that is more akin to Bertrand Russell's view than to the teaching of evangelical annihilationists. However, since these passages do not speak of judgment after death, they do not teach annihilationism and therefore pose no threat to the orthodox view of eternal punishment.

We turn now to a second Old Testament perspective on the fate of the ungodly—that provided by passages speaking of sheol.

Passages Concerning Sheol

The Hebrew word *sheol* occurs sixty-five times in the Old Testament and refers to the place of the dead. Bible translations reflect different understandings of the word. The King James Version renders *sheol* "grave" thirty-one times, "hell" thirty-one times, and "pit" three times. *The Revised Standard Version* and *The New American Standard Bible* simply put the Hebrew word into English letters as "Sheol." *The New International Version* usually translates it as "grave" (occasionally as "death") with a footnote "Sheol."

The variety in these translations points toward an even greater variety of approaches to sheol. One approach assumes that the Israelites shared the mythological ideas concerning the afterlife of Mesopotamia and Egypt: the Israelites' speculations, though restrained in comparison to those of their neighbors, merely reflect the mentality common to these ancient peoples.[3] Evangelicals reject this approach because it leaves God and his special revelation to Israel out of the picture.

Another approach is the so-called compartmental theory. This view, popular in the early church, holds that the righteous and the wicked alike go to sheol, where they are segregated into different compartments or "holding chambers" to await their respective fates. For Old Testament believers this amounts to a limbo from which the resurrected Christ later delivered them. This view is to be rejected because neither Testament supports the idea of a compartmentalized netherworld. (The relevant New Testament passages will be examined in chapters 4 and 8.)

A somewhat better approach is to hold that *sheol* has two meanings: originally it meant "grave" and it later came to mean "hell." The righteous share the former with the wicked, but only the wicked populate the latter. This was the solution adopted by the King James Version. Old Testament scholar Alexander Heidel offered a similar approach. He argued that *sheol* always means "grave" when referring to the righteous and "netherworld" (with negative connotations) when referring to the wicked.[4] Heidel has been criticized for arbitrarily handling the biblical data.[5] The same criticism could be leveled against the translators of the King James Version.

Old Testament professor R. Laird Harris offers still another possibility. He points out that *sheol* most often occurs in poetry (in fifty-
seven cases out of sixty-five) and suggests that it is just a poetic
synonym for the common Hebrew word for "grave" (*qeber*). *Sheol* does
not refer to a netherworld but means "grave."[6] Although he persuaded
the translators of *The New International Version*, some have criticized
his ideas as being theologically motivated and as not accounting for all
the facts.[7]

A full discussion of the problems associated with these approaches
lies beyond the scope of this book, so I will here summarize only the key
points and draw implications for our study. Whatever sheol may be, it is
clear that both the righteous and the unrighteous go there. Examples of
the former are Jacob (Gen. 37:35; 42:38; 44:29, 31) and Hezekiah (Isa.
38:10, 17–18). Examples of the latter are Korah (Num. 16:30) and the
king of Babylon (Isa. 14:9, 11, 15). The attempt to keep the righteous
from sheol by claiming that Jacob and Hezekiah (in the passages cited
above) feared going to the final abode of the wicked is unconvincing.[8]

Harris makes a good case for his thesis by showing that many
passages commonly taken to refer to the underworld actually speak of
the grave. For example, concerning the judgment of Korah (in Num.
16:30–33) one writer contends, "The descent of all the rebels with
their households into Sheol implies more than mere descent into the
grave."[9] Harris, however, has an apt reply: "Not only did Korah and his
fellows go to Sheol, his houses and goods also went down. His tents and
things surely did not go to the place of departed spirits! The obvious
meaning is that he and his goods were all buried alive in the earth."[10]

Even Isaiah 14 and Ezekiel 31 and 32, chapters traditionally
understood as referring to hell, make better sense if we take them as
speaking of the tomb. The pictures of the king of Babylon with
maggots and worms covering him (Isa. 14:11) and of Pharaoh lying
among fallen warriors with their swords placed under their heads
(Ezek. 32:27) speak not of hell but of the humiliation of the grave.

Nevertheless, Harris's position also has difficulties. His explanations of Deuteronomy 32:22 ("For a fire is kindled in My anger, and
burns to the lowest part of Sheol" [NASB]) and Psalm 49:14–15 ("As
sheep they are appointed for Sheol; death shall be their shepherd.
. . . But God will redeem my soul from the power of Sheol; for He will

receive me" [NASB]) are not fully persuasive.[11] Where does this leave us? I confess that I cannot endorse any one view of sheol with confidence. The best I can do is to consider the ramifications of the two most likely views.

If Harris is correct and *sheol* only refers to the grave, then our conclusions are similar to those reached from our study of the judgment passages: the concern of the Old Testament is largely earthly and temporal. The negative connotations often associated with sheol reflect the fact that death is a punishment for sin, as we learned from the account of the fall in Genesis 3. But sheol tells us nothing about life after death.

According to the predominant evangelical view, however, *sheol* sometimes refers to a netherworld to which both godly and ungodly go at death. The Bible uses characteristics associated with the grave to describe this underworld: depth (Ps. 63:9), darkness (Ps. 88:6), silence (Ps. 31:17), and dust (Job 17:16). If this view is correct, then *sheol* forms a bridge between the judgment passages and the passages suggesting the eternal punishment of the wicked. *Sheol* speaks of life after death in vague terms. It moves beyond the judgment passages in affirming that there is life after death for the wicked, but it does not approach the clarity we find in the New Testament concerning their fate.

Generally, and especially in regard to the unrighteous, the Old Testament concentrates on this life. It is possible that *sheol* provides us with a shadowy glimpse of life after death. At least two passages, however, give us a clearer picture of the final destiny of the wicked: Isaiah 66:22–24 and Daniel 12:1–2.

Passages Suggesting Eternal Punishment

Isaiah 66:22–24

"As the new heavens and the new earth that I make will endure before me," declares the LORD, "so will your name and descendants endure. From one New Moon to another and from one Sabbath to another, all mankind will come and bow down before me," says the LORD. "And they will go out and look upon the dead bodies of those who rebelled against me; their worm will not die, nor will their fire be quenched, and they will be loathsome to all mankind."

The opening words harken back to Isaiah 65:17: "Behold, I will create new heavens and a new earth. The former things will not be remembered, nor will they come to mind." Here at the end of his prophecy Isaiah looks toward the distant future, when God will make all things new, even the heavens and the earth. His people's sorrow will be replaced with "delight" and "joy" (Isa. 65:18).

Specifically, God's people will rejoice over his accomplishments. He whose throne is in heaven and whose footstool is the earth will demonstrate his greatness to his humble people by vanquishing their adversaries (Isa. 66:1–5). God will grant peace and comfort to his own, and they will rejoice (Isa. 66:12–14). To his foes, however, "his fury will be shown." With bold strokes the prophet paints the divine warrior's punishment of the wicked: "See, the Lord is coming with fire, and his chariots are like a whirlwind; he will bring down his anger with fury, and his rebuke with flames of fire. For with fire and with his sword the LORD will execute judgment upon all men, and many will be those slain by the LORD " (Isa. 66:15–16).

God displays his glory by judging the wicked, but more so by spreading his fame among the countries. In addition, he will "gather all nations and tongues" to "come and see" his "glory." As a result, redeemed Jews will worship God, and even Gentiles will be brought to "Jerusalem as an offering to the LORD " (Isa. 66:18–21). Here in the language of the old dispensation is a prediction of the worldwide worship of God so characteristic of the new.[12]

Permanence Promised to God's People. The preceding context, then, speaks of God's creating the new heavens and earth. Now, in verse 22, the Lord makes a comparison: "As the new heavens and the new earth that I make will endure before me, so will your name and descendants endure." God assures his people that they will be part of the new order. He will grant them the permanence that belongs to the new heavens and earth.

What will occupy their time? "From one New Moon to another

and from one Sabbath to another, all mankind will come and bow down before" the Lord (v. 23). Here Isaiah predicts the ongoing adoration of God by redeemed Jews and Gentiles in the new earth. The prophet, of course, spoke in terms of Old Testament worship. He could hardly have said, "Each Sunday all will go to their local Christian churches to glorify the Trinity." He used the language of Israel's worship to foretell the worldwide worship of God in the last days.

The Terrible Fate of the Wicked. People from every nation will fulfill the supreme purpose of human existence—to worship and enjoy God forever. Not everyone will do so, however. Instead, the ungodly will suffer a terrible fate.

Isaiah envisioned worshipers leaving the temple and gazing upon the corpses of the Lord's enemies, probably in the Valley of Hinnom, as a comparison with Jeremiah 7:32–8:3 suggests. In this valley, another name for which is Topheth, human sacrifices were offered to the Ammonite god Molech during the reigns of Ahaz and Manasseh (2 Kings 16:3; 21:6). It was eventually desecrated by Josiah (2 Kings 23:10) but gained an evil reputation that continued into the first century A.D. when it was used as a designation for hell.[13] Isaiah wrote, "They will go out and look upon the dead bodies of those who rebelled against me" (Isa. 66:24).

The prophet, using battlefield imagery, pictured those slain by the divine warrior. Having rebelled against the living God, they will suffer the horrifying consequences. In fact, the consequences are so horrifying that the synagogue modified the order of verses 23–24 for public readings, repeating verse 23 after verse 24, so that the final words would speak of comfort rather than woe.[14]

Undying Worm and Inextinguishable Fire. The burning of corpses in the Old Testament is sometimes viewed as an act of desecration. Examples include the burning of Achan's body (Josh. 7:25) and the king of Moab's burning the bones of the king of Edom (Amos 2:1).

To show contempt, a victorious army would leave the bodies of its foes unburied on the battlefield. To be subject to such exposure was considered a disgrace. It denied the deceased a proper burial. Worse, the birds would feast on the remains. Worst of all, what the birds

began, the worms would finish. This explains the valiant efforts of the
people of Jabesh Gilead to recover the dead bodies of Saul and his sons
from the Philistines (1 Sam. 31:11–13). It also explains Rizpah's
concern to protect her sons' corpses from the birds and wild animals
(2 Sam. 21:10).

With these images in mind we can better understand Isaiah's
words: "They will go out and look upon the dead bodies of those who
rebelled against me; their worm will not die, nor will their fire be
quenched, and they will be loathsome to all mankind" (66:24). The
prophet used imagery from the present world to describe the future
order. For exposed corpses to be eaten by worms or burned was a
disgrace. Here was the ultimate disgrace. In all other cases the maggots
would die when they had finished their foul work (cf. Isa. 14:11), and
the fire would go out once its fuel was consumed. But in the prophet's
picture of God's judgment of those who rebel, the worm does not die
and the fire is not quenched! The punishment and shame of the
wicked have no end; their fate is eternal. It is no wonder that "they will
be loathsome to all mankind."

Isaiah here does not give us (as the New Testament does) a
developed doctrine of hell. He doesn't speak of the resurrection of the
dead, or of the Last Judgment. Instead, he uses earthly imagery—
corpses, worm, and fire—to point to the final doom of the wicked. He
gives us "an early description of eternal punishment: though dead, the
rebels will continue to suffer for ever."[15]

Daniel 12:1–2

The second Old Testament passage that speaks to the final destiny of
the wicked is Daniel 12:1–2.

> At that time Michael, the great prince who protects your
> people, will arise. There will be a time of distress such as has
> not happened from the beginning of nations until then. But
> at that time your people—everyone whose name is found
> written in the book—will be delivered. Multitudes who
> sleep in the dust of the earth will awake: some to everlasting
> life, others to shame and everlasting contempt.

The words "at that time" (v. 1) connect these two verses to the end of chapter 11. There Daniel records how God predicted events in the lives of Israel's prominent northern and southern neighbors, from the time of Cyrus to the reign of the Syrian king Antiochus Epiphanes (vv. 2–35), and how he spoke of the distant future (vv. 35–45).

Daniel 11:35–45 points to "the appointed time," "the time of wrath," and "the time of the end" (11:35, 36, 40). These verses describe the evil and destruction of the Antichrist. Therefore, when Daniel 12:1 says, "at that time," it refers to the last times.

Deliverance in a Time of Unparalleled Trouble. In Daniel 12:1 the prophet predicts a time of unprecedented trouble, the great tribulation spoken of by Jesus: "There will be great distress, unequaled from the beginning of the world until now—and never to be equaled again" (Matt. 24:21). In spite of this coming adversity God's people can rest assured that he will deliver them. In fact, God emphasizes the help by mentioning it before the announcement of unparalleled trouble. Michael, a mighty angel earlier spoken of as fighting on behalf of God's kingdom (Dan. 10:13), will arise to do battle for "everyone whose name is found written in the book." Daniel uses the image of the citizen list of the true Jerusalem (cf. Ps. 69:28; Mal. 3:16) to show that in the last days God will rescue spiritual Israel.

We are not told the logical connection between Daniel 12:1 and 2. It seems most likely that, although God will deliver his own in the dreadful times predicted by Daniel, both the wicked and the righteous will suffer casualties. Since God is Lord even over death, however, his conquest extends beyond the grave. He will resurrect the dead—his martyrs to glory and his enemies to shame.

"Multitudes Who Sleep . . . Will Awake." Verse 2 begins with the words "Multitudes who sleep." How are we to understand the word "multitudes" (Heb.: *rabbim*)? Some say that it is a Hebrew way of saying "all." God will raise all—not merely some—from the grave. We find this usage in, for example, Isaiah 2:3: "Many peoples will come and say, 'Come, let us go up to the mountain of the LORD" (see also Deut. 7:1). Nevertheless, this is not the most likely meaning of Daniel 12:2. The particular Hebrew construction[16] here rendered "multitudes

of" most commonly means "many" in the Old Testament. Daniel writes of the resurrection of the martyrs and their foes who will have died during the horrible times predicted in verse 1. Of course, he is not denying that God will raise *all* of the dead; he is just focusing here on a part of that whole.[17]

Notice how the prophet uses language from everyday activities of this life—awakening those who sleep—to depict the bodily resurrection of the last day: "Multitudes who sleep . . . will awake." God rouses the deceased from the "slumber" of death as easily as we awaken someone from sleep. Before his power death is only a temporary state of "sleep" from which people "awake."

"The Dusty Earth." Furthermore, the slumberers are said to "sleep in the dust of the earth" (or "dusty earth"). Here is an allusion to the divine Potter's original work: "The LORD God formed the man from the dust of the ground and breathed into his nostrils the breath of life and the man became a living being" (Gen. 2:7). We also cannot help but recall the Lord's words to Adam and Eve after their fall into sin: "By the sweat of your brow you will eat your food until you return to the ground, since from it you were taken; for dust you are and to dust you will return" (Gen. 3:19). The Creator who made Adam from the dust of the earth and in whose providence humans return to dust at death will raise the bodies of those who have died.

Two Groups, Two Fates. The resurrected will be divided into two groups that will experience different fates: "Multitudes who sleep in the dust of the earth will awake: some to everlasting life, others to shame and everlasting contempt." This passage teaches the resurrection of the dead. In addition, it contrasts the destinies of the righteous and the wicked (epitomized in the martyrs and enemies of God).

"Everlasting" Does Not Always Mean "Everlasting." This is the only occurrence of the words "everlasting life" in the Old Testament, although the concept of God's people enjoying life in his presence after death is taught in passages such as Job 19:26, Psalm 73:23–24, and Isaiah 26:19. Here in Daniel 12:2 the word "everlasting" (Heb.: *olam*) is used to describe the fates of the just and unjust. This word

deserves careful study, as it does not always mean "everlasting." It is an adjective signifying long duration with limits set by the context. For example, Exodus 21:6 describes the period of time a willing bondslave could choose to serve his master: "Then he will be his servant for *life*."

When used of God, however, as in Psalm 90:2 ("from *everlasting* to *everlasting* you are God"), *olam* means "eternal." In this case the limits of the long duration indicated by *olam* are set by the eternal life of God himself. That happens frequently in the Old Testament, which uses this word to speak of the eternal God's (Gen. 21:33) eternal name (Ex. 3:15), eternal attributes (love: 1 Kings 10:9; glory: Ps. 104:31; faithfulness: Ps. 117:2; righteousness: Ps. 119:142), eternal reign (Ex. 15:18), eternal salvation (Isa. 51:6, 8), eternal covenants (Gen. 9:16; 17:7, 13, 19), and eternal word (Isa. 40:8) and the eternal praise due him (Pss. 89:53; 135:13).

In Daniel 12:2 this word is used of the destinies of both the righteous and the wicked. It is difficult to limit either of these destinies; they are both "everlasting."[18] As we will see when we study the New Testament, the state of affairs after the resurrection of the dead is characterized by the life of God himself; the age to come lasts as long as he does—forever. So we see that even though *olam* does not always mean "eternal," the context here indicates that it must.

Everlasting Life and Everlasting Disgrace. The godly will be raised to "everlasting life." "Life" is used in the Old Testament to speak of welfare and happiness in the presence of the king (Prov. 16:15, contrasted with the king's wrath in v. 14). Being in the presence of the Great King brings never-ending "life," that is, true welfare and happiness. The wicked, however, are not raised to life; they are raised to shame and contempt. The first word speaks of "reproach," "shame," and "disgrace" in passages such as 2 Samuel 13:13, Lamentations 5:1, and Daniel 9:16. The second word occurs only here and in Isaiah 66:24, where, as we saw, it describes the final fate of the wicked as "*loathsome* to all mankind."

Daniel assures his believing readers that God will not abandon them, not even in death. God will raise them to their reward, even as the Lord promises Daniel himself in the last verse of the book that bears his name: "As for you, go your way till the end. You will rest, and then at the end of the days you will rise to receive your allotted inheritance" (12:13). God will raise his people to eternal life. The wicked, however, will find no escape from the God who defends his people. The enemies of God will suffer a terrible fate: they will be raised to eternal disgrace.

Conclusion

In our study of the Old Testament witness to the fate of the ungodly, we first investigated the primary judgment passages and reached two conclusions: (1) Contrary to modern assumptions, God is just and punishes sinners. (2) God's destruction of the wicked resulted in physical death, not in the obliteration espoused by annihilationists.

Second, we explored the possible meanings of *sheol* and considered ramifications of the two most likely views. If R. Laird Harris is correct and *sheol* always refers to the grave, then *sheol* tells us nothing about life after death. If the predominant evangelical view is correct, however, *sheol* sometimes refers to a netherworld to which all go at death. *Sheol*, therefore, takes us beyond the primary judgment passages and speaks of life after death, although in vague terms.

Third, we examined two passages that paint a clearer picture of the destiny of the wicked. Isaiah uses earthly images of corpses beset by undying worms and inextinguishable fire to point to the final doom of the wicked—eternal punishment (Isa. 66:24). Daniel teaches that whereas the godly will be raised to never-ending life, the wicked will be raised to never-ending disgrace (Dan. 12:2).

Our study of the Old Testament raises questions as we turn to the New Testament: Do the testaments agree in their portrayal of God as holy and just, or does the New Testament offer a kinder, gentler theology as some claim? What do Jesus and the apostles say happens to the wicked? Are they all finally saved? Are they annihilated after resurrection and punishment? We will seek answers to these questions and more in chapters 3, 4, and 5.

Notes

1. So Sierd Woudstra, "The Old Testament on the Afterlife," *Vox Reformata* 20 (1973): 1–21.

2. Examples include Edward W. Fudge, *The Fire That Consumes: A Biblical and Historical Study of Final Punishment* (Houston: Providential Press, 1982), 116–17; and Clark H. Pinnock, "The Destruction of the Finally Impenitent," *Criswell Theological Review* 4.2 (1990): 250–52.

3. Othmar Keel, *The Symbolism of the Biblical World: Ancient Near Eastern Iconography and the Book of Psalms* (New York: Seabury, 1978).

4. Alexander Heidel, *The Gilgamesh Epic and Old Testament Parallels* (Chicago: University of Chicago Press, 1949), 170–207.

5. Desmond Alexander, "The Old Testament View of Life After Death," *Themelios* 11.2 (1986): 44.

6. R. Laird Harris, "The Meaning of the Word Sheol as Shown by Parallels in Poetic Texts," *Bulletin of the Evangelical Theological Society* 4 (1961): 129–35; and "sheol" in R. Laird Harris, ed., *Theological Wordbook of the Old Testament*, 2 vols. (Chicago: Moody Press, 1980), 2:892–93.

7. Alexander, "The Old Testament View of Life After Death," 43; and Hans Scharen, "The Development of the Concept of Gehenna and Its Use in the Synoptics" (Th.D. dissertation, Dallas Theological Seminary, 1991), 55–56.

8. Alexander, "The Old Testament View of Life After Death," 44.

9. Scharen, "The Development of the Concept of Gehenna," 56.

10. Harris, "The Meaning of the Word Sheol," 130.

11. Ibid., 130–31.

12. For a stirring defense of the thesis that "the ultimate goal of God in all of history is to uphold and display his glory for the enjoyment of the redeemed from every tribe and tongue and people and nation," see John Piper, *Let the Nations Be Glad! The Supremacy of God in Missions* (Grand Rapids: Baker, 1993).

13. For this summary I am indebted to my former student William L. Klousia, "Jesus' Teaching Concerning the Final Destiny of the Wicked with Special Reference to Annihilationism" (Th.M. thesis, Covenant Theological Seminary, 1993).

14. So R. N. Whybray, *Isaiah 40–66*, New Century Bible Commentary (Grand Rapids: Eerdmans, 1975), 293.

15. Ibid., 294.

16. When *rabbim* is followed by the preposition *min*, normally it is partitive, according to Gerhard Hasel, "Resurrection in the Theology of Old Testament Apocalyptic," *ZAW* 92 (1982): 279.

17. E. J. Young (*The Prophecy of Daniel* [Grand Rapids: Eerdmans, 1973], 256) and Joyce G. Baldwin (*Daniel*, Tyndale Old Testament Commentaries [Downers Grove, Ill.: InterVarsity, 1978], 204) agree.

18. So Edmund F. Sutcliffe, *The Old Testament and the Future Life*, 2d ed. (Westminster, Md.: The Newman Bookshop, 1947), 115–18.

3

The Witness of the Redeemer (1): According to Matthew

Theodore Parker, a mid-nineteenth–century Unitarian minister in New England, expressed his opinion of hell (and other doctrines) in a November 1852 address.

> I take not the Bible for my master, nor yet the church; nor even Jesus of Nazareth for my master. . . . I am ready to believe that Jesus taught, as I think, eternal torment, the existence of a devil, and that he himself should ere long come back in the clouds of heaven. I do not accept these things on his authority.[1]

Kenneth Kantzer, one of the most respected evangelical leaders of our time, agrees with Parker that Jesus taught eternal torment, but that is where their agreement ends.

> I have read the speculations of Schleiermacher, Bultmann, Tillich, Brunner, Barth, and Moltmann, to say nothing of

Plato, Kant, Hume, Feuerbach, Lenin, and Bertrand Russell. All offer logical explanations used to discredit the notion of eternal punishment. . . .While I am deeply impressed by the arguments of brilliant thinkers like Schleiermacher, Tillich, and others, I prefer our Lord's words to theirs. Those who acknowledge Jesus Christ as Lord cannot escape the clear, unambiguous language with which he warns of the awful truth of eternal punishment.[2]

Parker and Kantzer agree that Jesus Christ taught eternal punishment. From that common starting point, however, they diverge sharply. Parker rebelled against the idea of eternal condemnation, even though Jesus taught it! Although Kantzer doesn't like the thought of sinners suffering forever in hell any more than Parker, he submits to the authority of Christ and believes the terrible truth of eternal punishment.

In this chapter the star witness in defense of eternal punishment, Jesus Christ, takes the stand. We will listen carefully to Jesus' testimony about hell as recorded in the gospel of Matthew. Then, we will be called upon to answer the question, If Jesus teaches eternal punishment, will we side with Parker or Kantzer?

We will examine Jesus' teaching on hell in Matthew under four main headings:

- Hell Is Real (Matt. 5:21-22, 27-30; 23:15, 33)
- Hell Is Ruled by God (Matt. 10:28; 25:41, 46)
- Hell Involves Rejection (Matt. 7:23; 8:11-12; 22:13; 25:30)
- Hell Involves Pain (Matt. 13:30, 40–43, 49–50; 18:6–9; 24:51)

Hell Is Real

Matthew 5:21–22

You have heard that it was said to the people long ago, "Do not murder, and anyone who murders will be subject to

judgment." But I tell you that anyone who is angry with his
brother will be subject to judgment. Again, anyone who says
to his brother, "Raca," is answerable to the Sanhedrin. But
anyone who says "You fool!" will be in danger of the fire of
hell.

In one of Jesus' most famous messages, the Sermon on the
Mount, he shocks his hearers with the statement, "I tell you that
unless your righteousness surpasses that of the Pharisees and the teachers of the law, you will certainly not enter the kingdom of heaven"
(Matt. 5:20). The people looked up to the Pharisees, a lay group noted
for their dedication to God, as exemplified by their giving, praying,
and fasting more than the law required (see Luke 18:11–12). The
people also looked up to the teachers of the law, experts in the Old
Testament who devoted their lives to its study and teaching. It is these
highly respected teachers of the law and these Pharisees that Jesus of
Nazareth, an itinerant preacher, excludes from the kingdom of God!

Jesus points out the deficiency in the righteousness of Israel's
leaders. The Pharisees and teachers rightly quote the sixth commandment, which prohibits murder. At the same time, however, they
display sinful anger and use hateful words. They keep the letter of the
law but violate its spiritual purpose. Outwardly they appear holy, but
inwardly they flagrantly break the sixth commandment, thus showing
that they lack the purity of heart that Jesus says characterizes those
who will see God (Matt. 5:8).

Jesus warns that if Israel's leaders persist in their hypocrisy, they
have more to fear than the local courts and even the Sanhedrin, the
Jewish supreme court. Above all, they should fear the living God! In
fact, they are "in danger of the fire of hell" (Matt. 5:22). According to
Jesus, hell is real.

The word Jesus here uses for hell is *gehenna*, the English render-
ing of a Greek word that comes from the Hebrew *Ge Hinnom*, meaning "Valley of Hinnom." In this valley human sacrifices were offered
to the Ammonite god Molech during the reigns of Ahaz and Manasseh
(2 Kings 16:3; 21:6). Josiah later desecrated the valley (2 Kings 23:10),
but it had already gained an evil reputation, which continued into the
first century A.D.

Here, then, is a ready-made designation for hell. When Jesus warns of "gehenna," his hearers understand that he speaks figuratively of the fate of the wicked. The "fire of gehenna" means terrible suffering at the hands of almighty God. It is the opposite of entering the kingdom of heaven (Matt. 5:20).

Matthew 5:27–30

> You have heard that it was said, "Do not commit adultery." But I tell you that anyone who looks at a woman lustfully has already committed adultery with her in his heart. If your right eye causes you to sin, gouge it out and throw it away. It is better for you to lose one part of your body than for your whole body to be thrown into hell. And if your right hand causes you to sin, cut it off and throw it away. It is better for you to lose one part of your body than for your whole body to go into hell.

Again Jesus exposes the hypocrisy of Israel's leaders. They not only violate the sixth commandment, but the seventh as well. Although they think they are morally pure as long as they do not take another man's wife, Jesus reminds them that adultery begins in the heart. To desire a woman with one's eyes is to violate the spiritual intent of the seventh commandment.

Jesus speaks figuratively when he commands gouging out eyes and cutting off hands;[3] he is not teaching that his hearers should mutilate their bodies. In fact, such mutilation would not accomplish his ends. A blind man, for example, can still lust in his heart. Rather, Jesus warns his hearers to restrict themselves, to perform radical spiritual "surgery," rather than yield to their sinful desires. The reason? Because the Savior loves sinners and wants them to avoid the terrible reality of hell.

Matthew 23:15, 33

> Woe to you, teachers of the law and Pharisees, you hypocrites! You travel over land and sea to win a single convert,

and when he becomes one, you make him twice as much a
son of hell as you are. . . . You snakes! You brood of vipers!
How will you escape being condemned to hell?

These verses are included in Jesus' seven woes against Israel's
hypocritical leaders in Matthew 23. In verse 15 Jesus laments the
results of the Pharisees' fanatical zeal to make converts, which are
disastrous because the Pharisees themselves do not know the way to
eternal life. "The Pharisees' interpretations and the rules deduced from
Scripture became so fully those of their converts that they 'out-
Phariseed' the Pharisees."[4] Their disciples, therefore, are more lost
than they are, since they follow unreliable guides. Tragically, the
Pharisees' bad theology leads their followers to reject Jesus.

In verse 33 Jesus denounces the hypocrisy of the Jewish leaders,
who build tombs to commemorate the prophets but fail to heed their
messages. The teachers and Pharisees claim that if they had lived in
their forefathers' time, they would not have taken part in killing the
prophets. The actions of these Jewish leaders, however, belie that
claim; they have already determined to arrest Jesus, the great prophet
of God, and will shortly conspire to kill him (Matt. 21:46; 26:3–4).

With irony Jesus tells them, "Fill up, then, the measure of the sin
of your forefathers!" (Matt. 23:32). God tolerates only so much sin,
and then, when the measure is full, he responds in wrath. The irony
is that this Old Testament idea (see Gen. 15:16), common in the
intertestamental literature, had never before been applied to Israel.[5]
Now the leaders of the covenant nation are outstripping the Gentiles
in provoking God to anger! Because of such sin, Jesus warns, the
Pharisees and teachers of the law will not escape the condemnation of
hell. How pathetic! The leaders of God's people are heading for hell
and taking their converts with them!

Conclusion

Jesus Christ taught that hell is real. Contrary to Bertrand Russell's view
that life after death is unlikely, there is an afterlife, and all who die
unforgiven will experience God's awful judgment in hell. Jesus also contradicts John Hick's universalism. It simply is not true that ultimately all

will belong to the kingdom of heaven. Many people, even religious people, will be "thrown into hell" by almighty God (Matt. 5:29).

In light of Jesus' condemnation of the Pharisees' and teachers' hypocrisy, an examination of our hearts is in order. Do we sincerely trust Christ as Lord and Savior? Or are we frauds like many of the religious leaders of the Israel of old? We must not take these questions lightly. Hell is as real as the rule of almighty God.

Hell Is Ruled by God

Matthew 10:28

> Do not be afraid of those who kill the body but cannot kill the soul. Rather, be afraid of the One who can destroy both soul and body in hell.

When sending out his twelve disciples to minister, Jesus warns them that they will suffer persecution because of him (Matt. 10:1–25). This is no reason for them to shrink back from their mission, however, for he assures them that their enemies "cannot kill the soul." Rather than fear human beings, who can harm only their physical lives, they should "be afraid of the One who can destroy both soul and body in hell." The disciples are not to fear mere mortals. God alone is able to destroy sinners in this life and the next. Death removes us from the jurisdiction of men, but not from that of God.

Taken by themselves, this verse and similar ones that speak of "destruction" are compatible with annihilationism, the teaching that God will blot the wicked out of existence. In the light of all of Scripture's teaching, however, it is clear that the "destruction" spoken of here is God's punishment of the ungodly with forfeiture of all that is worthwhile in human existence.

That Jesus is not speaking here of literal annihilation is corroborated by a similar passage in Luke. In Luke 12:5 Jesus warns: "Fear him who, after the killing of the body, has power to throw you into hell." The destruction mentioned in Matthew 10:28, therefore, is equivalent to being thrown into hell.[6]

Moreover, when Jesus warns his disciples to "be afraid of the One who can destroy both soul *and body* in hell," he implies that there will be a resurrection of the dead. God will raise the wicked from the dead to experience the ruin of their whole persons. It is no wonder that, as the ruler of hell, God is to be revered.

Matthew 25:41, 46

Then he will say to those on his left, "Depart from me, you who are cursed, into the eternal fire prepared for the devil and his angels." . . . Then they will go away to eternal punishment, but the righteous to eternal life.

When Christ returns in glory with his angels, he will sit as king on his glorious throne (Matt. 25:31). Then the entire human race ("all the nations") will stand before him; no one will escape the Final Judgment. After the nations are gathered in his presence, "he will separate the people one from another as a shepherd separates the sheep from the goats" (v. 32).

As a result of this separation people will experience one of two contrasting fates: God's blessing or his wrath. To his people King Jesus will declare, "Come, you who are blessed by my Father; take your inheritance, the kingdom prepared for you since the creation of the world" (v. 34). He bids those saved by the sovereign grace of God to enter into their reward.

They demonstrated their faith in Christ by performing deeds of mercy for God's children. The reason for their surprise (vv. 37–39) is sometimes misunderstood. These people are not surprised that Jesus accepts them, but at the reason he gives for doing so—he welcomes them because they treated him well without realizing it when they showed compassion to his people.[7]

Not so the wicked! Because they failed to show mercy to King Jesus, represented by his people, he rejects them. "Depart from me, you who are cursed, into the eternal fire prepared for the devil and his angels" (v. 41). Jesus banishes them from his presence and his kingdom; theirs is the awful fate of ultimate renunciation by God.

Furthermore, instead of inheriting the kingdom of heaven, they will enter eternal fire. This fire was originally prepared for the punishment of the Devil and his evil angels. How tragic that human beings also rebelled against God and share their lot!

Annihilationists insist that Jesus here speaks of the obliteration of the wicked by fire. That interpretation is erroneous, however, as a comparison of Matthew 25:41 with Revelation 20:10 makes clear. There John describes the condemnation of the Devil: "The devil . . . was thrown into the lake of burning sulfur." He also explains what this means for Satan: he "will be tormented day and night for ever and ever." John's words are unambiguous. The Devil's being cast into eternal fire means that he will be perpetually tormented. When Jesus, therefore, says that wicked human beings will share the Devil's fate, he means that they too will suffer eternal torment.

Jesus' final words in Matthew 25 lead to the same conclusion: "Then they [the wicked] will go away to eternal punishment, but the righteous to eternal life" (v. 46). Our Lord here draws a parallel between the respective destinies of the wicked and the righteous. Augustine noted this parallel long ago.

> Is it not folly to assume that eternal punishment signifies a fire lasting a long time, while believing that eternal life is life without end? For Christ, in the very same passage, included both punishment and life in one and the same sentence when he said, "So those people will go into eternal punishment, while the righteous will go into eternal life" (Matt. 25:46). If both are "eternal", it follows necessarily that either both are to be taken as long-lasting but finite, or both as endless and perpetual. The phrases "eternal punishment" and "eternal life" are parallel and it would be absurd to use them in one and the same sentence to mean: "Eternal life will be infinite, while eternal punishment will have an end." Hence, because the eternal life of the saints will be endless, the eternal punishment also, for those condemned to it, will assuredly have no end.[8]

Notice that Jesus depicts the destiny of the wicked as eternal *punishment* (v. 46). In spite of the modern aversion to the use of legal categories in religion, the Bible depicts God as Judge, sin as violation of his law, Christ's saving work as paying the penalty of sin, and the end of the wicked as eternal punishment. In so doing the Bible sits in judgment on the rebellion of many modern people.

In fact, even if Matthew 25:41 and 46 were the only verses to describe the fate of the wicked, the Bible would clearly teach eternal condemnation, and we would be obligated to believe it and teach it on the authority of the Son of God.

Conclusion

God rules over everything, including heaven and hell. The popular idea that hell is Satan's kingdom over which he rules is proved false by the passage we just studied. Jesus described the destiny of wicked humans as "the eternal fire prepared for the devil and his angels" (Matt. 25:41). Instead of reigning over hell, Satan will suffer the worst punishment there.

Moreover, Jesus taught that we are not to fear human beings, but rather God, "who can destroy both soul and body in hell" (Matt. 10:28). In fact, since God is Lord over all, he alone "is able to save and destroy" (James 4:12). Jesus, therefore, tells us to reverence God alone. Oh, that modern men and women would fear the living God, repent of their sins, and turn to him for forgiveness! Tragically, those who do not will be rejected by their Maker forever.

Hell Involves Rejection

Matthew 7:23

> Then I will tell them plainly, "I never knew you. Away from me, you evildoers!"

These words of Jesus are among the most shocking in the whole Bible. After warning his disciples of false prophets who look good but whose sinful lives ultimately will give them away, Jesus addresses the topic of false disciples. "Not everyone who says to me, 'Lord, Lord,' will enter the kingdom of heaven," he warns, "but only he who does the will of my Father who is in heaven" (Matt. 7:21). Only those who produce good fruit, thereby demonstrating that they are good trees, will be admitted into God's kingdom.

Nevertheless, on Judgment Day many will fervently but falsely claim to belong to Jesus. They will present as evidence of their knowing him the mighty deeds that they performed in his name. These include prophesying, casting out demons, and performing many miracles (v. 22). Jesus the all-knowing Judge will not deny that they did these things. Instead, he simply will say: "I never knew you. Away from me, you evildoers!"

Jesus repudiates the false disciples' claim that they know him as Lord. In addition, he disowns them by denying that he ever entered into a personal relationship with them. Their claim to know him, therefore, is invalid. Finally, he exiles the wicked from his blissful presence.

Jesus' words astonish many readers, who assume that people who do such great deeds in his name are saved. The truth is that performing miracles is an insufficient sign of salvation. What Jesus accepts as evidence of salvation is true faith showing itself in obedience to the Father's will.

Matthew 8:11–12

> I say to you that many will come from the east and the west, and will take their places at the feast with Abraham, Isaac and Jacob in the kingdom of heaven. But the subjects of the kingdom will be thrown outside, into the darkness, where there will be weeping and gnashing of teeth.

The occasion for Jesus' words is the remarkable demonstration of faith of a centurion, a Roman military officer nominally in charge of a hundred soldiers. This man comes to Jesus in Capernaum and begs him to help his servant, who is paralyzed and in great suffering. When Jesus agrees to go and heal the servant, the centurion protests: "Lord, I do not deserve to have you come under my roof. But just say the word, and my servant will be healed" (Matt. 8:8). The centurion explains that he is used to merely speaking a directive and having those under his command carry out his orders. Jesus is amazed at the centurion's confidence in him: "I have not found anyone in Israel with such great faith" (v. 10).

Jesus' prophetic words about a feast then follow. This is the feast foretold by Isaiah: "On this mountain the LORD Almighty will prepare a feast of rich food for all peoples, a banquet of aged wine— the best of meats and the finest of wines. . . . In that day they will say, . . . 'This is the LORD, we trusted in him; let us rejoice and be glad in his salvation'" (Isa. 25:6–9). Good food and laughter will abound at the banquet God is preparing for his people. Those who will come from the east and the west are Gentiles, like the centurion, whom Jesus distinguishes from "the subjects of the kingdom," the Jews. The tragedy is that many of the covenant people, Israel, will not partake of the feast with their own patriarchs. Instead, unbelieving Jews will "be thrown outside, into the darkness" of hell (v. 12).

Jesus' meaning is unmistakable. If sitting at the feast means belonging to God and enjoying his presence, then being excluded from the banquet means being rejected by God and cut off from his blessed presence. It is to go from the light of the feast "outside into the darkness" (see also Matt. 22:13). When Jesus adds, "There will be weeping and gnashing of teeth" (v. 12), he is describing hell as a place of terrible sorrow, "extreme suffering and remorse."[9]

Matthew 25:30

> Throw that worthless servant outside, into the darkness, where there will be weeping and gnashing of teeth.

In Jesus' parable of the talents, the "good and faithful" servants prove trustworthy stewards of the resources God entrusts to them. By contrast the "wicked, lazy servant" fails to use his resources for God (Matt. 25:14–30). When the master returns, he rewards the good servants but orders the "worthless" one "thrown outside into the darkness" (v. 30). These words, reminiscent of Matthew 8:12 and 22:13, indicate that God rejects those who are unfaithful to him. Such people are excluded from the joy of God's gracious presence. Instead, they go "into the darkness, where there will be weeping and gnashing of teeth." This is one of five times in Matthew's gospel that Jesus speaks of the damned in hell crying and grinding their teeth in pain (see also Matt. 8:12; 13:42, 50; 22:13; 24:51).

Conclusion

Such horrible pictures of suffering shock our sensibilities. Upon reflection, however, we realize that the Redeemer paints such pictures out of kindness. By announcing the fate of the wicked before the Last Judgment, he affords them opportunity to escape that fate. In fact, all who heed his warnings, repent, and cast themselves upon his mercy will be delivered from hell.

It is the same Lord Jesus who dies and rises again to save sinners who tells them plainly what their sins deserve. Jesus' preaching about hell, therefore, is part of his gracious ministry to a lost world. It is his way of showing unbelievers their need of him. They, in turn, inevitably make one of two responses. Some display ingratitude for his warnings and reject him. Others, however, gratefully own him as the One who alone can rescue them. Instead of experiencing the wrath their sins deserve, they will taste the sweet victory won by his death and resurrection.

Hell Involves Pain

Matthew 13:30, 40–43

> At that time I will tell the harvesters: First collect the weeds and tie them in bundles to be burned; then gather the wheat and bring it into my barn. . . . As the weeds are pulled up and burned in the fire, so it will be at the end of the age. The Son of Man will send out his angels, and they will weed out of his kingdom everything that causes sin and all who do evil. They will throw them into the fiery furnace, where there will be weeping and gnashing of teeth. Then the

righteous will shine like the sun in the kingdom of their Father. He who has ears, let him hear.

These words conclude Jesus' parable of the weeds and his interpretation of that conclusion. Here, as in Matthew 5:22, Jesus employs fire imagery to describe hell. What does the hell-fire signify? Consumption of the wicked, as annihilationists claim? Let us study Jesus' interpretation of the parable in an attempt to answer these questions.

Notice that Jesus builds the burning of the weeds into the parable (Matt. 13:30). If he wants to teach that the fires of hell consume the wicked, here is an excellent opportunity to do so. All he has to do is say, "They will throw them into the fiery furnace, *and they will be no more.*" But Jesus never says that. Instead, when he interprets the burning of the weeds, he speaks of pain, not consumption: "They will throw them into the fiery furnace, where there will be weeping and gnashing of teeth" (Matt. 13:42).

The doom of the ungodly, "the fiery furnace" of hell, therefore, will be a place of great sorrow and suffering. By contrast, the godly "will shine like the sun in the kingdom of their Father" (Matt. 13:43). Jesus quotes Daniel 12:3 to predict that the righteous will "radiate perfections and experience bliss in the consummation of their hopes."[10]

Matthew 13:49–50

> This is how it will be at the end of the age. The angels will come and separate the wicked from the righteous and throw them into the fiery furnace, where there will be weeping and gnashing of teeth.

This is the way Jesus ends his parable of the net. He likens the kingdom of heaven to a net that is let down into the sea and catches many varieties of fish. When the net is full, the fishermen pull it to shore, save the good fish, and discard the bad ones. Jesus equates the fishermen with angels, and the time of harvesting the fish with the end of the age: the good fish are the righteous and the bad fish are the wicked. The destiny of the ungodly, as in the parable of the weeds, is the fiery furnace. Here again, by speaking of crying and grinding of teeth, Jesus describes hell as a place of untold grief and agony.

Matthew 18:6–9

> If anyone causes one of these little ones who believe in me to sin, it would be better for him to have a large millstone hung around his neck and to be drowned in the depths of the sea. Woe to the world because of the things that cause people to sin! Such things must come, but woe to the man through whom they come! If your hand or your foot causes you to sin, cut it off and throw it away. It is better for you to enter life maimed or crippled than to have two hands or feet and be thrown into eternal fire. And if your eye causes you to sin, gouge it out and throw it away. It is better for you to enter life with one eye than to have two eyes and be thrown into the fire of hell.

In response to the disciples' asking, "Who is the greatest in the kingdom of heaven?" Jesus uses a little child for an object lesson. "Unless you change and become like little children," he teaches, "you will never enter the kingdom of heaven. Therefore, whoever humbles himself like this child is the greatest in the kingdom of heaven" (Matt. 18:1–4). Childlike humility, not a desire for greatness, is highly esteemed by God. The disciples must repent of their selfish ambition and instead adopt the submissive attitude of God's true children.

After forcing his hearers to look within their hearts, Jesus turns their focus outward. They must carefully weigh their influence on others. If someone receives "a child" in Jesus' name, he receives Jesus. If, however, someone causes "a child" to sin, he is headed for God's judgment. By "a child" Jesus means one who humbles himself, a true disciple, as the previous verses indicate.

Jesus uses the image of a person being drowned to depict God's punishment of sinners. Jesus graphically portrays a huge millstone, the kind pulled by a donkey, being hung about someone's neck and that person being drowned in the Mediterranean Sea.

He then warns, "Woe to the world because of the things that cause people to sin!" The Savior recoils at the wickedness of sin and at the terror of God's wrath. Nevertheless, he acknowledges God's sovereignty, even over sin, when he says, "Such things must come." He also underscores human responsibility as he continues, "But woe to the man through whom they come!"[11]

Preachers frequently recycle their illustrations and Jesus is no exception. He returns to the hyperbole of Matthew 5:29-30 when he speaks of cutting off the offending hand or foot, or gouging out the offending eye. He means that his hearers should take drastic action, rather than continue to sin and face the horrors of hell.

Our Lord contrasts entering life with being thrown into "the fire of hell," even "eternal fire" (Matt. 18:8–9). Here are opposite destinies. The righteous will enter eternal life in God's joyous presence. The unrighteous, however, will be cast by God into hell. Jesus paints a picture of hell-fire to warn his listeners of the pain of God's judgment. When he speaks of "eternal fire," he means that the torments of hell will have no end. Once more, then, the Savior compassionately warns his hearers of the dread of eternal punishment at the hands of almighty God.

Matthew 24:51

> He will cut him to pieces and assign him a place with the hypocrites, where there will be weeping and gnashing of teeth.

Jesus exhorts his hearers to be ready for his second coming: "Therefore, keep watch, because you do not know on what day your Lord will come. . . . So you also must be ready, because the Son of Man will come at an hour when you do not expect him" (Matt. 24:42–44). He then tells the parable of the faithful and unfaithful servants (vv. 45–51). In the parable the "master" obviously represents God. When the master returns, he will find the faithful and wise servant treating the servants under his charge fairly. However, the wicked servant, who abuses his fellow servants, will not be prepared for his master's return.

God will reward the faithful servant with greater responsibility, but he will punish the unfaithful one. Specifically, "he will cut him to pieces and assign him a place with the hypocrites." Both Testaments speak of being cut in pieces as a severe punishment. In Deuteronomy 32:41, for example, the Lord warns, "When I sharpen my flashing sword and my hand grasps it in judgment, I will take vengeance on my adversaries and repay those who hate me" (see also Heb. 11:37).

The wicked servant is allotted "a place with the hypocrites where there will be weeping and gnashing of teeth" (Matt. 24:51). He will join other false believers in the place of torment and regret—hell.

Our Lord hereby bestows great significance upon this life, for in it decisions are made that have momentous consequences. There will be no opportunity for salvation after his return.

Conclusion

Jesus often and undeniably depicted hell as involving terrible pain and suffering. At the end of both the parable of the weeds and the parable of the net he speaks of unbelievers' being thrown into a fiery furnace. In Matthew 18:6–9 he warns his hearers of a fate worse than being drowned in the depths of the sea with a large millstone hung around one's neck. In the same passage he threatens unbelievers with "eternal fire," even "the fire of hell" (Matt. 18:8–9). Finally, at the conclusion of the parable of the faithful and unfaithful servants he speaks of human beings' being cut to pieces (Matt. 24:51). It is time to integrate these conclusions with those previously reached in this chapter.

Conclusion

Jesus Christ says more about the fate of the wicked than anyone else in the Bible. The twelve passages that we have studied from Matthew's gospel introduce us to Jesus' teaching. Despite the protests of many, hell is real. Contrary to popular opinion, God alone rules over hell. The wicked face a dreadful fate—rejection by their Creator and eternal pain!

Having examined Jesus' abundant testimony, it is now time to respond. We must answer the question with which this chapter began:

if Jesus teaches eternal punishment, will we side with Theodore Parker, and reject Jesus' teaching, or with Kenneth Kantzer, and accept it? For all who know Jesus as Lord and Savior there can be only one answer. It is inconsistent for us to confess him as Lord and yet reject any aspect of his teaching. We must bow before his authority and accept his terrible teaching on hell. Although it is not easy to adjust our thinking and emotions to that doctrine, we need to submit every area of our lives to Christ's Lordship, including what we believe about the after-life.

An additional question begs for an answer: *Why* does Jesus speak so often about hell? Matthew's first chapter suggests an answer. Before Jesus' birth, God appeared to Joseph in a dream and told him to name the child "Jesus, because he will save his people from their sins" (Matt. 1:21). Jesus speaks frequently of hell because he is the Savior of the world. He warns of unspeakable torment in order to move his hearers to flee from the wrath to come. We who name his name should not shrink from following his good example. We must tell people the truth: without Jesus as Lord and Savior they are headed for the eternal judgment of God.

Francis Schaeffer understood this well, for when asked at seventy-one years of age what kept him serving God with great intensity, in spite of his battle with cancer, he replied:

> . . . sorrow for all the lost, and this should press us on to be faithful tellers, regardless of the cost. . . . to teach the eternal lostness of the lost without tears would be a cold and dead orthodoxy indeed. And to teach this without then a great emphasis upon the responsibility, in the light of this, to do all we can regardless of the cost that men might know the gospel, would be totally ugly and opposed to the biblical message that those who are lost are my kind.[12]

NOTES

1. Theodore Parker, *Two Sermons* (Boston: Benjamin B. Mussey, 1853), 14.
2. Kenneth Kantzer, "Troublesome Questions," *Christianity Today*, 20 March 1987, 45.
3. It is possible that "hand" is a euphemism for the male sexual organ. See D. A.

Carson, *Matthew, Mark, Luke,* The Expositor's Bible Commentary (Grand Rapids: Zondervan, 1984), 8:151.

4. Ibid., 479.

5. Ibid., 483–84.

6. This point is made by Hans Scharen, "Gehenna in the Synoptics: Part 2," *Bibliotheca Sacra* 149 (October–December 1992): 461.

7. Carson, *Matthew, Mark, Luke,* 522.

8. Augustine, *The City of God* 21.23–24. D. A. Carson extends Augustine's argument: "The same word 'eternal' (*aionion*) modifies 'punishment' as modifies 'life.' *Aionion* can refer to life or punishment in the age to come, or it can be limited to the duration of the thing to which is refers (as in 21:19). But in apocalyptic and eschatological contexts, the word not only connotes 'pertaining to the [messianic] age' but, because that age is always lived in God's presence, also 'everlasting' (cf. BAGD2, s.v.; and esp. DNTT, 3:826–33)" (*Matthew, Mark, Luke,* 522).

9. *The New International Dictionary of New Testament Theology,* ed. Colin Brown 3 vols. (Grand Rapids: Zondervan, 1976), 2:421.

10. Carson, *Matthew, Mark, Luke,* 327.

11. See Hans Scharen, "Gehenna in the Synoptics: Part 1," *Bibliotheca Sacra* 149 (July–September 1992): 334.

12. Schaeffer to the Rev. David H. Bryson, 14 January 1983.

4

The Witness of the Redeemer (2): According to Mark, Luke, and John

Why does anyone believe in hell in these enlightened days? Because Jesus plainly taught its existence. He spoke more often about hell than he did about heaven. We cannot get around this fact. We can understand that there are those who do not like the idea of hell. I do not like it myself. But if we are serious in our understanding of Jesus as the incarnate Son of God, we must reckon with the fact that he said plainly that some people will spend eternity in hell. He knew that while this present life is important, it is not all-important. We face eternal issues, and it would have been no kindness had he left his hearers in doubt about that. He spoke plainly about hell as well as about heaven, about damnation as well as about salvation.[1]

These sobering words, penned by Australian biblical scholar Leon Morris, raise a key issue: that of the popularity of belief in hell.

Living at the end of the twentieth century, we expect skeptics and unbelievers to reject the Bible's message of condemnation. Today, however, some very successful Christian *preachers* emphasize the positive aspects of the faith and almost never mention sin, wrath, and hell. But as Morris reminds us, Jesus spoke more often about hell than about heaven. Why was Jesus so negative in his preaching? Why didn't he take a more positive approach? In this chapter we will address these questions, examining the Redeemer's testimony about hell in the Gospels of Mark, Luke, and John. The following outline will help orient the reader:

- Hell and Demons (Mark 1:24; 3:11; 5:7)
- Hell and Eternity (Mark 9:42–48)
- Hell and Scripture (Luke 16:19–31)
- Hell and the Present (John 3:16–21; 3:36)
- Hell and the Future (John 5:28–29; 8:21, 24)

Hell and Demons

Mark 1:24

> What do you want with us, Jesus of Nazareth? Have you come to destroy us? I know who you are—the Holy One of God!

Near the middle of Jesus' ministry he visits Capernaum, and on the Sabbath, as is his custom, teaches in the local synagogue. The people are astonished at his words. The reason? He teaches with prophetic authority, not as the teachers of the law, who often merely appeal to the traditions of the elders. Jesus brings a word from God, probably similar to that of Mark 1:15, "The kingdom of God is near. Repent and believe the good news!" Here is something the people are not used to hearing: a summons to decide, issued with the authority of God himself![2]

As Jesus teaches, a man possessed by an evil spirit cries out to him: "What do you want with us, Jesus of Nazareth? Have you come to destroy us? I know who you are—the Holy One of God!" That this man is in a pitiful condition, controlled by a demon, is evidenced by the fact that sometimes the demon speaks for him (notice the shift from the first person plural to the singular). The evil spirit recognizes a threat in the person of Jesus and reacts to his holiness and power. We must be careful not to misunderstand the demon's words. Although the demon knows Jesus' identity, he does not acknowledge Jesus' lordship. By uttering Jesus' name and title he attempts to gain control over the Lord and disarm him, in accordance with contemporary occult belief.[3]

"Be quiet!" Jesus commands, "Come out of him!" (v. 25). In response the evil spirit shakes his host violently and comes out of him with a shriek. The people are even more astounded. "What is this? A new teaching—and with authority! He even gives orders to evil spirits and they obey him" (v. 27).

Indeed, Jesus in his earthly ministry teaches with God's authority. In addition, he commands the unclean spirits and they yield to his power. By delivering many who are demon possessed, he anticipates not only the ultimate deliverance of his people, but also the final vanquishing of the Devil and his demons. They will be cast into "the eternal fire, prepared for" them (Matt. 25:41).

Mark 3:11; 5:7

> Whenever the evil spirits saw him, they fell down before him and cried out, "You are the Son of God."

> He shouted at the top of his voice, "What do you want with me, Jesus, Son of the Most High God? Swear to God that you won't torture me!"

These two passages further describe Jesus' encounters with demons. Mark 3:11 summarizes the results of many such encounters over the course of his ministry. The demons cry out, "You are the Son of God," not in worship, but in an attempt to strip him of his might. In reply, however, he shows his lordship over them by forbidding them to reveal his identity (Mark 3:12).

Power meets power when Jesus clashes with the personalities of evil. The result is victory for the Son of God as he silences the evil spirits. Why does he do so? "Jesus silenced the outcries of the demons because the time for the clear revelation of who he was had not yet come, and the demons were hardly appropriate heralds of him."[4]

Mark 5:7 is set in the context of Jesus' deliverance of the Gerasene demoniac (Mark 5:1–17). The man, who lives in the cavern tombs about two miles from the southeastern coast of the Sea of Galilee, is demon possessed and uncontrollable. In fact, he often cries out and cuts himself, apparently in attempts to kill himself. When Jesus comes to his region, this pathetic figure runs to him, kneels, and screams, "What do you want with me, Jesus, Son of the Most High God? Swear to God that you won't torture me!" (v. 7). Here is a desperate attempt on the part of demons to defend themselves against Jesus.

Nevertheless, this attempt proves futile. By prostration and proclamation the evil spirits acknowledge the Son of God's superior power. The demons know they are in the presence of the One who will one day consign them to eternal torment. Sensing great danger, they lash out at him in fear and hatred. Yet all this is to no avail, for Jesus controls the evil spirits, eventually permitting them to enter a herd of about two thousand pigs. The herd, agitated by the demons, "rushed down the steep bank into the lake and were drowned" (v. 13).

A point easily missed is that "Jesus allowed the demons to enter the swine to indicate beyond question that their real purpose was the total destruction of their host."[5] They meant to destroy the man, but since Jesus has thwarted their design, they settle for inciting dumb animals to rush to their doom. By thus exposing the demons' murderous intent, Jesus highlights the fact that he delivered the man from *evil* spirits, over which he, the Son of God, exercises authority.

Conclusion

What do we learn from studying these three passages in which Jesus proves victorious over evil spirits? First, that the Son of God always acts according to the Father's timetable. He knows that the time for the final demise of the demons has not yet come. Still, moved with compassion for those who are tortured by demons, he frees humans from demonic control, thereby prefiguring his people's ultimate salvation on the new earth. Jesus' expulsion of the unclean spirits also demonstrates the final destiny of the demons: everlasting torment in the lake of fire (Matt. 25:41; Rev. 20:10).

Second, we learn that the demons know who Jesus is. In fact, their theology is better than that of the crowds, the Jewish leaders, and even the disciples. They acknowledge, even if begrudgingly, his divine sonship. Ironically, the *unclean* spirits testify loudly that Jesus is the *Holy One* of God, offering unexpected testimony to the deity of Christ. In all of this, God, who is truly sovereign, uses the wrath of his sworn enemies to further the mission of his Son.

Third, we learn that although the evil spirits know what fate awaits them, blinded by sin they oppose Jesus with all their might. While their might is considerable compared to that of humans, it is puny in relation to that of the Son of God. The result, of course, is their defeat; Jesus drives them out of their human hosts so that the demons can no longer torment them. God thereby assures all who believe in his Word that he will one day punish sin and give his enemies what they deserve.

In our day Christians in various places are encountering satanic opposition to the ministry of God's Word, opposition second only to that experienced by Jesus and the apostles. Believers' confidence today must be the same as that of the people of God of old: "You, dear children, are from God and have overcome them, because the one who is in you is greater than the one who is in the world" (1 John 4:4).

Hell and Eternity

Mark 9:42–48

> If anyone causes one of these little ones who believe in me to sin, it would be better for him to be thrown into the sea with a large millstone tied around his neck. If your hand causes you to sin, cut it off. It is better for you to enter life maimed than with two hands to go into hell, where the fire never goes out. And if your foot causes you to sin, cut it off.

> It is better for you to enter life crippled than to have two feet
> and be thrown into hell. And if your eye causes you to sin,
> pluck it out. It is better for you to enter the kingdom of God
> with one eye than to have two eyes and be thrown into hell,
> where "their worm does not die, and the fire is not quenched."

Jesus admonishes his hearers to weigh carefully their influence
on others. Woe to that person who causes Jesus' followers, described
as "little ones," to stumble! In fact, the fate of such an evildoer will be
worse than being forcibly drowned in the sea (v. 42). What could be
worse than such a terrible death? Being thrown into hell by God
himself!

In light of the disastrous wages of sin, Jesus urges drastic action.
Rather than indulge in sin, his listeners must perform "spiritual surgery" on their lives (vv. 43, 45, 47). It is better to "cut off" the
offending hand or foot and to "pluck out" the transgressing eye than
to be whole but go to hell! Keeping with Palestinian custom, Jesus does
not "refer to an abstract activity but to the specific member of the body
which is responsible for it."[6]

Jesus, therefore, is not enjoining bodily mutilation. Such action would insult the Creator. And it would not be an effective
remedy against sins of the heart: A person without limbs can still
steal by coveting. Instead of commanding mutilation, Jesus prods
his hearers to limit themselves severely rather than live in sin and
end up in hell.

Our Lord talks positively and negatively. On the positive side he
speaks of entering "life" (vv. 43, 45), even life with God after death.
He tells of entering the final stage of God's kingdom and thereby hints
at the blessings of those privileged to come into the King's presence (v.
47). On the negative side he warns of hell three times (vv. 43, 45, 47).
He thus draws attention to both divine sovereignty and human responsibility. When he warns of being "thrown into hell" (vv. 45, 47),
he directs his hearers' thoughts to God's control of all, including the
fates of human beings. It is God and God alone who casts people into
hell. But when Jesus warns of going into hell (v. 43), the accent falls
on human accountability. If people sow sin with abandon in this life,
they will reap hell in the next.

We must not miss Jesus' purpose for including positive and negative elements in his preaching. His "main concern . . . is not his listeners' consignment to Gehenna, but his urging . . . people to take drastic steps to avoid at all costs such a dreaded destiny."[7] Jesus came to save, not to condemn, and preaching hell is one of his means of saving his people from their sins.

Jesus' vivid description of hell merits study. He says that hell is a place "where the fire never goes out" (v. 43), thereby distinguishing the fires of hell from those on earth, all of which die. Even mighty forest fires, which may burn for weeks, eventually burn out. Hell-fire, however, is inextinguishable.

It is unwise to press Jesus' words concerning the fires of hell by asking about the temperature of the flames, for example. His main point is crystal clear: the pains of hell last forever. Jesus reinforces this point at the end of the passage when he again warns of being cast "into hell, where 'their worm does not die, and the fire is not quenched'" (vv. 47–48). The Redeemer here depicts hell in the words of Isaiah 66:24.

Annihilationist Edward Fudge interprets Isaiah's words as depicting the complete destruction of the corpses of the wicked, with the result that the wicked cease to exist. He then reads this meaning into Jesus' words in Mark 9, and in fact, into many New Testament passages.[8]

Fudge's methodology is flawed on two counts. First, it misinterprets Isaiah 66:24. Isaiah pictures God's judgment of the wicked as issuing in endless punishment when he says, "their worm will not die, nor will their fire be quenched." William L. Lane affirms that "as the final word of the prophecy of Isaiah the passage was thoroughly familiar to the disciples as a vivid picture of a destruction which continues endlessly."[9]

Second, proper theological methodology involves allowing the New Testament writers to move beyond their Old Testament background in keeping with the progress of revelation. Fudge errs by reading his supposed meaning of Isaiah 66:24 into the New Testament, where it does not fit.

In fact, Jesus sharpens Isaiah's preview of hell when he says that it is a place where the "worm does not die." What Isaiah saw dimly from afar Jesus broadcasts to all who will hear—hell has no end. Normally, maggots feed on their prey until it is consumed, then they die. The "worms" of hell, however, will never complete their work. Of course, Jesus is not teaching that there will be worms in hell, but he paints a picture describing the endlessness of sinners' torment.

Jesus does the same when he asserts that hell is a place where "the fire is not quenched" (Mark 9:48). Although all earthly fires eventually consume their fuel and go out, the fire of hell never comes to an end because its work is never done. In the context of hell, fire speaks of torment. Jesus here teaches, therefore, that the torment of hell will never cease.

In sum, the Lord Jesus teaches in Mark 9:42–48 that it is abundantly preferable to suffer temporally and be saved eternally than to enjoy sin in this life and to endure its effects forever. The reason? Because of the horror of hell's eternal torments.

Graciously, the living Christ still uses his message of hell to save sinners today. Listen to the published testimony of a friend of mine, Larry Dixon.

> A faithful youth worker thirty years ago challenged a small, insecure, pimpled group of adolescents with a simple question: "If you were to die tonight, where would you spend eternity?" It's the kind of question we see brightly painted on large rocks on interstate highways. But like only a few of the many questions which we hear in life, this one sunk deep into my heart on that Friday night so long ago.
>
> I knew the Gospel, but had not yet come to know the Person of that good news. That question of eternity burned in my mind all the way home that night, and I barely made it to my room before dropping on my knees beside my bed and receiving Christ. It was a teenager's sense of guilt—and rightfully deserved judgment in hell—but I'm not ashamed to acknowledge that the Holy Spirit used *fear* to bring me to Christ.[10]

What about you? Are you faithfully sharing the bad news of hell so that others will come to know the Good News of the Savior too?

Hell and Scripture

Luke 16:19–31

There was a rich man who was dressed in purple and fine linen and lived in luxury every day. At his gate was laid a beggar named Lazarus, covered with sores and longing to eat what fell from the rich man's table. Even the dogs came and licked his sores. The time came when the beggar died and the angels carried him to Abraham's side. The rich man also died and was buried. In hell, where he was in torment, he looked up and saw Abraham far away, with Lazarus by his side. So he called to him, "Father Abraham, have pity on me and send Lazarus to dip the tip of his finger in water and cool my tongue, because I am in agony in this fire." But Abraham replied, "Son, remember that in your lifetime you received your good things, while Lazarus received bad things, but now he is comforted here and you are in agony. And besides all this, between us and you a great chasm has been fixed, so that those who want to go from here to you cannot, nor can anyone cross over from there to us." He answered, "Then I beg you, father, send Lazarus to my father's house, for I have five brothers. Let him warn them, so that they will not also come to this place of torment." Abraham replied, "They have Moses and the prophets; let them listen to them." "No, father Abraham," he said, "but if someone from the dead goes to them, they will repent." He said to him, "If they do not listen to Moses and the prophets, they will not be convinced even if someone rises from the dead."

With his parable of the rich man and Lazarus, Jesus rivets his hearers' attention on the need to live now with a view to life after death. He warns of the possible reversal of fortunes in the next life. The beggar was covered with sores and starving, and "the dogs aggravated the sores by licking them."[11] By contrast, the rich man "lived in luxury every day" (v. 19). Their lots in this world were at opposite ends of the spectrum, and would be in the next world as well—though not as popular Jewish piety would expect.

The Jews viewed the rich as blessed by God in this life and heading for greater blessing in the next. Not necessarily so, Jesus warns, because riches are a terrible temptation towards idolatry. So it is with the rich man in the parable. He has taken no thought of preparation for life after death, as is evident from his realization, after it is too late, of his brothers' need for repentance (v. 30). Consequently, although the beggar dies and goes to the place of blessing, the rich man dies and finds himself in hell.[12]

We must be careful not to derive from this parable things that God never intended. For example, it is tempting to teach that fates are sealed at death because verse 26 says that a "great chasm has been fixed" that prohibits movement in either direction. This is indeed a biblical truth, but was Jesus intending to teach it here? I think not. We simply cannot milk every detail of a parable for meaning. This interpretive principle is best illustrated by citing preposterous examples. Shall we glean from this parable that there will be prayer in hell, that the wicked in hell will be able to see the righteous in heaven, that poor people are automatically saved, that people will want to be able to travel from heaven to hell, or that Abraham will speak for God on the other side? We can readily agree that we are not supposed to draw these ridiculous conclusions from the parable. But this raises important questions: How can we avoid such excess in the interpretation of parables? What controls should we employ to avoid squeezing too much out of them?

Fortunately, scholars who have studied the parables offer us help. Here I will employ two principles of interpretation, one from Craig Blomberg and another from Robert Stein. First, Blomberg argues that we should derive one point for each major character in a parable. He shows that this rule helps us understand Jesus' main points in many parables and keeps us on track. The three main characters in the parable before us are, of course, Abraham, the rich man, and Lazarus.

Abraham stands for God. The rich man represents not all wealthy people, but unrepentant ones (we know this from the emphasis on repentance in verse 30 and from the fact that Abraham himself was rich). Similarly, Lazarus, whose name means "God helps," signifies not all the poor, but those whom God helps.[13]

If we follow Blomberg's lead, we may draw one point from each of the three major characters. First, "Like Lazarus, those whom God helps will be borne after their death into God's presence." Jesus teaches that there is life after death for God's people. His focus here is probably on the intermediate, rather than the final, state.[14] Second, "Like the rich man, the unrepentant will experience irreversible judgment." The wicked survive death too, only to endure "torment" and "agony" (vv. 23, 24, 25, 28). Third, through Scripture, "God reveals himself and his will so that none who neglect it can legitimately protest their subsequent fate."[15]

This last point is based upon the rich man's final request of father Abraham: that Lazarus be permitted to return from the dead and warn his brothers, lest they too come to hell (vv. 27–28). God replies (through Abraham), "They have Moses and the prophets; let them listen to them" (v. 29). At this the rich man protests, "No, father Abraham, but if someone from the dead goes to them, they will repent" (v. 30). But God objects, "If they do not listen to Moses and the prophets, they will not be convinced even if someone rises from the dead" (v. 31).

This final point, then, is that God's Word is necessary and sufficient for salvation; to neglect it is to commit spiritual suicide. This becomes the main point of the parable if we take into account a principle taught by Robert Stein, "the rule of end-stress," whereby what comes last is considered most important.[16] The thinking here is that Jesus saves his main idea for last in order to leave it ringing in his hearers' ears. Indeed, this is the case for many of his parables. Jesus' main concern, therefore, in the parable of the rich man and Lazarus is to draw attention to the folly of ignoring the Bible's message.

Application

In light of Jesus' message in the parable of the rich man and Lazarus, the questions haunt us: Are we listening to "Moses and the Prophets"? Are we reading and heeding the Scriptures we own? A measuring stick lies close at hand to help us answer these questions: "Lazarus and his heartless neighbors depict . . . those who demonstrate by their attitudes to material possessions a proper or improper relationship to God."[17] Do our attitudes toward material possessions demonstrate a proper relationship to God? I fear that in general we do not measure up. Regardless of our professions of faith, our love for material things betrays an improper relationship to God. If neglecting the Bible's warnings about hell is as dangerous as Jesus says, then on the whole Christendom is in serious trouble.

Moreover, our predicament is compounded, as we observe in the parable's theme of being "too late." "The rich man pays attention to Lazarus too late, he sees the unbridgeable chasm too late, he worries about his brothers too late, and he heeds the law and the prophets too late."[18] Woe unto us prosperous professing Christians if we fail to respond in time to the message of God's Word. If we postpone repentance until it is "too late," all that will await is the wrath of God.

Hell and the Present

John 3:16–21

> For God so loved the world that he gave his one and only Son, that whoever believes in him shall not perish but have eternal life. For God did not send his Son into the world to condemn the world, but to save the world through him. Whoever believes in him is not condemned, but whoever does not believe stands condemned already because he has not believed in the name of God's one and only Son. This is the verdict: Light has come into the world, but men loved darkness instead of light because their deeds were evil.

Martin Luther called John 3:16 the gospel in a nutshell because it encapsulates God's loving the world of sinners by giving his Son so that they will not perish, but have eternal life. The next verse is more emphatic: God did not send his Son into the world to condemn the lost, but to rescue them from hell (v. 17). Here we learn of God's heart;

he loves sinners and commissions his Son as a missionary to reach them. Jesus comes to them in love, offering salvation freely to all who will receive it.

Believers in Christ need not wait for the Judgment Day to learn God's verdict (v. 18). The Judge has come before that day as the Savior. In this capacity he announces the rulings of the Last Day ahead of time. All who trust Jesus as Savior, therefore, have already received God's verdict of no condemnation.

Unbelievers, however, receive the opposite verdict—that of condemnation (v. 18). They too need not wait for the Last Day; based upon their rejection of God's Son they can know now that they are heading for hell. Oh that they would heed God's warning, turn from their sins, and accept Jesus' gift of salvation!

The Son of God did not come into the world to condemn sinners any more than missionaries go into other cultures to condemn people. In both cases the motivation for going is love! Nevertheless, because greater knowledge brings with it greater responsibility, a by-product of the missionaries' ministry is worse condemnation for those who reject their message.

It is the same for the ministry of the Son of God. He came to save, not to condemn. Regardless, those who spurn him—since they have rejected God's ultimate revelation—will reap worse condemnation than if they had never heard his name. Verse 19 summarizes the majority's response to Jesus: although he caused God's light to blaze upon a dark world, most people refused the light. Why? The reason is moral: They "loved darkness instead of light because their deeds were evil." These are some of the saddest words in the Bible. Let us, however, not forget their purpose in context. God designed his words to drive us to his love as it is offered in his Son. May God's good purpose be fulfilled in us and in those to whom we minister.

John 3:36

> Whoever believes in the Son has eternal life, but whoever rejects the Son will not see life, for God's wrath remains on him.

Here John casts human responses to Jesus' message in terms of two alternatives. Either one believes in the Son of God or one rejects him; there is no middle ground. Furthermore, John presents "the last things" as both already fulfilled and as yet to be fully consummated. John 5:28–29 and 8:21, 24, for example, speak of events that are still future. In John 3:36, however, eternal life and God's wrath are depicted as present realities.

All who trust God's Son have eternal life now. Nevertheless, this does not deny that eternal life is still a future hope. Although this idea is rare in John's gospel, we see it in 12:25: "The man who loves his life will lose it, while the man who hates his life in this world will keep it for eternal life."

Eternal life is not only present and future; it is also qualitative and quantitative. John 12:25, by contrasting "eternal life" with "life in this world," emphasizes the quantitative aspect, that eternal life lasts forever. Jesus brings out the qualitative dimension when he describes eternal life as knowing the Father and the Son: "Now this is eternal life: that they may know you, the only true God, and Jesus Christ, whom you have sent" (John 17:3).

The wrath of God likewise is present and future, qualitative and quantitative. John writes, "Whoever rejects the Son will not see life, for God's wrath remains on him" (3:36). A holy God already directs his anger toward those who despise his Son, and that anger stays with them forever, for they will not "see," that is, experience, eternal life in the future. Moreover, unbelievers will not know spiritual life in its qualitative or quantitative aspects. They will not know the Father and Son now, or enjoy life with God forever.

Application

John's teaching that eternal life and condemnation are present realities gives urgency to evangelism. We must plead with the unsaved not to wait until the Last Judgment to find out their fate. They can know their eternal destiny now, based on their relationship to Jesus. If they die unforgiven, a terrible fate awaits, as the next two passages reveal.

Hell and the Future

John 5:28–29

> Do not be amazed at this, for a time is coming when all who
> are in their graves will hear his voice and come out—those
> who have done good will rise to live, and those who have
> done evil will rise to be condemned.

At first glance Jesus' words in John 5:25 seem outlandish: "I tell
you the truth, a time is coming *and has now come* when the dead will
hear the voice of the Son of God and those who hear will live"
(emphasis added). Does Jesus claim to bring about the general resurrection of the dead during his earthly ministry? No, he is not speaking
of physical resurrection in John 5:25 but of spiritual resurrection, as the
preceding verse confirms. "I tell you the truth, whoever hears my word
and believes him who sent me has eternal life and will not be condemned; he has crossed over from death to life" (v. 24).

Accordingly, Jesus raises believers spiritually by giving them
eternal life in the present. In addition, he will raise the just and the
unjust bodily in the future. Indeed, "a time is coming when all who are
in their graves will hear his voice and come out" (vv. 28–29). At Jesus'
summons the dead will rise from their graves. Moreover, Jesus' command will usher all to their eternal destinies: "Those who have done
good will rise to live, and those who have done evil will rise to be
condemned" (v. 29).

Some have been troubled that this verse might teach salvation
by works. It does not. It teaches judgment based on works. The
righteous will be rewarded with eternal life for the good they have
done, the good produced in them by "God who works in [his people]
to will and to act according to his purpose" (Phil. 2:13). These good
works are the fruit the Holy Spirit produces (Gal. 5:22–23) in those
saved freely by God's grace (Rom. 3:24).

The resurrected wicked, however, will be condemned for the evil
they have done. It is just of God to base his judgment of the unsaved
on their deeds, rather than on whether or not they have heard the
gospel. Though no one is saved apart from believing the gospel, it is

fair for God to judge people according to their deeds. And the wicked get what they deserve for their evil deeds—damnation.

In sum, John here teaches that the Son of God by his power will summon all people from their graves to one of two destinies. Those whose lives evidence that God saved them by his grace will rise to eternal life. The wicked, however, whose lives betray the fact that they do not know God, will rise to condemnation.

John 8:21, 24

> I am going away . . . and you will die in your sin. Where I go you cannot come. . . . I told you that you would die in your sins; if you do not believe that I am the one I claim to be, you will indeed die in your sins.

According to the fourth gospel, Jesus performs unprecedented miracles, as the former blind man attests: "Nobody has ever heard of opening the eyes of a man born blind" (John 9:32). In addition, Jesus preaches messages unlike any other, as even the temple guards sent to arrest him realize: "No one ever spoke the way this man does" (John 7:46). Jesus' signs and sermons testify that the Father sent him into the world. Despite this abundant testimony, however, "the world did not recognize him" (John 1:10). And though he came especially as Messiah to Israel, sadly, "his own did not receive him" (1:11).

In John 8, Jesus responds to the Pharisees' refusal to accept his testimony (v. 13) by pointing to the root of their problem. He frankly tells them that they do not know him or his Father (v. 19). Furthermore, Jesus reveals that the Pharisees' ignorance of God has disastrous consequences: Israel's religious leaders will depart this life without having their sins forgiven.

Jesus repeats these awful words twice more: "I told you that you would die in your sins; if you do not believe that I am the one I claim to be, you will indeed die in your sins" (v. 24). His repetition under-scores the gravity of the utterance. In addition, he distinguishes be-tween the singular "sin" in verse 21 and the plural "sins" in verse 24. The former refers to the sin of rejecting Jesus, the latter "to the diverse and ugly forms of corruption that mushroom from the one sin of unbelief."[19]

Furthermore, the third time Jesus asserts that the Pharisees will die unforgiven, he specifies the reason for their condemnation—they reject him and his claims. Here is the heart of the matter. Israel's leaders will perish because they refuse to acknowledge that Jesus speaks the truth when he claims to be the unique Son of God, the only Savior of the world. As a result, they will die in their sins, that is, they will be damned.

John's sobering testimony concerning Jesus' preaching present and future condemnation points us back to the issue with which this chapter began: the unpopularity of belief in hell.

Conclusion

Judging from the responses Jesus received to his sermons, hell was no more popular in the first century than it is in the twentieth. Nevertheless, that did not deter him from often bringing up the topic. Consider the evidence: We have studied twenty-one passages from the four Gospels in which Jesus warns the unrepentant of the horrors of hell.

We are now in a position to answer the questions raised at the beginning of this chapter: Why is Jesus so negative in his preaching? Why doesn't he adopt a more positive approach? Because he is the Savior of the world. Because he loves sinners. And because he desires to alert his hearers to the coming wrath that they might turn to him and be saved. Seen in this light, people's aversion to Jesus' preaching hell is folly and ingratitude, as Martin Luther aptly relates.

> If a doctor, able to help, were at the side of a sick person and promised to help him from his trouble and advised him how to combat his ailment or the poison he had taken, and if the sick person knew that the doctor could help him but nonetheless said: Oh, get out, I won't accept your advice; you are no doctor, but a highwayman; I am not sick, nor have I taken poison; it will not hurt me; and if the sick person wanted to kill the doctor, would you not say that this fellow,

who persecuted and wanted to kill his doctor, was not only
sick but demented, mad, and irrational as well? . . . But this
spiritual madness—that we do not want to accept help
when God's Son wants to help us—is ten times worse.
Should our Lord God not be angry and let hell-fire, sulphur,
and pitch rain upon such ingrates? For besides being sinners,
we are also so wretched as to reject help and chase away and
kill those who urge us to accept it.[20]

Notes

1. Leon Morris, "The Dreadful Harvest," *Christianity Today*, 27 May 1991, 34.
2. William L. Lane, *Commentary on the Gospel of Mark*, New International Commentary on the New Testament (Grand Rapids: Eerdmans, 1974), 71–72.
3. Ibid., 73–74 and 74 n. 118.
4. Walter W. Wessel, *Matthew, Mark, and Luke*, The Expositor's Bible Commentary (Grand Rapids: Zondervan, 1984), 641.
5. Lane, *Mark*, 186.
6. Ibid., 347.
7. Hans Scharen, "Gehenna in the Synoptics: Part 1," *Bibliotheca Sacra* 149 (July–September 1992): 333.
8. Edward W. Fudge, *The Fire That Consumes* (Houston: Providential Press, 1982), 110–14, 160, 177, 185, 187, 198, 283, 298. For criticism of Fudge's methodology at this point see Kendall S. Harmon, "The Case Against Conditionalism: A Response to Edward William Fudge," in *Universalism and the Doctrine of Hell*, ed. Nigel M. de S. Cameron (Grand Rapids: Baker, 1992), 206–10.
9. Lane, *Mark*, 349; cf. 349 n. 81.
10. Larry Dixon, *The Other Side of the Good News: Confronting Contemporary Challenges to Jesus' Teaching on Hell* (Wheaton, Ill.: Victor, 1992), 9.
11. I. Howard Marshall, *The Gospel of Luke*, New International Greek Testament Commentary (Grand Rapids: Eerdmans, 1978), 636.
12. Notice that "after describing each in turn (vv. 19, 20–21), Jesus relates their deaths in reverse order, highlighting the reversal of their status in the life to come" (Craig L. Blomberg, *Interpreting the Parables* [Downers Grove, Ill.: InterVarsity Press, 1990], 203).
13. Ibid., 205.
14. Marshall agrees, *Luke*, 636–37.
15. Blomberg, *Parables*, 206.
16. Robert H. Stein, *An Introduction to the Parables of Jesus* (Philadelphia: Westminster, 1981), 56, 123, 127. Blomberg agrees, when he writes with reference to the third point, "The parable's climax then makes this principle the dominant of the three" (*Parables*, 208).
17. Blomberg, *Parables*, 205.

18. Ibid., 204.

19. D. A. Carson, *The Gospel According to John* (Grand Rapids: Eerdmans, 1991), 342.

20. Ewald M. Plass, *What Luther Says*, 3 vols. (St. Louis: Concordia, 1959), 2:695.

5

The Witness of the Apostles

After listening to the Redeemer's testimony concerning the fate of the
wicked, we now consider the witness of his apostles. Two differences
will be apparent. First, although the apostles write often about hell,
they tend to be less pointed in their descriptions of it than Jesus was.
Second, they tend to speak of God's wrath in general terms and give
fewer particulars than Jesus did. In fact, they are often content merely
to use theological shorthand. How are we to explain these tendencies?
W. G. T. Shedd offers this explanation:

> The strongest support of the doctrine of Endless Punish-
> ment is the teaching of Christ, the Redeemer of man. . . .
> The Apostles enter far less into detailed description, and are
> far less emphatic upon this solemn theme, than their divine
> Lord and Master. And well they might be. For as none but
> God has the right, and would dare, to sentence a soul to
> eternal misery, for sin; and as none but God has the right,
> and would dare, to execute the sentence; so none but God
> has the right, and should presume, to delineate the nature
> and consequences of the sentence.[1]

Shedd is correct. Jesus is the author of the doctrine of hell. Nevertheless, his apostles bear important testimony to this doctrine. Therefore, we will study passages that speak of hell in Paul's letters, Hebrews, Jude, and Revelation:

- Paul: (1) God's Wrath, (2) God's Justice
- Hebrews: The Importance of the Doctrine of Hell
- Jude: The Eternity of Hell
- Revelation: (1) God's Wrath, (2) The Lake of Fire and the Second Death, (3) Banishment from the City of God

Paul

God's Wrath: Romans 2:5

> But because of your stubbornness and your unrepentant heart, you are storing up wrath against yourself for the day of God's wrath, when his righteous judgment will be revealed.

Paul, after announcing the theme of Romans in 1:16–17, the revelation of God's saving righteousness, immediately speaks of the revelation of God's wrath. His strategy, in fact, is to present the "bad news" (1:18–3:20) as the essential background for a proper understanding of the Good News (3:21–5:21).

Whereas the evildoers of Romans 1:32 flaunt their sinful lifestyle, the sinners Paul takes to task in Romans 2:1–6 are hypocrites; they indulge in sins themselves even while they condemn the same sins in others. Such arrogance exasperates Paul: "So when you, a mere man, pass judgment on them and yet do the same things, do you think you will escape God's judgment?" (Rom. 2:3).

This hypocrisy draws some of Paul's strongest words: "Because of your stubbornness and your unrepentant heart, you are storing up wrath against yourself for the day of God's wrath, when his righteous judgment will be revealed" (Rom. 2:5). Paul accuses the hypocrites of stubborn refusal to admit their sins to a holy God. Indeed, he summarizes the condition of their hearts with a single word: "unrepentant." Although they think themselves moral, their spiritual fraud progressively adds to their condemnation; they are storing up wrath against themselves.

This wrath will accumulate until the Judgment Day, "the day of God's wrath, when his righteous judgment will be revealed" (v. 5). Paul, in harmony with the Old Testament and Jesus, teaches that a day is coming when the divine Judge will be acknowledged as righteous. Then sin will be exposed for what it is—rebellion against him—and it will receive its due punishment. In all of this God will be glorified in his qualities of holiness and righteousness, and in his work of judgment.

The wrath of God, his holy hatred of sin, is a major theme of Paul's letters. God has not appointed his people for wrath but for salvation through Christ (1 Thess. 5:9). Although they were "by nature objects of wrath" (Eph. 2:3) and spiritually dead, God gave them new life in Christ (v. 5). Indeed, through Jesus' death and resurrection he "rescues" them "from the coming wrath" (1 Thess. 1:10; see also Rom. 5:9).

Paul mercifully proclaims "the wrath of God . . . revealed . . . against all the godlessness and wickedness of men" (Rom. 1:18), to show them their need for Christ. In spite of this, many of the ungodly refuse to acknowledge their sins and believe the gospel. As a result, "God's wrath is coming" (Col. 3:6) upon them.[2]

Compassionate readers can only shudder when they contemplate such a prospect for any human being, let alone for family members and friends.

God's Justice: 2 Thessalonians 1:5–10

All this is evidence that God's judgment is right, and as a result you will be counted worthy of the kingdom of God, for which you are suffering. God is just: He will pay back trouble to those who trouble you and give relief to you who are troubled, and to us as well. This will happen when the Lord Jesus is revealed from heaven in blazing fire with his powerful angels. He will punish those who do not know God and do not obey the gospel of our Lord Jesus. They will be punished with everlasting destruction and shut out from the presence of the Lord and from the majesty of his power on the day he comes to be glorified in his holy people and to be marveled at among all those who have believed.

Paul has just boasted in verse 4 of the Thessalonians' steadfastness while enduring persecutions. Indeed, due to their response to affliction, God counts them worthy of his future salvation (v. 5). Furthermore, the apostle reminds them that God is just and will demonstrate his justice in two ways: (1) in retribution he will punish the believers' enemies as they deserve, and (2) he will bless the Thessalonians (vv. 6–7).

When will God do these things? "This will happen when the Lord Jesus is revealed from heaven in blazing fire with his powerful angels" (v. 7). At Christ's second coming he will deliver his people and punish their oppressors. Paul, thus, after discussing the particular case of the Thessalonians and their foes, moves to a discussion of all believers and unbelievers.

The apostle elaborates on the fate of the wicked. God "will punish" them (v. 8). This statement and those in verses 6 ("[God] will pay back trouble. . .") and 9 (lit. "[the wicked] will pay the penalty") are among the clearest assertions of God's retributive justice in Scripture. Plainly, the Lord will not leave sinners unpunished for their rebellion against him.

God's enemies are further described as "those who do not know God and do not obey the gospel of our Lord Jesus" (v. 8). We are probably to understand these words as referring to one group rather than two. The wicked are condemned for their ignorance of God, as manifested in their rejection of the message of salvation.[3]

Paul spells out their destiny: "They will be punished with everlasting destruction" (v. 9). Although "destruction" could refer to either annihilation or eternal punishment, three reasons suggest that it here refers to the latter.

First, the expression "*eternal* destruction" seems an unlikely way to denote the obliteration of the wicked. If extinction were meant, why not just say "destruction"?[4]

Second, Charles A. Wanamaker correctly states, "As there is no evidence in Paul (or the rest of the New Testament for that matter) for a concept of final annihilation of the godless, the expression 'eternal destruction' should probably be taken in a metaphorical manner as indicating the severity of the punishment awaiting the enemies of God."[5]

Third, Paul's next words rule out annihilation: ". . . and [they will be] shut out from the presence of the Lord and from the majesty of his power" (v. 9). Unbelievers will be excluded from the gracious presence of the Lord. This cannot be annihilation, for their separation *presupposes* their existence.[6]

Consequently, unbelievers should bemoan the second coming of Christ because for them it signals "everlasting destruction," a condition of complete ruin, being out of fellowship with God forever. By contrast, believers eagerly await his return because he will come "to be glorified in his holy people and to be marveled at among all those who have believed" (v. 10).

We could liken Christ's return to a rescue team storming a school building to subdue terrorists and free their hostages. To the terrorists the coming of the team means punishment, but to the captives their coming means relief and deliverance.

Application

Paul's doctrine of hell teaches three lessons. First, it helps us to understand God's wrath better in relation to his justice. In 1973, J. I. Packer wrote, "The subject of divine wrath has become taboo in modern society, and Christians by and large have accepted the taboo and conditioned themselves never to raise the matter."[7] Sadly, Packer's words still ring true today. The apostle Paul, however, will not let us get away with such cowardice. Why? Because he knows that God's glory is at stake. That is why he calls Judgment Day "the day of God's wrath, when his righteous judgment will be revealed" (Rom. 2:5). That is why he says: "God is just. He will pay back . . . those who trouble you" (2 Thess. 1:6). And that is why he states, "He will punish those who do not know God. . . . with everlasting destruction" (vv. 8–9).

Simply put, the Last Judgment is necessary and good. It is necessary because there is a holy God in heaven. If God did not punish sin, he would deny himself, and that he cannot do. The Last Judgment is good because it involves a revelation of God's justice that will glorify him. On that day he will balance the scales of justice and set all things right.

How difficult it is for modern men and women to accept these truths! In fact, the degree of difficulty we experience in accepting them is a measure of how deeply we have imbibed the spirit of this evil age, rather than the Spirit of God. When it comes to speaking about God's wrath, I fear that most Christians have lost their nerve.

Second, Paul's message of condemnation, like that of his Master, underscores the awfulness of hell. It is awful in what its inhabitants miss and in what they endure. The damned miss the joy of "the presence of the Lord and the majesty of his power" (2 Thess. 1:9). Instead they endure God's "wrath" (Rom. 2:5) and "everlasting destruction" (2 Thess. 1:9). May God use Paul's revolting descriptions of hell to break us until we love the unsaved more than we love ourselves.

This leads us to the third application. Paul doesn't preach hell for its own sake, any more than Jesus did. The apostle preaches it to show sinners their need of the Savior. Do we do the same? Or do we too lack the spiritual backbone needed to tell poor sinners the truth? I pray that God will move us to prayerfully, tactfully, and lovingly look for opportunities to share the bad news and the Good News with lost people. After studying Paul's doctrine of hell, how can we do less?

Hebrews

The Importance of the Doctrine of Hell: Hebrews 6:1–3

> Therefore let us leave the elementary teachings about Christ and go on to maturity, not laying again the foundation of repentance from acts that lead to death, and of faith in God, instruction about baptisms, the laying on of hands, the resurrection of the dead, and eternal judgment. And God permitting, we will do so.

These verses conclude a section (Heb. 5:11–6:3) in which the writer chides his readers for their lack of spiritual progress. In fact, though enough time has elapsed since they professed faith in Christ that they ought to be teachers of the Word, they themselves need to be taught the spiritual abc's because they have not consistently obeyed the truth they know (5:12–14).

The writer, therefore, exhorts his readers to "go on to maturity" (6:1). He desires that they build upon the foundation of repentance, faith, and elementary doctrines. He divides these doctrines into two categories (v. 2). The first deals with Christian initiation and includes instruction about baptism and the laying on of hands. The second category concerns future things: the general resurrection and eternal punishment. Moreover, the writer expresses confidence that God will enable them to grow: "And God permitting, we will do so" (v. 3).

This passage shows the importance of the doctrine of hell to the early church. It was a part of the foundational teaching given to new converts. It was, therefore, considered basic to a Christian view of life. Indeed, people looked at the world differently after embracing the doctrine of hell. They saw human beings as creations of God who live forever, either with him in joy or apart from his bliss in conscious torment. This in turn made them thankful to God for granting them the former fate and sparing them the latter. In addition, belief in hell caused them to see themselves as stewards of God's grace. God was gracious to them so that they might in turn share his love with those outside the faith.

Jude

The Eternity of Hell

Jude 7.

In a similar way, Sodom and Gomorrah and the surrounding towns gave themselves up to sexual immorality and perversion. They serve as an example of those who suffer the punishment of eternal fire.

Jude begins his epistle by explaining that although he wanted to write about the salvation that believers share, he feels constrained to urge his readers to fight for Christianity (v. 3). Why the change? False teachers "have secretly slipped in among" his readers and are spreading ungodliness (v. 4).

Still, Jude assures his readers that the heretics will not escape condemnation. He does this by citing three Old Testament examples of how God punishes rebels. First, he recalls God's destruction of the disobedient Israelites who were ungrateful for their deliverance from Egypt (Num. 26:64–65).

Second, Jude reminds his readers that God holds captive the angels who rebelled.[8] "These he has kept in darkness, bound with everlasting chains for judgment on the great Day" (v. 6). These evil angels are now incarcerated and await a worse fate on Judgment Day: the fire of gehenna (Matt. 25:41).

Third, Jude cites the classic case of divine judgment—that of Sodom and Gomorrah. These cities indulged in the "perversion" of homosexuality. As a result God made an "example" of them (v. 7). Genesis specifies: "The LORD rained down burning sulfur on Sodom and Gomorrah. . . . Thus he overthrew . . . all those living in the cities—and also the vegetation in the land." In fact, the next morning Abraham looked down toward the cities and "saw dense smoke rising from the land, like smoke from a furnace." In this way "God destroyed the cities of the plain" (Gen. 19:24–29).

Referring to this event Jude says that these cities "serve as an example of those who suffer the punishment of eternal fire" (v. 7). Notice that "eternal fire" is a "punishment." Jude here sounds like his half-brother, the Lord Jesus, who taught that God would punish sin with "eternal fire" (Matt. 25:41, 46).

What does Jude mean when he says that Sodom and Gomorrah "serve as an example of those who suffer the punishment of eternal fire"? That their citizens were totally obliterated, as Fudge insists? "There is no biblical hint that Sodom and Gomorrah's inhabitants presently endure conscious torment; several passages, in fact, make a point of their abiding extinction."[9] If that is correct, then it proves more than annihilationists want to prove—that the inhabitants of those cities were destroyed at death, never to exist again. That, however, is not the teaching of evangelical annihilationism, which holds that the wicked dead will be resurrected to face terrible judgment before their extinction.

Jude does not teach annihilationism in verse seven. He teaches that God's judgment of Sodom and Gomorrah furnishes an earthly, temporal example of the final fate of the damned. British church historian Richard J. Bauckham concurs.

> The idea is that the site of the cities . . . a scene of sulfurous devastation, provided ever-present evidence of the reality of divine judgment. . . . According to Philo [a first-century Jewish writer] "even to this day the visible tokens of the indescribable disaster are pointed out in Syria—ruins, cinders, brimstone, smoke and murky flames which continue to rise from the ground as from a fire still smoldering beneath.". . . Jude means that the still burning site of the cities is a warning picture of the eternal fires of hell.[10]

The destruction of Sodom and Gomorrah "became a proverbial object-lesson of God's vengeance on sin: Isa. 1:9; Jer. 23:14; Ezek. 16:48–50; Amos 4:11 . . . Matt. 10:15; 11:24; Rom 9:29."[11] A much worse fate awaits the false teachers of Jude's day and all the unrepentant: the punishment of eternal fire!

Jude 13.

> They [false teachers] are wild waves of the sea, foaming up their shame; wandering stars, for whom blackest darkness has been reserved forever.

Jude has a fondness for triads (groups of three). He begins his epistle by describing believers as those "called . . . loved . . . and kept" (v. 1). He ends it by ascribing glory to the Father through the Son "before all ages, now, and forevermore" (v. 25). In between he often uses triads, including two in verses 12–13, in which he denounces the false teachers.

In the first triad (v. 12) Jude compares the heretics to blemishes (or hidden reefs; the meaning of the word is debated), shepherds, and clouds. The apostates are out of place at believers' love feasts because they are not Christians. Although they profess to shepherd the flock, in reality they care only for themselves. In addition, they make big promises but don't deliver, like "clouds without rain" (v. 12).

In the second triad Jude likens the false teachers to autumn trees, wild waves, and wandering stars. They are trees that should be full of fruit but instead are "without fruit and uprooted," and hence are "twice dead." This tree metaphor has the same meaning as the picture of clouds: the heretics fail to make good on their boasts.

When Jude says that the apostates "are wild waves of the sea, foaming up their shame," he refers to Isaiah 57:20: "The wicked are like the tossing sea, which cannot rest, whose waves cast up mire and mud." J. N. D. Kelly explains the comparison: "Scraps of filth and debris collect in foam and are cast up on the foreshore; and in the same way the false teachers spread everywhere traces of their corruption and impurity."[12]

Finally, Jude calls the false teachers "wandering stars" (v. 13), that is, "stars which go astray from their God-ordained courses . . . misleading those who look to them for guidance."[13] Although they claim to bring spiritual light, they are really blind guides. On Judgment Day, however, their masquerade will be over and God will consign them to "blackest darkness." As in his use of fire imagery (v. 7), when Jude pictures hell in terms of darkness, he echoes the teaching of Jesus (see Matt. 8:12; 22:13; 25:30).

Regardless of the apostates' audacity, their fate is sure. That is why Jude says that the darkness of hell "has been reserved" for them (v. 13). Furthermore, since it has been "reserved *forever*," their deprivation of God's grace will have no end.

Jude uses two different images to depict the fate of the wicked: fire (v. 7) and darkness (v. 13). Moreover, via both of these images he teaches that hell is endless. In verse 7 he speaks of "eternal fire," and in verse 13 he says that condemnation has been reserved for the heretics "forever." In stressing the eternality of hell Jude again follows in the footsteps of the Lord Jesus, who spoke of "eternal fire" (Matt. 18:8; 25:41) and "eternal punishment" (Matt. 25:46).

Revelation

God's Wrath: Revelation 14:9–11

> If anyone worships the beast and his image and receives his mark on the forehead or on the hand, he, too, will drink of the wine of God's fury, which has been poured full strength into the cup of his wrath. He will be tormented with burning sulfur in the presence of the holy angels and of the Lamb. And the smoke of their torment rises for ever and ever. There is no rest day or night for those who worship the beast and his image, or for anyone who receives the mark of his name.

The last book in the canon, the final revelation of Jesus Christ, says much about the doom of the lost. In fact, Revelation 14:9–11 is one of the Bible's two most revealing passages on hell (the other being Matt. 25:31–46). Here an angel proclaims the fate of idolaters: They will drink from the cup of God's wrath. This picture is found in the Old Testament, for example in Isaiah: "Awake, awake! Rise up, O Jerusalem, you who have drunk from the hand of the LORD the cup of his wrath, you who have drained to its dregs the goblet that makes men stagger" (Isa. 51:17). Isaiah likens Jerusalem's experience of God's judgment to getting drunk on strong wine.

It is the same in Revelation 14: those who worship false gods "will drink of the wine of God's fury, which has been poured full strength into the cup of his wrath" (v. 10). This means that they will personally endure God's fierce anger. John's use of the words "fury," "full strength," and "wrath" emphasize the terror of falling into the hands of the living God!

Next, John borrows language from God's judgment of Sodom and Gomorrah: The damned "will be tormented with burning sulfur" (Rev. 14:10; cf. Gen. 19:24). This refutes the annihilationists' claim that the main purpose of fire in judgment is to destroy. To the contrary, its main purpose is to inflict pain, as this text shows. We need not, however, insist that there is literal fire in hell. "Such language . . . must be taken as symbolical of a fearful and final reality which no man can describe."[14]

Shockingly, this torment takes place "in the presence of the . . . Lamb" (Rev. 14:10). Not many Christians think that Christ is present in hell. Nonetheless, he is there, as the word "Lamb" suggests. In fact, John uses the symbol "lamb" to refer to Christ in twenty-seven out of twenty-eight occurrences in Revelation (the exception is 13:11, where the Beast from the earth has "horns like a lamb"). However, Christ does not bring grace to hell, but rather "the wrath of the Lamb" (6:16).

Thus far John paints a dreadful picture of hell. Alas, it is even worse, for he says that "the smoke of their torment rises for ever and ever," signifying that hell's sufferings are endless (v. 11). The church through the ages has taught, especially on the basis of this passage, that hell never ends. Some, however, contend that the church has erred by overlooking John's intended contrast between the fire and the smoke; he does not say that the fire endures forever but that the smoke does. Moreover, they argue, the perpetually rising smoke testifies to God's complete destruction of the wicked.[15]

How are we to evaluate this argument? First, by examining the proposed distinction between fire and smoke. How could smoke rise forever if the fire had used up its fuel? Would not the smoke cease if the fire went out? The distinction is an attempt to get around a difficult text. John does not distinguish fire and smoke. Rather, when he says, "The smoke of their torment rises for ever and ever," he means that the torment of the damned with "burning sulfur" is endless. Indeed, the perpetually rising smoke bears witness to the continual suffering of the lost.

The second reason for rejecting the alleged distinction between fire and smoke is found in the next sentence of verse 11: "There is no rest day or night for those who worship the beast." John explicitly says that the damned will have no relief at any time ("day or night"). The annihilationist interpretation that John means the wicked will find no relief "so long as their suffering lasts"[16] is far from convincing.

I conclude, therefore, that despite attempts to prove otherwise, Revelation 14:9–11 unequivocally teaches that hell entails eternal conscious torment for the lost. In fact, if we had only this passage, we would be obligated to teach the traditional doctrine of hell on the authority of the Word of God.

This obligation raises an important issue. It is dangerous to resort to various maneuvers to avoid aspects of the Bible's teaching that we don't like. A far better course is to submit to the teaching of Scripture, even when that teaching offends us. As one who often struggles to submit to the challenges of God's Word, I call on those Christians who espouse annihilationism to repent and give glory to God by submitting their minds to his truth.

The Lake of Fire and the Second Death

Revelation 20:10, 14–15.

> The devil, who deceived them, was thrown into the lake of burning sulfur, where the beast and the false prophet had been thrown. They will be tormented day and night for ever and ever. . . . Then death and Hades were thrown into the lake of fire. The lake of fire is the second death. If anyone's name was not found written in the book of life, he was thrown into the lake of fire.

Revelation 19:20 supplies background for this passage: The Beast and the False Prophet "were thrown alive into the fiery lake of burning sulfur." In 20:10 Satan also meets his doom, as God casts him into the lake of fire to join the other two. John continues, "They will be tormented day and night for ever and ever." It is plain, therefore, that the Devil, the Beast, and the False Prophet will endure eternal torment.

Attempts to show that being "tormented day and night for ever and ever" signifies annihilation are not persuasive.[17] For example, the assertion that Revelation 20:10 has nothing to do with the fate of lost *human beings* is false for two reasons. First, Jesus taught that unsaved humans suffer the Devil's fate: "Depart from me, you who are cursed, into the eternal fire prepared for the devil" (Matt. 25:41). Second, the verses that follow in Revelation 20 depict resurrected humans being thrown into the lake of fire: "If anyone's name was not found written in the book of life, he was thrown into the lake of fire" (v. 15).

After speaking of Satan's doom, John sees God seated on "a great

white throne" with "the dead, great and small, standing before" him
(vv. 11–12). We know that these people who come before God are
resurrected because John writes of the sea, death, and hades giving up
the dead (v. 13). Since it makes no sense to speak of the sea containing
souls, John must mean that God will raise the bodies of all who died
at sea. In addition, God will raise all who were buried ("hades" here
means the grave). Indeed, God will raise *all* the dead, since the term
"death" covers all those not included in the categories of those who are
buried or who died at sea.

John speaks of hell from the perspectives of divine sovereignty
and human responsibility. In terms of the divine sovereignty, "If
anyone's name was not found written in the book of life, he was
thrown into the lake of fire" (v. 15). "The book of life" is the register
of the city of God, in which all of God's elect are recorded. John also
speaks in terms of human responsibility: "The dead were judged according to what they had done. . . . each person was judged according
to what he had done" (vv. 12–13). The wicked get what they deserve
for their sins—the wrath of God.

When John says that "death and Hades were thrown into the
lake of fire" (v. 14), he indicates that the intermediate state gives way
to the final one. He also does this by revealing that the "lake of fire
is the second death" (v. 14). As death means the separation of the soul
from the body, so the second death denotes the ultimate separation of
the ungodly from their Creator's love. Accordingly, God reunites the
souls of the unsaved dead with their bodies to fit the lost for eternal
punishment. If eternal life entails forever knowing the Father and the
Son (John 17:3), its antithesis, the second death, involves being
deprived of God's fellowship for all eternity.

To summarize: in the span of six verses John teaches that wicked
human beings will share the Devil's fate. This fate, here called "the
lake of fire" and "the second death," is synonymous with what Jesus
called "hell" (*gehenna*). As a faithful servant of Christ, John echoes the
teaching of his Master. Moreover, God deems this terrible truth of
condemnation important enough to be taught in each of the last three
chapters of the book that closes the canon. Having studied the relevant passage from the first of these chapters, we now turn our attention to the other two.

Revelation 21:8.

> The cowardly, the unbelieving, the vile, the murderers, the
> sexually immoral, those who practice magic arts, the idola-
> ters and all liars—their place will be in the fiery lake of
> burning sulfur. This is the second death.

In Revelation 21 John sees "the Holy City, the new Jerusalem"
descending from God (v. 2). Next, John interprets the vision: "Now
the dwelling of God is with men, and he will live with them" (v. 3).
No longer will God dwell temporarily with Israel in tabernacle or
temple. Rather, "From this point on God remains with [all] his people
throughout eternity."[18]

In fact, heaven is God's presence on the new earth in such close
communion with believers that John describes it with the most inti-
mate of human relationships, that between bride and groom and that
between father and children (vv. 2, 7). What will God's presence
mean to his own? "He will wipe every tear from their eyes. There will
be no more death or mourning or crying or pain" (v. 4). God will
personally meet the needs of his people as they have never been met
before; never again will they face death, grief over the loss of loved
ones, sadness, or anguish.

However, not all will experience these joys. Not everyone will
find his or her place in God's family. Many will have another place:
"But the cowardly, the unbelieving, the vile, the murderers, the sexually immoral, those who practice magic arts, the idolaters and all
liars—their place will be in the fiery lake of burning sulfur" (v. 8). Is
it possible to conceive of a greater disparity: the family of God and the
lake of fire?

John's description of the wicked is ugly. They are: "cowardly,"
lacking the courage to stand for God; "unbelieving," rejecting his
truth; "vile," loving what he hates; "murderers," destroying people
made in his image; "sexually immoral," rebelling against his sexual
standards; "practicing magic arts," which he forbids; "idolaters," worshiping other gods; and "liars," lying as a way of life. John paints such
a portrait to show his readers that the damned deserve condemnation.
It is right for a holy and just God to punish sinners.

Graciously, John prefaces these hard words with an invitation: "To him who is thirsty I will give to drink without cost from the spring of the water of life" (v. 6). John desires that unbelievers read his words of woe and repent. In addition, he summons professing believers to persevere so as to overcome and ultimately inherit the kingdom of God (v. 7).

Banishment from the City of God: Revelation 22:15

> Outside are the dogs, those who practice magic arts, the sexually immoral, the murderers, the idolaters and everyone who loves and practices falsehood.

The Bible's last chapter promises joy to all who trust Jesus to atone for their sins: "Blessed are those who wash their robes, that they may have the right to the tree of life and may go through the gates into the city" (Rev. 22:14). Eating of the tree of life means enjoying eternal life in its fullness. Entering the city means having eternal access to the joy of God's presence.

By contrast, "Outside are the dogs, those who practice magic arts, the sexually immoral, the murderers, the idolaters and everyone who loves and practices falsehood" (v. 15). The only characterization of the wicked found here but not in Revelation 21:8 is "dogs." By this term John teaches that "only the redeemed inhabit the holy city, while the wicked, like dogs cowering at the city gates, are excluded from the holy city and find their destiny somewhere in the final order outside."[19]

So, near the end of his prophecy John speaks of unbelievers' banishment from the city of God. Next, however, John tenderly invites people of faith to come: "Whoever is thirsty, let him come; and whoever wishes, let him take the free gift of the water of life" (Rev. 22:17).[20]

Conclusion

Paul, the writer to the Hebrews, Jude, and John in Revelation are faithful disciples of Jesus regarding the fate of the damned. Although they do not go into as much detail as Jesus did, his message of judgment reverberates in their writings.

Paul includes God's wrath as part of the gospel of grace, and thereby sits in judgment on much modern Christian preaching and teaching. If "any interpretation of the New Testament gospel which does not include the wrath of God is an attenuated and apocopated message,"[21] then many messages today are seriously deficient.

Moreover, according to Hebrews, "eternal judgment" (6:1–2) deserves a place in our instruction of new converts. How do our discipleship booklets measure up compared to the apostolic standard? As a former pastor who worked in the area of discipleship, I must answer, "Not very well." Indeed, the apostles' testimony summons us to repentance.

Jude assures his troubled readers that false teachers will not escape judgment. Today, no less than in Jude's day, the church is besieged by heresy. On a recent flight I sat next to a man who told me he was a Christian—in fact, an evangelist. As our conversation progressed, however, I was troubled by aspects of his teaching. And by the time the plane landed, I was saddened by the man's denial of the doctrine of the Trinity and depreciation of grace. Subsequently, I learned that his denomination makes thousands of converts yearly, largely from orthodox Christian churches. This sad tale underscores the need to train new believers in God's truth and to warn them of false teachers. The end of such heretics, converts need to know, is "the punishment of eternal fire" (Jude 7).

The book of Revelation paints some of the most graphic pictures of hell found in the Bible. The wicked will drink from the cup of God's wrath, and be tortured endlessly with burning sulfur (Rev. 14:10–11). They will be thrown into the lake of fire to suffer eternal torment (20:14–15; 21:8). Moreover, they will be excluded forever from the city of God (21:15).

Such pictures of hell take our breath away. Why does the apostle John paint them? First, he, like Jesus and Paul, knows that sinners must realize their plight in order to come to the Savior. For that reason, in the immediate contexts of threats of hell, he graciously offers his readers "the eternal gospel" (Rev. 14:6) and "the water of life" (21:6 and 22:17).

Second, John writes of hell to motivate persecuted Christians to persevere. "This calls for patient endurance on the part of the saints who obey God's commandments and remain faithful to Jesus" (14:12).

Third, John comforts believers by assuring them that they will not suffer the pains of hell. "Blessed are the dead who die in the Lord from now on" (Rev. 14:13). This true happiness contrasts with the eternal torment of the lost (14:10–11). Similarly, John's consolation to the redeemed in verse 13 ("'Yes,' says the Spirit, 'they will rest from their labor'") is the converse of his statement to the damned in verse 11 ("There is no rest day or night"). The Lord calms his people in the same passages where he threatens the unbelieving with damnation in order to move his people to thanksgiving for their deliverance from hell.

Fourth, the judgment passages in Revelation assure Christians of eventual victory. Although persecuted believers, like John's original readers, are tempted to think that the church's prospects are bleak, John assures them that such is not the case. Instead, the Devil and all other enemies of God are heading for the lake of fire. Whereas the Evil One is powerful compared to puny humans, he is nevertheless under the authority of the sovereign God, and is subject to his purpose. In fact, "In the last analysis the Devil has to contribute to that purpose. It is beyond his power to frustrate it. For the original readers of the Revelation that will have been a source of no little comfort. It should provide that for the people of God in all ages."[22]

The apostles, therefore, faithfully proclaimed Jesus' doctrine of hell to those whom they served. As a result, the church possesses rich resources to enable believers to reach out to a needy world with Good News and to equip the saints for the work of the ministry. May God give us grace that we might use those resources—including the doc- trine of eternal punishment—as he intended and for his glory.

NOTES

1. W. G. T. Shedd, *The Doctrine of Endless Punishment* (1885; reprint, Carlisle, Pa.: Banner of Truth, 1986), 12–13.

2. William V. Crockett aptly summarizes the outcome of God's wrath according to Paul: "At the final judgment God no longer is willing to operate on behalf of the wicked. Love would not be concealed in wrath. There would be nothing

but wrath for the wicked. To put it another way, God would no longer 'love' them. His wrath at the end would be final. . . . For Paul *orge* [wrath] is the opposite of love, and once life is over, God's wrath is final" ("Wrath That Endures Forever," *Journal of the Evangelical Theological Society* 34.2 [June 1991]: 210–12).

3. F. F. Bruce, *1 & 2 Thessalonians*, Word Biblical Commentary (Waco, Tex.: Word, 1982), 151; Leon Morris, *The First and Second Epistles to the Thessalonians*, The New International Commentary on the New Testament (Grand Rapids: Eerdmans, 1959), 204–5.

4. Some annihilationists have argued their case from Paul's use of the same word for "destruction" in 1 Thess. 5:3 (see Basil Atkinson, *Life and Immortality* [n.p., n.d], 101; Edward W. Fudge, *The Fire That Consumes* [Houston: Providential Press, 1982], 242). This argument is flawed, however, because Paul writes, "destruction will come on them *suddenly.*" If, therefore, 1 Thess. 5:3 teaches that God annihilates the wicked, he does so at Christ's return and not after the resurrection and punishment of the wicked, as evangelical annihilationists hold.

5. Charles A. Wanamaker, *Commentary on 1 & 2 Thessalonians*, New International Greek Testament Commentary (Grand Rapids: Eerdmans, 1990), 229.

6. Scot McKnight argues that "the emphasis here is on the nature of that final judgment: it is eternal, it is destructive, and it excludes one from the presence of God. Eternal separation from God is the essence of God's punishment on the wicked, as eternal fellowship with God is the essence of God's final deliverance of the faithful. But separation from God's presence must be defined as nonfellowship, not annihilation. In other words, it could be argued that since God is omnipresent, then banishment from his presence means extinction. It is more likely, however, that Paul has in mind an irreversible verdict of eternal nonfellowship with God. A person exists but remains excluded from God's good presence" ("Eternal Consequences or Eternal Consciousness?" in *Through No Fault of Their Own? The Fate of Those Who Have Never Heard*, ed. William V. Crockett and James G. Sigountos [Grand Rapids: Baker, 1991], 155–56).

7. J. I. Packer, *Knowing God* (Downers Grove, Ill.: InterVarsity Press, 1973), 134.

8. For the two main views on the rebellion see Richard J. Bauckham, *Jude, 2 Peter*, Word Biblical Commentary (Waco, Tex.: Word, 1983), 50–53; and Simon J. Kistemaker, *Peter and Jude*, New Testament Commentary (Grand Rapids: Baker, 1987), 377–80.

9. Fudge, *The Fire That Consumes*, 286–87.

10. Bauckham, *Jude, 2 Peter*, 55.

11. J. N. D. Kelly, *A Commentary on the Epistles of Peter and Jude* (Grand Rapids: Baker, 1969), 259.

12. Ibid., 274.

13. Bauckham, *Jude, 2 Peter*, 92.

14. George Eldon Ladd, *A Commentary on the Revelation of John* (Grand Rapids: Eerdmans, 1972), 196.

15. So Stott, in David L. Edwards and John Stott, *Evangelical Essentials: A Liberal-Evangelical Dialogue* (Downers Grove, Ill.: InterVarsity Press, 1988), 318.

16. Fudge, *The Fire That Consumes*, 300. Annihilationists also appeal to the destruction of "Babylon" in Rev. 18:8, 18; 19:3 as proof that annihilation is taught in Rev. 14:11. This argument fails because, in the nature of the case, the city of Babylon cannot survive the creation of the new heaven and new earth (Rev. 21:1), whereas the damned do survive, as Rev. 21:8; 22:15 bear witness.

17. See Atkinson, *Life and Immortality*, 99–100; Fudge, *The Fire That Consumes*, 304; Harold E. Guillebaud, *The Righteous Judge* [n.p., n.d.], 25–26. Guillebaud later concedes that Rev. 20:10 "certainly appears" to "teach the everlasting torment of the trinity of evil," 44.

18. Robert H. Mounce, *The Book of Revelation*, The New International Commentary on the New Testament (Grand Rapids: Eerdmans, 1977), 372.

19. Ladd, *Revelation of John*, 293.

20. I was stimulated in my study of these passages in Revelation by my former Th.M. student Thomas McCort.

21. Ibid., 196.

22. G. R. Beasley–Murray, *Revelation*, The New Century Bible Commentary, rev. ed. (Grand Rapids: Eerdmans, 1978), 298.

6

The Witness of Church History (1): The Early Church Through the Reformation

Until the nineteenth century almost all Christian theologians taught the reality of eternal torment in hell. Here and there, outside the theological mainstream, were some who believed that the wicked would be finally annihilated. . . . Even fewer were the advocates of universal salvation, though these few included some major theologians of the early church. Eternal punishment was firmly asserted in official creeds and confessions of the churches. It must have seemed as indispensable a part of universal Christian belief as the doctrines of the Trinity and the incarnation. Since 1800 this situation has entirely changed, and no traditional Christian doctrine has been so widely abandoned as that of eternal punishment.[1]

This overview by British church historian Richard Bauckham helps us to formulate the main purposes of this chapter and the next.

In this chapter we will seek the reasons for Christianity's near uniformity of belief in eternal conscious torment through the Reformation. In the next chapter we will survey the modern period to learn the causes for the widespread abandonment of belief in what was previously viewed as a cardinal and indispensable doctrine. Here we will consider the chief advocates of the orthodox view of hell in the early church, the Middle Ages, and the Reformation: Tertullian, Augustine, Aquinas, Luther, and Calvin. We will also examine the ideas of two men who departed from orthodoxy: Arnobius, the earliest proponent of annihilationism, and Origen, the most influential defender of universalism.

Tertullian

Tertullian (whose dates are estimated as 160/170–215/220) was a North African convert from paganism who became a theologian and produced the first significant body of Christian literature in Latin. In his writings he defended the faith, taught morals, and refuted false teachings. He is famous for coining theological terms, including the word *Trinity*.

About 208 he wrote *On the Resurrection of the Flesh* to affirm the resurrection against gnostic denials. In chapter 35 of this work he distinguishes the resurrection of the body from the immortality of the soul. They err, he teaches, who say that resurrection is merely another name for the ongoing existence of the soul after death. Rather, Christ would have us "believe that the flesh which has been consigned to the ground, is able in like manner to rise again by the will of the same God."[2]

Tertullian quotes Jesus' saying in Matthew 10:28: "He is rather to be feared, who is able to destroy both body and soul in hell, not those who kill the body, but are not able to hurt the soul." Tertullian, unlike others who think these words refer to Satan, correctly interprets their subject as "the Lord alone." He recognizes the vocabulary of destruction and opposes those who use it to teach the final obliteration of the wicked.

> If, therefore, any one shall violently suppose that the de-
> struction of the soul and the flesh in hell amounts to a final

annihilation of the two substances, and not to their penal treatment (as if they were to be consumed, not punished), let him recollect that the fire of hell is eternal—expressly announced as an everlasting penalty; and let him then admit that it is from this circumstance that this never-ending "killing" is more formidable than a merely human murder, which is only temporal.[3]

Tertullian holds to the orthodox view of hell for several reasons. First, notice how he regards consumption and punishment as mutually exclusive. Annihilationism is to be rejected precisely because it is not punishment. Indeed, it is an alternative to the punishment of eternal torment.

Second, Tertullian regards it as a scriptural given that eternal punishment lasts forever; it is "expressly announced as an everlasting penalty." On this basis he appeals to his readers to understand the word "destroy" in Matthew 10:28 figuratively—as a "never-ending 'killing'"—rather than literally—as an extinction of being.

Third, a little later, Tertullian points out what he considers the absurdity of annihilationism.

It would be most absurd if the flesh should be raised up and destined to "the killing of hell," in order to be put an end to, when it might suffer such an annihilation (more directly) if not raised again at all. A pretty paradox, to be sure, that an essence must be refitted with life, in order that it may receive that annihilation which has already in fact accrued to it![4]

Tertullian regards annihilationism as being inconsistent with Christian theology and as hopelessly confused. He chides it for seeking to unite two incompatible things: the belief that life ends at death and the Christian doctrine of the resurrection of the dead.

Elsewhere in his writings Tertullian positively sets forth his belief in eternal life and eternal punishment. He does this in his *Apology*, a work in which he argues for the superiority of Christianity over heathen philosophy: "The worshippers of God will be with God for ever, clothed with the proper substance of eternity; but the profane and all who are not wholly devoted to God, in the punishment of fire which is just as eternal."[5]

Here Tertullian draws a parallel between the eternity of bliss for the righteous and the eternity of sorrow for the unrighteous. In so doing, this early church father clearly affirms the everlasting punishment of the wicked.

Annihilationists have sometimes accused Tertullian of merely deducing the doctrine of eternal punishment from his belief in the immortality of the soul.[6] However, such an accusation is unjustified, as his arguments above demonstrate.

Origen

Origen (whose approximate dates are 185–254), born of Christian parents in Egypt, demonstrated such ability that he became the head of a catechetical school at the age of eighteen and later became a brilliant theologian. He studied Hebrew and Greek manuscripts of the Bible, produced biblical commentaries, defended the faith, and wrote a systematic summary of Christian doctrine. In spite of his marvelous accomplishments, he is perhaps most remembered as the father of universalism and was judged heretical after his death.

In *Against Celsus*, written before 249, Origen countered the attacks on Christianity set forth in *The True Doctrine* by an educated Greek named Celsus. In response to Celsus' mockery that Christians say "God comes down bringing fire like a torturer," Origen admits that Scripture says "our God is a consuming fire." Nevertheless, when we inquire what is fit to be consumed by God, "we say that as fire God consumes evil and the actions resulting from it." Origen holds that the fires of hell are purifying.

> So also He enters "like the fire of a smelting-furnace" to mould the rational nature which has been filled by the lead of evil and other impure substances which adulterate the soul's golden or silver nature, so to speak. . . . since he makes the evil which has permeated the whole soul to disappear.[7]

Writing as one philosopher to another, Origen admits to Celsus that prudence must be exercised in handling the deeper things of the faith, lest uneducated people misunderstand them. These people read the Bible on the surface, fear everlasting punishment, and are thereby restrained from plunging headlong into depravity.

> It is risky to commit to writing the explanation of these matters, because the multitude do not require any more instruction than that punishment is to be inflicted upon sinners. It is not of advantage to go on to truths which lie behind it because there are people who are scarcely re-strained by fear of everlasting punishment from the vast flood of evil.[8]

One of the "truths which lie behind" the Bible's doctrine of judgment and which is accessible to spiritual interpreters is that, through God, "punishments . . . are transformed into the means by which certain souls are purified through torment."[9]

Written earlier, Origen's systematic theology, *On First Principles*, provides a framework for understanding the remedial punishment he spoke about in *Against Celsus*. Each individual's fate is only properly understood, Origen insists, in light of the consummation: "The end of the world and the consummation will come when every soul shall be visited with the penalties due for its own sins."[10]

All these penalties will be paid eventually, however, for "the goodness of God through Christ will restore his entire creation to one end, even his enemies being conquered and subdued." This conquest and subduing does not involve eternal punishment, or even annihilation. Rather, it involves the ultimate restitution (*apocatastasis*) of all things. "For the word subjection, when used of our subjection to Christ, implies the salvation, proceeding from Christ, of those who are subject."[11]

The order and harmony of God's original creation, therefore, will be restored at the end:

> For the end is always like the beginning; as therefore there is one end of all things, so we must understand that there is

one beginning of all things, and as there is one end of many things, so from one beginning arise many differences and varieties, which in their turn are restored, through God's goodness, through their subjection to Christ and their unity with the Holy Spirit, to one end, which is like the beginning.[12]

Though space prohibits us from thoroughly exploring Origen's system, two additional aspects deserve mention: (1) his speculation of successive cycles of worlds in which every member of the human race will ultimately choose God, and (2) his emphasis on the freedom of the will, by virtue of which all will eventually make the right choice.

How are we to evaluate Origen's vision of all things coming from God in the beginning and returning to him in the end? Despite his efforts to prove it from Scripture, "the final unity of all things with God is more Platonic than biblical in inspiration."[13] His theology was greatly shaped by his commitment to revived Platonic philosophy. This commitment influenced each doctrine, in this case casting a Christian view of last things in terms of the Platonic idea of flow and return via purifying punishments.[14]

In the following context Origen once again discusses the biblical language of "eternal fire." Calling God the physician of our souls, and sins our spiritual ills, Origen writes, "God our physician, in his desire to wash away the ills of our souls, which they have brought on themselves through a variety of sins and crimes, makes use of penal remedies of a similar sort, even the infliction of a punishment of fire on those who have lost their soul's health."[15]

In fact, this purifying fire burns within the soul, producing interior anguish.

> Every sinner kindles for himself the flame of his own fire. . . .
> Of this fire the food and material are our sins. . . . so when
> the soul has gathered within itself a multitude of evil deeds
> and an abundance of sins, at the requisite time the whole
> mass of evil boils up into punishment and is kindled into
> penalties; at which time also the mind or conscience . . . will

see exposed before its eyes a kind of history of its evil
deeds. . . . Then the conscience is harassed and pricked by
its own stings, and becomes an accuser and witness against
itself.[16]

To summarize, already in the third century one of the church's
brightest minds had concluded that all of the wicked will ultimately
be restored to God's favor. Although these teachings were condemned
in the anathemas of Emperor Justinian in 540, and were repudiated by
Augustine, Aquinas, Luther, and Calvin, Origen greatly influenced
the Christian tradition that followed. His influence was greater in the
long term than immediately, however, and during the Middle Ages
only John Scotus Erigena taught universalism. Nevertheless, Origen
continues to affect theologians to this day.

Arnobius

Arnobius was a teacher of rhetoric in North Africa and a convert from
paganism, whose dates are unknown, but did embrace A.D. 304–10.
Friends and foes alike describe him as a less-than-careful thinker.

In *Against the Pagans* Arnobius defended the Christian faith by
exposing the folly of pagan worship and mythology. In this work's
second of seven divisions (called "books") he talks about "hell and fires
which cannot be quenched." He shows great admiration for Plato,
who held correctly that the souls of the wicked "are cast into rivers
blazing with masses of flame, and loathsome from their foul abysses."
But Arnobius rejected Plato's doctrine of the immortality of the soul.
When souls are consigned to the fires of hell,

They are cast in, and being annihilated, pass away vainly in
everlasting destruction. . . . this is man's real death, this
which leaves nothing behind. For that which is seen by the
eyes is [only] a separation of soul from body, not the last
end—annihilation: this, I say, is man's real death, when
souls which know not God shall be consumed in long-
protracted torment with raging fire. . . .[17]

One of two fates awaits human beings: they will "perish if they have not known God," or "be delivered from death if they have given heed to his threats and [proffered] favours."[18]

At first glance, a later passage in *Against the Pagans* seems to contradict what we have just read.

> Your interests are in jeopardy, —the salvation, I mean of your souls; and unless you give yourselves to know the Supreme God, a cruel death awaits you when freed from the bonds of the body, not bringing sudden annihilation, but destroying by the bitterness of its grievous and long-protracted punishment.[19]

Does he here deny what he formerly affirmed, that the wicked will be annihilated in hell? Is this evidence of his not being a careful thinker? The answer to both questions is no. This passage is reconcilable with the preceding if we lay emphasis on his words "*sudden* annihilation." Apparently he here teaches that a "grievous and long-protracted punishment" sometimes precedes sinners' final obliteration. He points to a way to combine two ideas: (1) the Christian doctrine of the punishment of the ungodly and (2) annihilationism. The eradication of the wicked follows their judgment. Regardless, he can rightly be accused of lacking theological precision in his failure to take into account the resurrection of the body.

Here, in the early fourth century, is the first clear expression of annihilationism. Arnobius rejects the immortality of the soul and understands the biblical terms for the final fate of the wicked, such as "everlasting destruction," "perishing," and "death," to speak of their being burned up in the fires of hell. This final consumption, moreover, since it follows the punishment of unbelievers, is compatible with that punishment.

Augustine

Augustine of Hippo in North Africa (354–430) was the preeminent father of the early church. He excelled in commenting on Scripture, preaching, defending the faith, and penning theological works. His influence upon subsequent Christianity is incalculable.

After the Goths had captured and sacked Rome in 410, pagans blamed Rome's defeat on the Christians' infiltration of the city. Over a period of fourteen years Augustine composed his masterpiece, *The City of God* (413–26), to answer these pagan attacks on the Christian religion. He devoted book twenty-one of *City of God* to the fate of the wicked.

Enemies of the faith allege the impossibility of the resurrection of unbelievers and their everlasting punishment as taught by Christian doctrine. Augustine has two answers to these allegations. First, the answer to those who demand a rational explanation is that it is "the will of Almighty God. For God is certainly called 'Almighty' for one reason only; that he has the power to do whatever he wills." God's omnipotence enables him to raise and punish the ungodly. Augustine's second answer is that God, who is able to do these things, wills to do them. We know that because God has said so in his holy Word. "Therefore, what God said through the mouth of his prophet, about the eternal punishment of the damned, will come true; it will most certainly come true that 'their worm will never die and their fire will not go out.'"[20]

Augustine wrestles with educated pagans' attacks against the justice of eternal punishment. He offers two answers to the objection that eternal retribution is disproportionate to sins committed in time. First, the length of time it takes to commit a crime does not determine its punishment. In fact, "The offenses which are punished by the longest possible retribution are committed in the shortest possible time." No one argues that the punishments of the guilty should be limited to the time taken to commit homicide, adultery, or sacrilege. No! The enormity of these crimes is measured "by the magnitude of their wickedness and impiety."[21]

His second answer builds on the first.

Now the reason why eternal punishment appears harsh and unjust to human sensibilities, is that in this feeble condition of those sensibilities under their condition of mortality man lacks the sensibility of the highest and purest wisdom, the sense which should enable him to feel the gravity of the wickedness in the first act of disobedience.[22]

By disobeying his Maker, Adam "merited eternal evil, in that he destroyed in himself a good that might have been eternal." If we could escape the limitations of our own sinfulness, and from God's perspective could fathom the abomination of the first man's sin, we would accept the justice of eternal punishment.[23]

Augustine rejects the Platonic notion that "all punishments are directed towards purification." He admits that some punishments in this life are purificatory. But "penalties inflicted on those whose life is not improved thereby or is even made worse, are not purificatory." And it is common knowledge that such punishments occur daily. These "punishments, whether temporal or eternal, are imposed on every person in accordance with the treatment he is to receive from God's providence . . . in retribution for sins."[24]

Augustine reserves his strongest words for those who, like Origen, deny eternal punishment. He reminds his readers that "the Church has rejected Origen's teaching, and not without good reason." Augustine, a former teacher of rhetoric, puts his training to use by showing where the supposed "tenderness of heart" of Origen leads. In the name of compassion he claims that the miseries of judgment will be temporal, "whereas the felicity of all men, who are released after a shorter or longer period, will be everlasting."[25]

Augustine urges sarcastically, "Let the fountain of compassion be deepened and enlarged until it extends as far as the evil angels." With tongue in cheek he laments that "our friends cannot bring themselves to stretch out further in their compassion until they reach the liberation of the Devil himself! Nevertheless, if anyone could bring himself to go so far he would outdo them in compassion!"[26]

Augustine withstands "those who in their own defence attempt to oppose God's words with what purports to be a higher degree of compassion." He is convinced that denying eternal retribution is repudiating God's truth.[27]

As usual, he offers arguments for his position. He regards the teaching of our Lord in Matthew's gospel as especially clear and convincing. When Jesus said, "Out of my sight, accursed ones, into the eternal fire which is prepared for the Devil and his angels" (Matt. 25:41), he gave "a clear indication that the Devil and his angels are to burn in eternal fire." And we are not left to guess how long the Devil's punishment will last, for the book of Revelation tells us: "The Devil, who seduced them, was consigned to the lake of fire and sulphur. . . . and they will be tortured day and night for ever and ever" (Rev. 20:10).[28]

Referring to the two passages just cited, Augustine reasons:

"Eternal" in the first passage is expressed in the second by "for ever and ever", and those words have only one meaning in scriptural usage: the exclusion of any temporal end. And this is why there cannot conceivably be found any reason better founded or more evident for the fixed and immutable conviction of true religion that the Devil and his angels will never attain to justification and to the life of the saints. There can be, I say, no stronger reason than this: that the Scriptures, which never deceive, say that God has not spared them.[29]

Remember, in Matthew 25:41 Jesus likened the fate of the "accursed" humans to that of the Devil and his angels. Augustine's conclusion, therefore, is compelling: unrepentant sinners will suffer everlasting condemnation.

Augustine is not through with Matthew 25, however. He next points out that "Christ, in the very same passage, included both punishment and life in one and the same sentence when he said, 'So those people will go into eternal punishment, while the righteous will go into eternal life'" (Matt. 25:46). Augustine contends:

If both are "eternal", it follows necessarily that either both are to be taken as long-lasting but finite, or both as endless and perpetual. The phrases "eternal punishment" and "eternal life" are parallel and it would be absurd to use them in one and the same sentence to mean: "Eternal life will be infinite, while eternal punishment will have an end." Hence, because the eternal life of the saints will be endless, the eternal punishment also, for those condemned to it, will assuredly have no end.[30]

It is easy to see why Augustine is regarded as one of the church's greatest theologians. We would do well to imitate his esteem for Holy Scripture, his toiling to understand its meaning, and his willingness to submit his mind and heart to its teachings. In addition, we must heed his admonitions lest we follow the pattern of those who "while not slighting the authority of the sacred Scriptures . . . nevertheless interpret them wrongly and suppose that what is to happen will be not what the Scriptures speak of, but what they themselves would like to happen."[31]

Thomas Aquinas

Thomas Aquinas (1224–74) was the greatest philosopher and theologian of the medieval church. He generated an enormous literary output, although his work at first did not receive the acclaim it eventually would. His two most famous works were the *Summa Contra Gentiles* and the *Summa Theologiae*.

The former, written during 1261–64, was a manual designed to equip missionaries to understand and defend the faith. Aquinas addresses the topic of punishments in chapters 140–46 of the *Summa Contra Gentiles*: Because God is just, he punishes or rewards people's actions with the correct degree of punishment or reward. In chapter 144 he affirms the endless punishment of the wicked.

> We set aside the error of those who say that the punishments of the wicked are to be ended at some time. In fact, this view seems to have originated from the theory of certain philosophers who said that all punishments are for purposes of purification and so are to terminate at some time.[32]

This, of course, was the view of Origen. Thomas says that this view seems "persuasive on the basis of human custom. Indeed, the punishments under human law are applied for the remedy of vices, and so they are like medicines." This argument is not as convincing as it first appears, however, "for even according to human laws some people are punished with death, not, of course, for their own improvement, but for that of others." So too, God, for the maintaining of the divine government, inflicts a penalty that is not remedial, even eternal punishment on the wicked.[33]

The *Summa Theologiae*, begun in 1265 and still not complete at the time of Aquinas's death in 1273, was his most outstanding work. In a section dealing with guilt he again argues for eternal punishment. To those who claim that everlasting punishment is out of proportion with sins committed in time, Aquinas has an apt reply. "The duration of a punishment does not match the duration of the act of sin but of its stain; as long as this lasts a debt of punishment remains. The severity of the punishment matches the seriousness of the sin."[34]

This prompts another question: What makes sins committed in this life so serious that they deserve a never-ending penalty? Once more Aquinas has a ready response:

> The magnitude of the punishment matches the magnitude of the sin. . . . Now a sin that is against God is infinite; the higher the person against whom it is committed, the graver the sin—it is more criminal to strike a head of state than a private citizen—and God is of infinite greatness. Therefore an infinite punishment is deserved for a sin committed against him.[35]

Aquinas makes a distinction that is of great importance for the history of the doctrine of hell. The pains of hell involve both "the pain of loss" (*poena damni*) and "the pain of sense" (*poena sensus*).[36] The former is the deprivation of the joyful vision of God, while the latter is the suffering of positive punishments in body and soul. In the *Summa Contra Gentiles* he concisely sums up these two aspects of the sufferings of the damned: "Those who sin against God are not only to be punished by their exclusion from perpetual happiness, but also by the experience of something painful."[37]

Aquinas notes that the Bible itself reflects this distinction: "Divine Scripture not only threatens sinners with exclusion from glory, but also with affliction from other things. For it is said, in Matthew (25:41): 'Depart from me you cursed into everlasting fire, which was prepared for the devil and his angels.'"[38] Jesus' commanding the damned to depart from his presence is the pain of loss; his ordering them into the eternal fires of hell is the pain of sense.

The most eminent of medieval theologians joins Tertullian and Augustine in teaching the orthodox view of the fate of the wicked. So do the major Reformers, as we shall see.

Luther

Martin Luther (1483–1546) was the father of the Reformation. His impact on history can be measured by the incredible fact that "in most big libraries, books by and about Martin Luther occupy more shelf room than those concerned with any other human being except Jesus of Nazareth."[39]

Luther views hell both as a present and a future reality. Already in the present God strikes sinners with the pains of hell through their bad consciences: "Everyone carries his own hell with him wherever he is, as long as he does not feel the final disasters of death and God's wrath."[40]

In addition, Luther agrees with Tertullian, Augustine, and Aquinas that the future destiny of the wicked involves eternal punishment, as we learn from Luther's commentary on Psalm 21:

> The fiery oven is ignited merely by the unbearable appearance of God and endures eternally. For the Day of Judgment will not last for a moment only but will stand throughout eternity and will thereafter never come to an end. Constantly the damned will be judged, constantly they will suffer pain, and constantly they will be a fiery oven, that is, they will be tortured within by supreme distress and tribulation.[41]

Hell's torments will be worse than anyone could imagine, as Luther asserts in his exposition of Jonah 2:3: "It is of little importance whether a person holds hell to be what men now paint or picture it to be. No doubt it now is, and will be, far worse than anyone is able to describe, picture, or think it to be." In fact, Luther preaches, this punishment is so terrible that "no one understands but the damned, who feel it." He therefore warns his unrepentant hearers, "You will suffer more than words can tell and thoughts can grasp."[42]

In one sense hell is so terrible because it entails separation from God's grace. This is the meaning of the biblical image of darkness used to describe the fate of the lost, as Luther explains in a sermon preached in his home in 1533. Those who have heard the gospel but have not believed "must lie in darkness, cut off from God's light, that is, from all comfort, in eternal torment, anguish, and sadness, so that they will nevermore see one spark of light."[43]

Yet, in another sense it is God's very presence that makes hell so dreadful. Although he is not present in grace and blessing, he is present in holy wrath, as Luther warns the readers of his commentary on the Psalms: "Not as though the ungodly see God and His appearance as the godly will see Him; but they will feel the power of His presence, which they will not be able to bear, and yet will be forced to bear." Indeed, "This chief and unbearable punishment God will inflict with His mere appearance, that is, with the revelation of His wrath."[44]

Luther is not surprised, therefore, that evildoers resent hell. In his comments on Psalm 90 he tells how even death is no escape from God's sovereign power: "Therefore, man, as he is by nature, cannot do otherwise than become obsessed with fear and be indignant at the thought that after death God, of whom one must be afraid, still rules over us."[45]

Nevertheless, for the people of God hell can actually be the cause of praise for God's justice, as Luther writes to his ailing Christian prince, Frederick the Wise, in 1520.

> Since God is a just Judge, we must love and laud His justice and thus rejoice in God even when He miserably destroys the wicked in body and soul; for in all this His high and inexpressible justice shines forth. And so even hell, no less than heaven, is full of God and the highest Good. For the justice of God is God Himself; and God is the highest Good.

Therefore even as His mercy, so His justice or judgment must be loved, praised, and glorified above all things.[46]

Thankfully, Christians have a greater reason to praise God—he has conquered their enemies, hell included. Speaking of the words of institution of the Lord's Supper, Luther says, "For him who believes in this all sins are forgiven by such a father and he is a child of life and has conquered hell and death."[47]

This victory is ours, Luther insists, because God has delivered believers through the work of his Son, who "was made a curse for us" (Gal. 3:13) and was punished with our punishment (Isa. 53:5). Christ, therefore, suffered the pains of hell for us, in physical death and "also in the anxiety and terror of a frightened conscience, which feels God's eternal wrath as though it would be forsaken and rejected by God for all eternity."[48] As a result, Luther teaches in his *Small Catechism*, every Christian enjoys the privilege of believing "that God is truly our Father and we are truly his children."[49]

Calvin

John Calvin (1509–64) was the leader of the Reformed branch of the Reformation. Although he was a faithful pastor, as well as a gifted preacher and biblical commentator, he is best known for his systematic theology, *The Institutes of the Christian Religion*. In chapter 25 of book 3 of the *Institutes* Calvin takes up the matter of the fate of unbelievers. He recognizes that Scripture uses figurative language to describe the terrible suffering of the damned:

> Now, because no description can deal adequately with the gravity of God's vengeance against the wicked, their torments and tortures are figuratively expressed to us by physical things, that is, by darkness, weeping, and gnashing of teeth (Matt. 8:12; 22:13), unquenchable fire (Matt. 3:12; Mark 9:43; Isa. 66:24), an undying worm gnawing at the heart (Isa. 66:24). By such expressions the Holy Spirit certainly intended to confound all our senses with dread.[50]

Calvin further recounts the pains of hell by endorsing a distinction, made by Aquinas before him, between "the pain of loss" (*poena damni*) and "the pain of sense" (*poena sensus*). You will remember that "the pain of loss" involves forfeiture of the blessed vision of God, while "the pain of sense" involves positive punishments in body and soul.

> As by such details we should be enabled in some degree to conceive the lot of the wicked, so ought we especially to fix our thoughts upon this: how wretched it is to be cut off from all fellowship with God. And not that only but so to feel his sovereign power against you that you cannot escape being pressed by it.[51]

"Being cut off from all fellowship with God" is the pain of loss; feeling "his sovereign power against you" is the pain of sense. Together they depict unspeakable misery.

On that day evildoers also will find no place of escape from the wrath of God almighty, for "they to whom the Lord will openly show his wrath will feel heaven, earth, sea, living beings, and all that exists aflame, as it were, with dire anger against them, and armed to destroy them." This is because God will use the creation as his tool to bring woe to the unrighteous.[52]

Even worse, this woe knows no relief, as Calvin maintains via a rhetorical question: "What and how great is this, to be eternally and unceasingly besieged by him?" Calvin, therefore, as the orthodox before him, holds to the everlasting damnation of the lost.[53] Again, the eternity of hell's sufferings corresponds to the eternity of Christ's glory, as Calvin explains in his commentary on 2 Thessalonians 1:9.

> The phrase which he adds in apposition explains the nature of the punishment which he had mentioned—it is eternal punishment and death which has no end. The perpetual duration of this death is proved from the fact that its opposite is the glory of Christ. This is eternal and has no end. Hence the violent nature of that death will never cease.[54]

In light of these awful truths we would all despair were it not for Christ. And it is to Christ that Calvin directs us in his comments on John 3:16.

> Christ brought life because the heavenly Father does not wish the human race that He loves to perish. . . . The outstanding thing about our faith is that it delivers us from eternal destruction. . . . By it we receive Christ as He is given to us by the Father—the one who has freed us from the condemnation of eternal death and made us heirs of eternal life by expiating our sins through the sacrifice of His death, so that nothing shall prevent God acknowledging us as His children.[55]

Just as Luther had done before him, Calvin regarded hell as serving the glory of God. That is evident from Calvin's comments on 1 Corinthians 15:28: "But when Christ has carried out the judgement which the Father has entrusted to Him, and overthrown Satan and all the disobedient, then the glory of God will be seen in their destruction."[56]

Conclusion

This concludes our survey of the history of the doctrine of hell from the early church through the Reformation. Although space prevents us from examining the ideas of other figures, we have studied the views of the most important ones.

We have confirmed the truth of the quotation with which this chapter began: eternal punishment was the predominant view of the church through the time of the Reformation. Tertullian, Augustine, Aquinas, Luther, and Calvin stand united in teaching that the torments of the damned never end. Why do they share this conviction? Because they are persuaded that Holy Scripture teaches this terrible doctrine, and so they submit their minds, wills, and emotions to this teaching. May God grant us the courage to do the same.

We have witnessed two defectors from orthodoxy. The first,

Origen, was one of the most intelligent people in the history of the church. How are we to account for his teaching that ultimately all will be saved? Was it due to his painstaking study of the Bible? No, Origen's universalism was the product of the Platonic philosophy which had captured his mind. Under the influence of this philosophy he reached unbiblical conclusions in a number of areas, including the fate of the wicked.[57]

The other defector is Arnobius. He is included here because a better representative of annihilationism could not be found in the early church, Middle Ages, or Reformation. He does not make much appeal to the Bible, but that may be due to his purposes in writing his defense of the faith, *Against the Pagans*. His theological argumentation is not strong, but that doesn't mean that there are no good arguments for annihilationism. It does mean, however, that there are no good arguments for it in the period we have studied.

In the next chapter we extend our study of the history of the doctrine of hell into the modern period.

NOTES

1. Richard J. Bauckham, "Universalism: A Historical Survey," *Themelios* 4.2 (January 1979): 48.
2. Alexander Roberts and James Donaldson, eds., *The Ante-Nicene Fathers* (reprint; Grand Rapids: Eerdmans, 1973), 3:570. For an analysis of Tertullian's eschatology see Jaroslav Pelikan, "The Eschatology of Tertullian," *Church History* 21 (1952): 108–22.
3. Ibid.
4. Ibid., 571.
5. Henry Bettenson, ed. and trans., *The Early Christian Fathers* (London: Oxford University, 1976), 160; (cf. Tertullian, *Apologeticus*, 48).
6. So Edward W. Fudge, *The Fire That Consumes* (Houston: Providential Press, 1982), 336–38.
7. Origen, *Contra Celsum,* trans. Henry Chadwick (Cambridge: Cambridge University Press, 1965), 191–92 (4:13).
8. Ibid., 341 (6:26).
9. Ibid.
10. Origen, *On First Principles*, trans. G. W. Butterworth (Gloucester, Mass.: Peter Smith, 1973), 52 (6:1).
11. Ibid., 52–53 (6:1–2).
12. Ibid., 53 (6:2).
13. Bauckham, "Universalism: A Historical Survey," 49.

14. See J. N. D. Kelly, *Early Christian Doctrines*, 2d ed. (New York: Harper & Row, 1960), 469–74 for a summary of Origen's eschatology.

15. *On First Principles*, 143 (2.10.6).

16. *On First Principles*, 142 (2.10.4). For a rejection of the popular view that Origen taught the salvation of the Devil and a questioning of whether he clearly held to universalism, see Frederick W. Norris, "Universal Salvation in Origen and Maximus," *Universalism and the Doctrine of Hell*, ed. Nigel M. de S. Cameron, (Grand Rapids: Baker, 1992), 35–72.

17. Hamilton Bryce and Hugh Campbell, trans., *The Seven Books of Arnobius Adversus Gentes*, Ante–Nicene Christian Library, vol. 19; Edinburgh: T & T Clark, 1871), 79–81 (2:14).

18. Ibid., 80 (2:14).

19. Ibid., 130 (2:61).

20. Augustine, *The City of God*, ed. David Knowles (Penguin Books, 1972), 977, 983 (21.7, 9).

21. Ibid., 987–88 (21.11).

22. Ibid., 988 (21.12).

23. Ibid., 989 (21.12).

24. Ibid., 989–91 (21.13). Augustine here lays the groundwork for the doctrine of purgatory when he allows that some by suffering punishment after death will escape "the eternal chastisement of the world to come." Cf. his misunderstanding of Matt. 12:32 in 1003 (21.24).

25. Ibid., 995 (21.17).

26. Ibid.

27. Ibid., 1002 (21.24).

28. Ibid., 1000–1001 (21.23).

29. Ibid., 1001 (21.23).

30. Ibid., 1001–2 (21.23). Philip E. Hughes (*The True Image: The Origin and Destiny of Man in Christ* [Grand Rapids: Eerdmans, 1989], 403) mishandles Augustine's argument by reducing his contrast between "eternal life" and "eternal punishment" to one between "eternal life" and "eternal death."

31. *City of God*, 1021 (21.27).

32. Thomas Aquinas, *On the Truth of the Catholic Faith, Summa Contra Gentiles*, trans. Vernon J. Bourke, Bk. 3, Providence, Pt. 2 (Garden City, N.J.: Doubleday, 1956), 216 (144.8).

33. Ibid., 216–17 (144.9–11).

34. *Summa Theologiae*, Blackfriars (New York: McGraw-Hill, 1974), Ia2ae. 27.

35. Ibid., 25.

36. Ibid.

37. *On the Truth of the Catholic Faith*, 218.

38. Ibid., 219.

39. John M. Todd, *Luther: A Life* (New York: Crossroad, 1982), xvi; cited in James M. Kittelson, *Luther the Reformer* (Minneapolis: Augsburg, 1986), 13.

40. Cited by Paul Althaus, *The Theology of Martin Luther* (Philadelphia: Fortress,

1966), 177.

41. Ewald M. Plass, *What Luther Says*, 3 vols. (St. Louis: Concordia, 1959), 2:627.

42. Ibid., 2:625–26, 627.

43. Ibid., 2:627.

44. Ibid., 2:626–27.

45. Ibid., 2:628.

46. Ibid.

47. Cited by Hans Schwarz, "Luther's Understanding of Heaven and Hell," in *Interpreting Luther's Legacy*, ed. Fred W. Meuser and Stanley D. Schneider (Minneapolis: Augsburg, 1969), 89.

48. Quoted in Althaus, *Theology of Martin Luther*, 205.

49. *The Book of Concord*, ed. and trans. Theodore G. Tappert (Philadelphia: Fortress, 1959), 346.

50. John Calvin, *Institutes of the Christian Religion*, ed. John T. McNeill, trans. Ford Lewis Battles, The Library of Christian Classics, vols. 20–21 (Philadelphia: Westminster, 1960), 20:1007 (3.25.12).

51. Ibid., *Institutes* 20:1007–8 (3.25.12).

52. Ibid., *Institutes* 20:1008 (3.25.12).

53. Ibid.

54. D. W. Torrance and T. F. Torrance, eds., *Calvin's New Testament Commentaries: The Epistles of Paul to the Romans and Thessalonians* (Grand Rapids: Eerdmans, 1959), 392.

55. D. W. Torrance and T. F. Torrance, eds., *Calvin's New Testament Commentaries: The Gospel According to St. John 1–10.* (Grand Rapids: Eerdmans, 1959), 73–75.

56. D. W. Torrance and T. F. Torrance, eds., *Calvin's New Testament Commentaries: The First Epistle of Paul to the Corinthians* (Grand Rapids: Eerdmans, 1959), 328.

57. For a perceptive evaluation of the influence of philosophy on Origen's universalism, see Jerry Walls, "Universalism in Origen's First Principles," *The Asbury Seminarian* (April 1981):3–13.

7

The Witness of Church History (2): The Modern Period

Let me say again, as a matter of perfect honesty, that, if the doctrine of eternal punishment was clearly and unmistakably taught on every leaf of the Bible, and on every leaf of all the Bibles of all the world, I could not believe a word of it. I should appeal from these misconceptions of even the seers and the great men to the infinite and eternal Good, who only is God, and who only on such terms could be worshiped.[1]

These words, uttered by M. J. Savage in his book *Life Beyond Death* in 1899, would have been considered blasphemous if spoken by a professing Christian at any time prior to the eighteenth century. As we saw in the previous chapter, there was a uniformity of belief in the early church, Middle Ages, and Reformation concerning the fate of the wicked. Christians nearly unanimously confessed that the unsaved suffer endless punishment.

In this chapter we will study the roots of the modern abandonment of belief in the traditional doctrine of hell. Ultimately, this abandonment can be traced to intellectual movements in eighteenth-century England, France, and Germany. These diverse and complex movements had this in common—they exalted human reason. The term "Enlightenment," especially as used to describe the German movement, captures the essence of them all. Immanuel Kant gave this classic definition in 1793:

> Enlightenment is man's release from his self-incurred tutelage. Tutelage is man's inability to make use of his understanding without direction from another. Self-incurred is this tutelage when its cause lies not in lack of reason but in lack of resolution and courage to use it without direction from another. *Sapere aude!* "Have courage to use your own reason!"—that is the motto of enlightenment.[2]

Why did some figures hold to orthodoxy (Jonathan Edwards, E. B. Pusey, and W. G. T. Shedd), while others questioned it (F. D. Maurice and F. W. Farrar) and still others spurned it (William Whiston and Friedrich Schleiermacher)? A survey of the key representatives of those views will help us answer that question.

William Whiston

William Whiston (1667–1752) was a mathematician and scientist, best known today as the translator of Josephus. He was overshadowed by his more famous friends John Locke, Isaac Newton, and Samuel Clarke. All four of these early scientists rejected Christ's deity and the doctrine of eternal torment. We include Whiston here, and not his more prominent friends, because he alone had the courage of conviction to make his beliefs public; consequently, we know more about his views.[3]

Whiston succeeded Newton as professor of mathematics at Cambridge but in 1710 was expelled from the University for his defective view of Christ. (Note the difference in theological climate between the early eighteenth century and our day—we cannot imagine a university *theology* professor being dismissed for holding an unorthodox view of Christ, let alone a mathematics professor.) Although this resulted in financial hardship, it gave him time to propagate his religious ideas. He attempted to restore primitive Christianity by studying the Scriptures and Christian writers before the Council of Nicea (A.D. 325). Consequently, he rejected the formulations of later councils, including the definitive Christological conclusions reached at Chalcedon in 451. The result was his espousing Arianism, an early heresy that held that Christ was not equal with God but was his first creature.

In 1740 Whiston wrote *The Eternity of Hell Torments Considered,* in which he explains away the threats of eternal punishment by claiming that the word traditionally translated "eternal" (*aionios*) means only age-long. In so doing he suggests a novel interpretation of the parallelism in Matthew 25:46, "Then they will go away to eternal punishment, but the righteous to eternal life." He claims that the life of the righteous and the torments of the wicked are both age-long. Although the bliss of the godly will last longer than the suffering of the damned, it too is limited. Not surprisingly, this shocked his contemporaries.[4]

Whiston finds the "astonishing love of God" shown at Calvary

> absolutely inconsistent with these common but barbarous and savage opinions. . . . that the torments, the exquisite torments of these most numerous and most miserable creatures, are determined without the least pity, or relenting, or bowels of compassion in their Creator, to be in everlasting fire, and in the flames of Hell; without abatement, or remission, for endless ages of ages.[5]

Whiston replaces this hated doctrine with the following (in the words of D. P. Walker):

> At death all souls go to Hades, which is inside the earth, where until the resurrection and Last Judgment they have a chance of repentance and amendment. After judgment, the

just go to their long, but not eternal, life of bliss, and the still
unrepentant wicked to a period of torment, the duration of
which is graded in proportion to their sins, and at the end
of which they are annihilated.[6]

Thus William Whiston, one of the early scientists, publicly
espoused annihilationism. He presented little rational argument against
eternal punishment; instead, he was content to lash out at it with
invective. Indeed, his condemnation of hell was largely emotional.
(Unfortunately, the same could be said for many moderns.)

The rejection of the traditional doctrine of hell, however, was
not yet prevalent in the eighteenth century. In fact, our next figure
was one of its staunchest supporters.

Jonathan Edwards

Jonathan Edwards (1703–58) is recognized as America's greatest phi-
losopher-theologian, though on the question of hell he has frequently
been ridiculed and caricatured by modern writers. He epitomized the
union of consecrated head and heart. In addition, his powerful preaching helped generate the Great Awakening in the American colonies.

Edwards often preached on heaven and hell. Indeed, the two
were related, for it is God who makes heaven heaven and hell hell, as
he explained in a sermon on 2 Corinthians 4:18: "God will be the hell
of the one and the heaven of the other." Sinners and saints alike will
spend eternity in their respective destinies "in the immediate presence
and sight of God."[7]

Although Edwards cringed at the horror of hell, he was constrained to tell sinners the truth that "the bodies of wicked men as well
as their souls will be punished forever." Here was hell's worst feature—
its duration. In fact, "Eternity is the sting of the doctrine of hell
torments whereby chiefly it is that it stings the consciences of wicked
men and there is no other way to avoid the torment of it but to deny
it." Edwards plainly defined hell's eternity: "It is that duration that has
no end."[8]

The very eternity of hell caused Edwards to cry out to his congregation: "This doctrine is indeed awful and dreadful. It is dreadful to think of it, but yet tis what God the eternal God who made us and who has us soul and body in his hands has abundantly declared to us, so that so sure as God is true there will absolutely be no end to the misery of hell."[9]

Edwards, therefore, attacked annihilationism as a nemesis of the faith. The Bible teaches eternal condemnation because it uses the same word for eternal life as it does for eternal punishment. This punishment, moreover, involves pain. But, as Edwards reminded his hearers in a sermon on Revelation 6:15–16, annihilation is the end of pain: "Wicked men will hereafter earnestly wish to be turned to nothing and forever cease to be that they might escape the wrath of God." Furthermore, "the Scripture is very express and abundant in this matter that the eternal punishment is in sensible misery and torment and not annihilation."[10]

Living in a time characterized by the increasing elevation of reason, Edwards nonetheless submitted his mind to the Word and taught the doctrine of the eternal punishment of the wicked. He did not, however, imagine that he had fully understood hell. In fact, it was the very fact of hell's eternity that convinced him that ultimately hell was unfathomable. This is clear from the climax of his most famous sermon, "Sinners in the Hands of an Angry God," where he alerts unbelieving hearers.

> When you look forward, you shall see a long forever, a boundless duration before you, which will swallow up your thoughts, and amaze your soul; and you will absolutely de-spair of ever having any deliverance, any end, any mitiga-tion, any rest at all; you will know certainly that you must wear out long ages, millions of millions of ages, in wrestling and conflicting with this almighty merciless vengeance; and then when you have done so, when so many ages have actually been spent by you in this manner, you will know that all is but a point to what remains. So that your punish-ment will indeed be infinite. Oh who can express what the state of a soul in such circumstances is! All that we can possibly say about it, gives but a very feeble, faint represen-

tation of it; tis inexpressible and inconceivable. For, "who knows the power of God's anger."[11]

When asked why he was a "scare preacher," Edwards explained that he did not think he could frighten people into heaven but by God's grace he could be used of God to bring many to an awareness of their plight before God.

> Some talk of it as an unreasonable thing to fright persons to heaven, but I think it is a reasonable thing to endeavor to fright persons away from hell. They stand upon its brink, and are just ready to fall into it, and are senseless of their danger. Is it not a reasonable thing to fright a person out of a house on fire?[12]

Edwards inhabited an intellectual world different from that of many other thinkers who lived during the Enlightenment. He refused to exalt reason above the Word of God; instead, he submitted his mind and heart to the authority of Scripture. Therefore, contrary to the spirit of his day, he defended the doctrine of hell. The same cannot be said for Friedrich Schleiermacher.

Friedrich Schleiermacher

Friedrich Schleiermacher (1768–1834) emerged from a pietistic background, later engaging in pastoral ministry and becoming part of the leading intellectual circle in Berlin. He is commonly regarded as the father of modern theology. Seeking to avoid both abstract speculation and orthodoxy's emphasis on revealed doctrines, he studied the Christian faith by analyzing religious experience. In addition, he was the first major theologian of modern times to teach universalism.

In *The Christian Faith* (1821) Schleiermacher gave the fullest statement of his views, including a brief treatment of the consummation of the church. Unfortunately, a study of the last things lay outside his theological program. "Strictly speaking . . . from our point of view we can have no doctrine of the consummation of the Church, for our Christian consciousness has absolutely nothing to say regarding a condition so entirely outside our ken." Nevertheless, he examines some of the "prophetic pictures" of the church.[13]

Schleiermacher affirms the survival of personality following death, since "if we take the utterances of the Redeemer about His eternal personal survival as being imbued with His perfect truth, as His disciples undeniably did, then all we who are of human race can look forward to survival too." This, he argues, is confirmed by the incarnation of Christ: "If the soul of the Redeemer were imperishable, but our souls perishable, it could not justly be said that as man He was like us in all points, except sin."[14]

We, however, know little about this survival since Christ's words concerning it are "either purely figurative, or otherwise so indefinite in tenor that nothing can be gathered from them" except "the essential thing . . . the persistent union of believers with the Redeemer." The best we can do is to examine the biblical images to determine "their essential meaning" that is relevant for our faith today. The Bible's teaching on the resurrection of the flesh communicates the survival of personality. The doctrine of the Last Judgment represents the church's consummation.[15]

Schleiermacher cannot accept the idea of an intermediate state because "all the passages which might be reckoned in here are either of uncertain doctrinal character or of doubtful meaning." In fact, he reduces much of traditional teaching concerning the future to a single idea.

> The various ideas of how the future life is attached to the present are incapable of being made perfectly definite. As the essential content of the doctrine there remains only this, that the ascension of the risen Redeemer was possible only if all other human individuals too can look forward to a renovation of organic life which has links of attachment to the present state.[16]

Schleiermacher concludes that *all* will enjoy future life with God. He thus rejects the traditional view of the Last Judgment with its separation of good and evil. "The separation contemplated at the Last Judgment remains . . . both inadequate and superfluous." His reason for this rejection is very important. He repudiates as unacceptable to moderns "that familiar and widespread idea of the divine righteousness which in its one-sidedness looks so like caprice." In fact, the doctrine of the Last Judgment "can be traced to an all but vengeful desire to enhance the misery of unbelievers . . . ; it springs from an unpurified Christian temper."[17]

The "essential meaning" of the Last Judgment is that the church triumphant will be completely separated from evil. Its positive counterpart is the vision of God to be enjoyed by those dying in fellowship with Christ. "This we can only take to mean the completest fulness of the most living God-consciousness."[18]

If Schleiermacher relegates the "last things" to a place outside of his theology, he banishes the topic of "Eternal Damnation" to an appendix, concluding, "The figurative sayings of Christ, which have led to a state of irremediable misery for those who die out of fellowship with Christ being accepted as the counterpart of eternal bliss, will, if more closely scrutinized, be found insufficient to support any such conclusion."[19]

Schleiermacher has theological as well as textual reasons for rejecting hell. "Still less can the idea of eternal damnation itself bear close scrutiny. . . . If we now consider eternal damnation as it is related to eternal bliss, it is easy to see that once the former exists, the latter can exist no longer." This is because the knowledge that their fellow humans are suffering eternal torment would "be a disturbing element in bliss" for the blessed. The redeemed in heaven would not fail to feel sympathy for the damned in hell. This is turn would produce "bitter feelings" that would spoil their enjoyment of heaven. He then concludes with an appeal that Christians accept "the milder view, namely, that through the power of redemption there will one day be a universal restoration of all souls."[20]

Schleiermacher thus discards the orthodox doctrine of hell and replaces it with the view that all will be saved in the end. The ultimate theological reason for his universalism appears in an earlier section of *Christian Faith*, which deals with predestination. There he teaches that election "is solely determined by the divine good pleasure." Furthermore, this unconditional election is universal. God sovereignly chooses all to be finally saved. Consequently, "This result clearly emerges, that if we take the universality of redemption in its whole range . . . we must also take fore-ordination to blessedness quite universally; and that limits can be imposed on neither without curtailing the other."[21]

Schleiermacher is correctly regarded as the father of liberal theology. He represents a shift from God-centered to human-centered religion, for he locates his ultimate authority for faith not in Holy Scripture but within humanity. Therefore, he rejects the doctrine of hell because it does not appeal to modern notions of God and human sympathy. In its place he puts the doctrine of the restoration of all people.

Although liberal theology gained ground faster in Germany than in England, it made inroads there too, as the following controversy demonstrates.

F. D. Maurice

Frederick Denison Maurice (1805–72), son of a Unitarian minister, joined the Anglican Church, was ordained, and after pastoral ministry became professor of theology at King's College, London. A prolific writer, he merits inclusion here because of the controversy that eventually swirled around him.

According to Maurice, the main concern of a study of future things lay not with the distribution of rewards and punishments but with the knowledge of God, which is eternal life.[22] In his *Theological Essays* (1853) he tried to steer a middle course between a dogmatic universalism and a rigorous orthodoxy. He sought to achieve this by emphasizing the qualitative rather than the quantitative nature of eternal life and death.

> What, then, is Death Eternal, but to be without God? What is that infinite dread which rises upon my mind, which I cannot banish from me, when I think of my own godlessness and lovelessness,—that I may become wholly separated from

Love. . . . What dread can I have—ought I to have—besides this? What other can equal this? Mix up with this, the consideration of days and years and milleniums [sic], you add nothing either to my comfort or my fears. All you do is withdraw from me the real cause of my misery, which is separation from the sources of life and peace; from the hope which must come to me in one place or another, if I can again believe in God's love and cast myself upon it.[23]

Maurice's focus was not on the duration of eternal life or death. In fact, he defines these important terms thus: "Eternal life is the knowledge of God who is Love, and eternal death the loss of that knowledge."[24] Above all, we must not set limits on what God may do, but must acknowledge that Christ has already broken down the barriers of time.[25]

Maurice's *Theological Essays* received mixed reviews. The Unitarians appreciated his fair treatment of their position, but disagreed with much of his theology. The Wesleyans' official journal "warned its readers to steer clear of 'this new, complex and deadly heresy.'" The famous New Testament scholar F. J. A. Hort, however, agreed with Maurice "that eternity was independent of duration, that the power of repentance was not limited to this life; and that it was not revealed whether or not all will ultimately be saved."[26]

In 1853 the council of King's College dismissed Maurice from his chair. Earlier we learned that in 1710 William Whiston was expelled as professor of mathematics at Cambridge for his defective view of Christ. Now, almost a century and a half later, we see that a theology professor was discharged from a British college because of his views on eternal punishment. Clearly, eternal conscious punishment was still viewed as an essential doctrine of the Christian faith. It is noteworthy that Maurice was fired for a *modification* of the doctrine of hell; he neither condemned the traditional view nor asserted dogmatically that all would be saved. Instead, he condemned harsh expressions of orthodoxy and was hopeful that everyone would be redeemed.

Nineteenth-century British controversies over eternal punishment continued, as we see in the following debate.

F. W. Farrar and E. B. Pusey

Frederic W. Farrar (1831–1903), son of missionaries to India, studied at King's College, London, where he came under F. D. Maurice's influence. He gained renown as a writer by producing his acclaimed *Life of Christ* (1874), which went through twelve printings in one year, and the celebrated *Life and Epistles of St. Paul* (1879). For the last eight years of his life he was dean of Canterbury. Our chief concern here is with Farrar's preaching and the controversy it aroused.

At the end of 1877 Farrar preached a series of messages on eternal punishment that excited much interest. The sermons were published the following year with the title *Eternal Hope*, and as might be expected, the book also had a significant impact. In it Farrar attacked eternal conscious torment as unworthy of the love and fairness of God. "He cautioned his hearers against easy appeals to Scripture" and "believed the doctrine of an endless hell depended on a misunderstanding of *aionios*."[27]

It was easier, however, for Farrar to reject what he regarded as errors than plainly to state his position. He dismissed the doctrine of purgatory, spurned annihilationism, and was unable to embrace universalism wholeheartedly. "He preferred to maintain a reverent agnosticism, though he was prepared to affirm that the fate of man was not 'finally and irrevocably sealed at death.'" Nevertheless, he was commonly understood to have taught universalism.[28] He is probably best labeled a hopeful universalist, to distinguish him from the two leading dogmatic universalists of his day, Andrew Jukes and Samuel Cox.[29]

E. B. Pusey (1800–1882), after attending Oxford, studied biblical criticism in Germany during 1825–27. He is well known for his conservative commentaries on the Minor Prophets and the book of Daniel. In 1828 he was appointed Regius Professor of Hebrew at Oxford. He was a leader of the Oxford Movement, and after John Henry Newman left Anglicanism for the Roman Catholic Church, Pusey became the best-known figure in the Church of England.

Pusey was disturbed by Farrar's *Eternal Hope* because it had unsettled the faith of many. He hoped that a younger scholar would answer its arguments, but when he saw that no reply was forthcoming, he undertook the task himself. In 1880 his rebuttal appeared as *What Is of Faith as to Everlasting Punishment?* Unfortunately, for supporters of orthodoxy,

> Pusey's book was a dry and scholarly tome, not likely to have the same popular appeal as Farrar's emotional rhetoric. Surprisingly, on some points Farrar and Pusey were shown to be in agreement. There was, Pusey declared, no ground for believing that the majority of mankind were lost, nor could it be known who had died out of grace.[30]

Pusey, however, laid greater emphasis than Farrar on the time of death, being open to the possibility of many believing at the last moment. Pusey's response pushed Farrar to further defend his views in *Mercy and Judgment*. Here he judged Pusey's appeal to deathbed repentance to be a weak argument. In its place he confessed his hope that after death all "except the absolutely reprobate" will continue to make progress and improve.[31]

Farrar and Pusey clearly embody conflicting approaches to the issues. Their debate helps us understand why it is so difficult to believe in hell in our own day. Pusey represents the traditional orthodox appeal to Scripture; Farrar, the modern protest against what seemed a morally intolerable doctrine—that a loving God would send many, perhaps most, human beings to eternal hell. Many today, like Farrar in his day, simply cannot believe that God would condemn human beings. Others, like Pusey, are compelled by Scripture to believe a very unpopular doctrine.

Farrar breaks with traditional Christianity on another issue too. "Mainstream Christian orthodoxy has always regarded this life as decisive for a man's fate and hell as the *final* destiny of the wicked."[32] In the nineteenth century, however, these convictions were gradually eroded due in part to growing confidence in evolutionary progress. Farrar, as we have seen, held that the destiny of the lost was not fixed at death, but that most improve their lot in the intermediate state.

Unlike Farrar, our next figure could not be accused of questioning eternal punishment.

W. G. T. Shedd

William G. T. Shedd (1820–1894) was born and educated in New England. After pastoring several churches, he served as professor of English literature at the University of Vermont. He is best known, however, as professor of theology at Union Theological Seminary in New York.

He was the author of *Lectures on the History of Philosophy* (1856), *History of Christian Doctrine* (1863), and the three-volume *Dogmatic Theology* (1888–94). We are chiefly interested here in his *Doctrine of Endless Punishment*, first written in 1885.

Shedd begins with a sketch of the history of the doctrine of hell. An extended quotation serves as a summary:

> The common opinion in the Ancient church was, that the future punishment of the impenitent wicked is endless. This was the catholic faith; as much so as belief in the trinity. . . . The Mediaeval church was virtually a unit in holding the doctrine of Endless Punishment. The Reformation churches, both Lutheran and Calvinistic, adopted the historical and catholic opinion.
>
> Since the Reformation, Universalism, Restorationism, and Annihilationism, have been asserted by some sects and many individuals. But these tenets have never been adopted by those ecclesiastical denominations which hold, in their integrity, the cardinal doctrines of the trinity and incarnation, the apostasy and redemption, although they have exerted some influence within these denominations.[33]

Shedd then presents the biblical argument for eternal punishment, beginning with the words that denote hell. The words *sheol* in the Old Testament and *hades* in the New sometimes speak of the grave, and sometimes of the place of punishment for the wicked. The New Testament word *gehenna*, however, is used only to denote hell; Jesus uses this word eleven of the twelve times it occurs (it also appears in James 3:6).[34]

In fact, "The strongest support of the doctrine of Endless Punishment is the teaching of Jesus, the Redeemer of man." He speaks of the suffering in hades and gehenna "as 'everlasting punishment' (Matt. 25:46); 'everlasting fire' (Matt. 18:8); 'the fire that never shall be quenched' (Mark 9:45); and 'the worm that dieth not' (Mark 9:46)."[35]

Jesus' apostles add to this description: "'flaming fire' (2 Thess. 1:8); 'everlasting chains' (Jude 6); 'eternal fire' (Jude 7); 'the blackness of darkness forever' (Jude 13); 'the smoke of torment ascending up forever and ever' (Rev. 14:11; 19:3); 'the lake of fire and brimstone,' in which the devil, the beast, and the false prophet 'shall be tormented day and night forever and ever' (Rev. 20:10)."[36]

Next Shedd investigates the meanings of the important Greek words *aion* ("age") and *aionios* ("eternal"). The word *aion* denotes "age" and by itself does not indicate the length of the age. Therefore:

> Since the word "aeon" (*aion*), or age, in Scripture, may denote either the present finite age, or the future endless age, in order to determine the meaning of "aeonian" (*aionios*), it is necessary first to determine *in which of the two aeons*, the limited or the endless, the thing exists to which the epithet is applied; because anything in either aeon may be denominated "aeonian". . . . God, on the other hand, is a being that exists in the infinite *aion*, and is therefore *aionios* in the endless signification of the word. The same is true of the spirits of angels and men, because they exist in the future aeon, as well as in the present one.[37]

Shedd concludes that when applied to hell *aionios* means "endless" since it pertains to the future infinite age.[38]

The punishment of the wicked is not only endless, but it is also conscious. Here Shedd rejects annihilationism, contending that "the extinction of consciousness is not of the nature of punishment. The essence of punishment is suffering, and suffering is consciousness." Consequently, "the extinction of consciousness is not regarded by sinful men as an evil, but a good."[39]

Shedd's final chapter begins, "The chief objections to the doctrine of Endless Punishment are not Biblical, but speculative." He therefore concentrates on the rational argument.[40] The most important issue concerns the nature of punishment. Punishment must not be confused with chastisement. Punishment satisfies justice; chastisement seeks to develop character. Punishment looks to sins committed in the past; chastisement to moral improvement in the future. The ultimate fate of the wicked involves punishment, not chastisement, for Scripture says, "Vengeance is mine; I will repay, saith the Lord" (Rom. 12:19, KJV). And this punishment is eternal because "suffering that is penal can never come to an end, because guilt is the reason for its infliction, and guilt once incurred never ceases to be."[41]

Shedd responds to a common late-nineteenth-century protest. "The objection, that a suffering not intended to reform, but to satisfy justice, is cruel and unworthy of God, is refuted by the question of St. Paul: 'Is God unrighteous who taketh vengeance? God forbid: for how then shall God judge the world?' (Rom. 3:5, 6)."[42] Furthermore, to make such a protest betrays a defective understanding of sin and atonement. Moderns underestimate the enormity of sin: "Sin is an infinite evil; infinite not because committed by an infinite being, but against one." And the hideousness of sin is seen most clearly at the cross. "The incarnation and vicarious satisfaction for sin by one of the persons of the Godhead, demonstrates the infinity of the evil." It follows that "the doctrine of Christ's vicarious atonement, logically, stands or falls with that of endless punishment."[43]

Shockingly, the wicked are happier in hell than they would be in heaven because "the unsubmissive, rebellious, defiant, and impenitent spirit prefers hell to heaven." Nonetheless, this is no cause for the wicked to rejoice, for they will experience despair from the endlessness of their punishment. At this point Shedd attacks F. W. Farrar's teaching. "In Scripture, there is no such thing as *eternal* hope. Hope is characteristic of earth and time only. . . . Canon Farrar's phrase 'eternal hope' is derived from Pandora's box, not from the Bible." There is no hope in hell because there is no repentance there.[44]

Although hell is infinite in duration, it is finite in intensity. For this reason there will be a gradation of punishment in hell; degrees of punishment will be based on the resoluteness of wicked self-determination and the degree of light. Sinners must beware, therefore, lest they "treasure up wrath" against themselves for the Day of Judgment (Rom. 2:5).[45]

In spite of all he has said thus far, Shedd seeks to limit the scope of hell.

> It is only a spot in the universe of God. Compared with heaven, hell is narrow and limited. . . . The Bible teaches that there will always be some sin, and some death, in the universe. Some angels and men will forever be the enemies of God. But their number, compared with that of unfallen angels and redeemed men, is small.[46]

Although Shedd highlights God's wrath in *The Doctrine of Endless Punishment,* he concludes by accenting God's kindness. Shedd reveals his heart for the lost by eloquently (as befits a former professor of English literature) extolling God's mercy.

> Over against God's infinite antagonism and righteous severity toward moral evil, there stands God's infinite pity and desire to forgive. This is realized, not by the high-handed and unprincipled method of pardoning without legal satisfaction of any kind, but by the strange and stupendous method of putting the Eternal Judge in the place of the human criminal; of substituting God's own satisfaction for that due from man. In this vicarious atonement for sin, the Triune God relinquishes no claims of law, and waives no rights of justice. The sinner's Divine Substitute, in his hour of voluntary agony and death, drinks the cup of punitive and inexorable justice to the dregs. Any man who, in penitent faith, avails himself of this *vicarious* method of setting himself right with the Eternal Nemesis, will find that it succeeds; but he who rejects it, must through endless cycles grapple with the dread problem of human guilt in his own person, and alone.[47]

Conclusion

Yale church historian Williston Walker said that the Enlightenment characterized the atmosphere of the eighteenth century.

The Enlightenment was the conscious effort to apply the rule of reason to the various aspects of individual and corporate life. Its fundamental principles—autonomy, reason . . . —deeply influenced the thought and action of the modern world and conditioned the atmosphere into which Christianity moved.[48]

In this chapter we have charted the reactions of various modern thinkers to this new atmosphere. Some perpetuated the orthodox view of hell (Edwards, Pusey, and Shedd); others questioned it (Maurice and Farrar); still others rejected it (Whiston and Schleiermacher). All were affected by the Enlightenment.

It is significant that our first figure, William Whiston, was one of the early scientists. The free inquiry that spawned science also led to questioning of the historic faith. This questioning was epitomized by John Toland's defiant declaration in 1696, "I ACKNOWLEDGE NO ORTHODOXY BUT THE TRUTH."[49] Human reason had been "liberated" from the shackles of superstition and tradition, and was now "free" to evaluate the Bible.

It is unfair, however, to equate Whiston's views with Toland's. Whiston was no deist assessing the Bible by the light of unaided human reason. He endeavored to restore Christianity to the purity of the early church. He did not reject the authority of Scripture but rather sought to correct what he considered traditional misinterpretations of Scripture.

Nevertheless, we detect in Whiston a rebellious spirit, characteristic of the modern age, when he rejects the orthodox doctrines of Christ and of hell. His rejection of hell was based not on biblical exegesis but on emotional reaction to what he considered the immorality of eternal punishment.

This critical spirit is more pronounced in Schleiermacher. His work exemplified what Jaroslav Pelikan calls "the affectional transposition of doctrine" that accompanied the Enlightenment. Appeal to the light shining in the heart replaced appeal to chapter and verse of Scripture. "Miracle, mystery, and authority, whose validity as objective realities seemed to have reached a dead end, took on new life when they became, instead, ways of speaking about the subjective validity of inward experience."[50]

Schleiermacher's whole theological program was based upon the analysis of religious experience. He repudiated eternal punishment because it was out of step with modern ideas of God and human sympathy. Schleiermacher therefore epitomizes the modern attitude toward hell, when on the basis of reason and emotion he rejects the teaching of Scripture.

Rabbi Daniel Cohn-Sherbok informs us that Jewish scholars, influenced by Christians, have ignored the doctrine of hell in Judaism for reasons similar to Schleiermacher's, namely,

> the tendency to regard everlasting punishment as morally repugnant. Echoing doubts about the doctrine of Hell voiced by a number of Christians . . . Jewish theologians have maintained that it is a self-delusion to believe that a God of love could have created a place of eternal punishment.[51]

This is the chief reason for the wholesale forsaking of the doctrine of hell that continues today. Modern men and women simply refuse to believe in a God of wrath who will punish sinners eternally in hell. This refusal echoes in the quotation with which this chapter began. There M. J. Savage rejected the biblical description of God, putting in its place "the infinite and eternal Good, who only is God, and who only on such terms could be worshiped." Here is the problem in a nutshell: Moderns will only accept a god who will meet them on their terms.

One important question remains: Why did thinkers such as Jonathan Edwards and W. G. T. Shedd continue to believe in such an unpopular doctrine? Edwards admitted that the doctrine of hell "is indeed awful and dreadful." Nevertheless, the Puritan was constrained to preach this horrible doctrine. Why? Because "tis what God the eternal God who made us and who has us soul and body in his hands has abundantly declared to us."[52] And Shedd explains: "Neither the Christian ministry, nor the Christian church, are [sic] responsible for the doctrine of Eternal Perdition. It is given in charge to the ministry, and to the church, by the Lord Christ himself, in his last commission, as a truth to be preached to every creature."[53]

Edwards and Shedd subscribed to the despised doctrine of hell because they submitted their thoughts and feelings to the truth of the Word of God. May God give us courage to do the same.

NOTES

1. Minot Judson Savage, *Life Beyond Death* (New York and London: G. P. Putnam's Sons, 1899), 101.
2. Immanuel Kant, *Philosophical Writings*, ed. Ernst Behler (1784; reprint, New York: Continuum Publishing, 1986), 263.
3. For Whiston's ideas I am indebted to D. P. Walker's outstanding *Decline of Hell: Seventeenth-Century Discussions of Eternal Torment* (Chicago: University of Chicago Press, 1964), 93–103.
4. Ibid., 99.
5. Ibid.
6. Ibid., 100.
7. John H. Gerstner, *Jonathan Edwards on Heaven and Hell* (Grand Rapids: Baker, 1980), 57.
8. Ibid., 55, 73.
9. Ibid., 74.
10. Ibid., 75.
11. Ibid., 77–78.
12. Ibid., 85.
13. Friedrich Schleiermacher, *The Christian Faith* (1821–22; reprint, New York: Harper & Row, 1963), 697.
14. Ibid., 701–2.
15. Ibid., 706.
16. Ibid., 711, 713.
17. Ibid., 716.
18. Ibid., 716, 719.
19. Ibid., 720.
20. Ibid., 720–22.
21. Ibid., 551, 560.
22. I learned much about Maurice's theology from Geoffrey Rowell's *Hell and the Victorians: A Study of the Nineteenth-Century Theological Controversies Concerning Eternal Punishment and the Future Life* (Oxford: Clarendon Press, 1974), 62–89.
23. Ibid., 81.
24. F. D. Maurice, *Theological Essays* (New York: Redfield, 1854), 349. For a helpful study of Maurice's eschatology see Don Cupitt, "The Language of Eschatology: F. D. Maurice's Treatment of Heaven and Hell," *Anglican Theological Review* 54.4 (1972):305–17.
25. Rowell, *Hell and the Victorians*, 81.
26. Ibid., 82–83.
27. Ibid., 139–40.

28. Ibid., 140.

29. Andrew Jukes, *The Second Death and the Restitution of All Things* (1867), and Samuel Cox, *Salvator Mundi* (1877).

30. Rowell, *Hell and the Victorians*, 144.

31. Ibid., 144–46.

32. Bauckham, "Universalism: A Historical Survey," *Themelios* 4.2 (January 1979): 49.

33. W. G. T. Shedd, *The Doctrine of Endless Punishment* (1887; reprint, Carlisle, Pa.: Banner of Truth, 1986), 1, 4–5.

34. Ibid., 19–49.

35. Ibid., 76.

36. Ibid., 76–77.

37. Ibid., 84.

38. Ibid., 87–88.

39. Ibid., 92–93.

40. Ibid., 118.

41. Ibid., 120–21, 127–28.

42. Ibid., 128.

43. Ibid., 152–53.

44. Ibid., 142–43, 151, 153–54.

45. Ibid., 138, 146–47.

46. Ibid., 159.

47. Ibid., 162.

48. Williston Walker, *A History of the Christian Church*, 3d ed. (New York: Charles Scribner's Sons, 1970), 430.

49. Quoted in Jaroslav Pelikan, *Christian Doctrine and Modern Culture (Since 1700)* (Chicago: University of Chicago Press, 1989), 11.

50. Ibid., 119.

51. "The Jewish Doctrine of Hell," *Religion* 8 (1978):206.

52. Gerstner, *Jonathan Edwards on Heaven and Hell*, 55–56.

53. *Shedd, Doctrine of Endless Punishment*, v.

8

False Witnesses (1): Universalism

British evangelist John Blanchard has some hard words for the view that everyone eventually will be saved.

> Universalism originated in the Garden of Eden when Satan brushed aside God's warning and assured Eve, "You will not surely die" (Gen. 3:4). . . .
>
> All the ways to hell are one-way streets. The idea that those who go there will eventually be released and join the rest of humanity in heaven has not a shred of biblical evidence to support it.
>
> Children are sometimes told fictional adventure stories with the delightful ending: "And they all lived happily ever after." We call that kind of story a fairy tale.
>
> Universalism is exactly that.[1]

What are we to make of Blanchard's statements? Is universalism a lie of Satan? Does it lack even a shred of biblical evidence? Is it a fairy tale? Or can we dismiss his loaded language as the exaggerations of an evangelist? In this chapter we will consider the arguments advanced by the most persuasive modern universalist, John Hick. In addition, we will evaluate the view, held by Hick and others, that opportunity for salvation extends beyond the grave. Finally, we will examine the passages of Scripture that universalists use to argue their case.

John Hick: Justice Demands That God Win All to Himself

The Problem of Evil

The starting point for British philosopher of religion John Hick was "the theodicy issue, the question whether the reality of suffering and wickedness are compatible with the reality of a loving God."[2] Hick answered this question affirmatively in *Evil and the God of Love* (1966). He concluded that God has ordered a world that contains real evil as a means of attaining his goal of bringing all persons to perfection through a process involving their free response.[3] Here, however, we are not interested in the details of his theodicy, but in his case for universalism.

Hick thinks the traditional Christian view of hell inhibits a resolution of the question of evil. "I . . . believe that the needs of Christian theodicy compel us to repudiate the idea of eternal punishment." Why? Because "the sufferings of the damned in hell, since they are interminable, can never lead to any constructive end beyond themselves and are thus the very type of ultimately pointless and wasted anguish." Hick assumes that only remedial suffering comports with God's love.[4]

Rather than helping to solve the problem of evil, according to Hick, belief in eternal punishment only compounds the problem. "Indeed misery which is eternal and therefore infinite would constitute the largest part of the problem of evil." Notice that he rejects hell on moral grounds. For sin to exist forever insults the perfect goodness of God. The traditional view of hell, therefore, is a "grim fantasy" and "a serious perversion of the Gospel."[5]

Did Jesus Teach Eternal Punishment?

But what about the biblical passages upon which the church has based its view of hell? Can we simply dispense with them? Not at all, Hick assures us. In fact, that Jesus seems to teach eternal punishment constitutes "the most serious objection" to universalism. And his sayings must "be taken with the utmost seriousness." Furthermore, Jesus preached that "real suffering and misery . . . is to come upon men hereafter as a divinely ordained consequence of selfish and cruel deeds performed in this life."[6]

Nevertheless, "That our Lord taught that such misery is to continue through endless times in a perpetual torture inflicted by God cannot safely be affirmed." Again Hick buttresses his theological assertions with a moral argument: endless punishment opposes Jesus' message of love. "If we see as the heart of his [Jesus'] teaching the message of the active and sovereign divine love, we shall find incredible and even blasphemous the idea that God plans to inflict perpetual torture upon any of His children."[7]

Curiously, Hick asserts that in the hereafter there is suffering, though not eternal, for sins committed in this life. What is the nature of this suffering? It is redemptive. We will study this idea in more detail shortly, but first let's examine Hick's alternative to the doctrine of hell.

The Divine Therapist Will Eventually Heal Everyone

In rejecting hell, Hick opts for universalism, the view that "God will eventually succeed in His purpose of winning all men to Himself in faith and love." The Bible teaches that this is God's purpose when it speaks of "God our Savior, who wants all men to be saved and to come to the knowledge of the truth" (1 Tim. 2:3–4). Due to the reality of free will, however, it is logically possible that some may spurn God's offer of salvation. Nevertheless, we can be absolutely sure that "God will never cease to desire and actively work for the salvation of each created person."[8]

God will never abandon people, and therefore, salvation will always remain a possibility to which God attempts to draw them. Nevertheless, how do we know that he will succeed in his purpose? Once more Hick bases his case on moral grounds. "It seems morally (although still not logically) impossible that the infinite resourcefulness of infinite love working in unlimited time should be eternally frustrated, and the creature reject its own good, presented in an endless range of ways."⁹

Although logical certainty eludes Hick, he feels he has a practical certainty of the final restoration of all. He illustrates this by comparing God to "a psychiatrist trying to empower a patient to be himself and to cease frustrating his own desires." In fact, "The divine Therapist has perfect knowledge of each human heart, is infinitely wise in the healing of its ills, has unbounded love for the patient and unlimited time to devote to him." Hick concludes, "It remains theoretically possible that He will fail; but He will never cease to try, and we may (it seems to me) have a full practical certainty that sooner or later He will succeed."¹⁰

How can Hick claim that the divine psychiatrist has unlimited time to devote to his patients if they all eventually die? The answer lies in Hick's theory of "temporal and redemptive" suffering after death. He rejects the idea of instantaneous perfection of human beings at death: "It is far from clear that an individual who had been instantaneously perfected would be in any morally significant sense the same person as the frail, erring mortal who had lived and died." In order to maintain continuity of persons' identity, Hick posits "progressive sanctification after death" in "an existence or existences." Unlike the Roman Catholic view that only those who die in a state of grace go to purgatory, Hick believes that the divine Therapist would eventually succeed in helping *all persons* to face reality.¹¹

Hick develops these ideas further in *Death and Eternal Life* (1976). He continues to reject hell as "morally revolting" because it attributes "to God an unappeasable vindictiveness and insatiable cruelty." In fact, eternal torment "is totally incompatible with the idea of God as infinite love." It is true that due to Augustine's influence this doctrine "dominated the imagination of the west" until the Enlightenment. Nevertheless, Hick rejoices that "in the seventeenth, eighteenth and nineteenth centuries the christian mind gradually awoke from these nightmare imaginings."¹²

Jesus Versus Paul

Hick devotes more attention to the New Testament in *Death and Eternal Life* than he did in *Evil and the God of Love*. Contrary to popular opinion, although Jesus uttered "scattered sayings about life after death," in which he affirmed "the future resurrection and judgement of the dead," we cannot "say with full assurance" that Jesus taught eternal punishment.[13]

Hick's study of the New Testament reveals two sets of sayings: Jesus' warnings about hell and Paul's statements pointing to the final salvation of all. The former are "rather rare." In fact, "the parable of the sheep and the goats . . . is the only passage in the recorded teachings of Jesus in the synoptic gospels in which eternal punishment is threatened and a final and permanent division is asserted between the saved and the damned."[14]

Moreover, Hick argues, most of Jesus' judgment sayings, traditionally taken as speaking of unending retributive punishment, are capable of another interpretation. They "are equally capable of being understood in terms of temporal and therefore potentially educative and redemptive suffering." Hick uses moral criteria to determine truth when he concludes, "The divinely ordained moral order of the world would be extremely crude if all the judgment sayings were rightly held to involve eternal heaven and hell."[15]

Alongside Jesus' warnings of judgment, Hick sees several texts in Paul pointing to the final restoration of all people: 1 Corinthians 15:22; Romans 5:18; 11:32; Ephesians 1:10; and 1 Timothy 2:4.[16]

Can these apparently contradictory statements of Jesus and Paul be harmonized? Hick thinks they can, once we realize that they are of two different types. Jesus "was neither propounding a theological theory nor defining theological doctrines." Rather, he was a preacher "wrestling with individual men and women, trying to win them back from self-destructive sinfulness." His was "not academic teaching," but "practical and personal admonition and exhortation." But Paul "was writing theology in and for the christian community." He, therefore, wrote "in the more detached theological mode," when he spoke of "a final universal salvation."[17]

Hick concludes: "The two truths are formally compatible with one another because the one asserts that something will happen if a certain condition is fulfilled (namely, permanent non-repentance) while the other asserts that this same thing will not happen because that condition will not in fact be fulfilled." He thus claims to take seriously Jesus' warnings of hell, while giving priority to Paul's "theological propositions" that allegedly affirm universalism.[18]

Our "Inherent Gravitation" Toward God

In *Death and Eternal Life* Hick makes what he regards as a more mature proposal concerning divine sovereignty and human responsibility than he had made in *Evil and the God of Love*. In order to show the possibility for omnipotent divine love to save without violating human freedom Hick appeals to the doctrine of creation. The fact that God created us in his image means that "God has so made us that the inherent gravitation of our being is towards him."[19]

In light of this "capacity for God" that all human beings possess, Hick returns to the divine psychiatrist metaphor. Again, God is the Therapist and we are the patients.

> The divine therapy is a matter of healing, of enabling us to fulfil our own selves and to become more truly what our nature cries out to be. The present life sees the beginning of this process of the bringing of human personality to maturity and wholeness. . . . We must suppose that beyond this life the process continues in other environments offering other experiences and challenges which open up new opportunities of response and growth.[20]

As he did in *Evil and the God of Love*, Hick argues for postmortem progressive sanctification: "If there *is* continued life after death, and if God *is* ceaselessly at work for the salvation of his children, it follows that he will continue to be at work until the work is done." Hick, as previously, rejects the idea of a final decision at death "determining the individual's destiny." In its place he puts the opportunity for "further personal growth" and "development in response to further experiences" after death.[21]

Hick reaffirms, "There must, then, be further time beyond death in which the process of perfecting can continue." Next, he takes a remarkable step. He engages in what he calls "global theology," and listens to the religious wisdom of both the East and the West. Indeed, his primary source for his startling proposal is the Tibetan Book of the Dead: there will be "a series of lives, each bounded by something analogous to birth and death, lived in other worlds in spaces other than that in which we now are."[22]

Religious Pluralism

In *God and the Universe of Faiths* (1973) and *God Has Many Names* (1980) Hick moves beyond his previous ideas to religious pluralism, the view that all faiths lead to God. "Somewhere around 800 B.C. there began . . . the golden age of religious creativity." This consisted in "a remarkable series of revelatory experiences." Indeed, "the divine Spirit came upon the human spirit" of many, including Old Testament prophets, Zoroaster, Confucius, Gotama the Buddha, the writers of the Bhagavad Gita, Socrates, Plato, Jesus, and Mohammed. These all bear witness that "the same divine reality has always been self-revealingly active towards mankind."[23]

Hick's Doctrine of Christ

From these premises Hick concludes that Christianity is one way of salvation among many. Furthermore, Hick candidly admits that this "shift from a Christianity-centered or Jesus-centered to a God-centered model of the universe of faiths" affects his view of Christ. "If Jesus was literally God incarnate, the Second Person of the Trinity living a human life, so that the Christian religion was founded by God-on-earth in person, it is then very hard to escape from the traditional view that all mankind must be converted to the Christian faith."[24]

Hick concludes, "The idea that Jesus proclaimed himself as God incarnate, and as the sole point of saving contact between God and man, is without adequate historical foundation and represents a doctrine developed by the church."[25] To put it bluntly, "That Jesus was God the Son incarnate is not literally true." Instead, Christians over the centuries expressed the significance of Jesus as "the exaltation of a human being to divine status." In reality, however, he was "a human being called to be God's special servant and agent on earth."[26] Accordingly, in 1977 Hick edited an influential book entitled *The Myth of God Incarnate.*[27]

John Hick espouses a pluralism of the world's religions and is confident that after death all people will experience many subsequent lives until all eventually attain salvation.

Evaluation

Hick's Moral Criticism

An evaluation of Hick's universalism is in order.[28] We have observed that Hick consistently employs a moral criterion as the test of theological truth. Specifically, as Nigel Cameron points out, Hick's "moral criticism of the doctrine of hell" is characteristic of "his moral approach to theology" generally.[29] Accordingly, Hick regards eternal torment as incompatible with God's infinite love. In fact, the traditional view of hell must be rejected because it is "morally revolting" and "morally intolerable."[30]

It should not surprise us, therefore, when Hick argues that anything less than universalism is "morally impossible," even if it is "*still not* logically impossible"[31] (emphasis added). For Hick, moral criticism is the master, and logic the servant. As an obedient servant, logic will unerringly follow Hick's moral judgment. Indeed, Hick reaches his conclusion on the basis of a moral criterion and then reasons so as to achieve the desired result.

Hick's moral criticism even functions as a principle of biblical interpretation. Hick interprets Jesus' judgment sayings as speaking of postmortem redemptive punishment, rather than of eternal punishment. Why? Because "the divinely ordained moral order of the world would be extremely crude if all the judgment sayings were rightly held to involve eternal heaven and hell."[32]

Hick's Interpretation of the Bible

This leads us to evaluate Hick's handling of the New Testament. His attempt to harmonize Jesus' "challenging warning" of hell with Paul's "theological proposition" of universalism fails miserably.[33] As Stephen Travis asks, "What is the use—or the morality—of an existential threat which turns out to have no corresponding reality?"[34] (Don't miss the irony of Travis taking Hick to task for creating *moral* problems for Jesus' preaching). Indeed, Hick's claim that "the two truths" (warnings about hell and statements assuring universalism) are logically compatible does not pass careful scrutiny, as Paul Helm has demonstrated.

> The serious threat of hell entails the possibility of hell, and the possibility of hell is inconsistent with there being no possibility of hell. Professor Hick has therefore failed to establish, by interpreting the synoptic sayings of Jesus as he does, that there is no possibility of hell according to the teaching of Jesus.[35]

Hick is able to have his cake (universalism) and eat it too (claiming to handle Scripture with integrity) only "by selecting certain statements from Paul, and then arranging the rest of Paul's own sayings and others around them," in an eclectic manner. In fact, ultimately, "There is no necessity for Holy Scripture to back up his theological proposals. . . . After all, this is the man who holds . . . a doctrine of purgatorial re-incarnation."[36]

Hick's Views Unbiblical

It is not hard to show that many of Hick's doctrines cut against the grain of the Bible. His insistence that suffering after death is remedial rather than retributive squares neither with Jesus' warning concerning "eternal punishment" (Matt. 25:46) nor with the words of Paul (the universalist!): "God is just: He will pay back trouble to those who trouble you. . . . the Lord Jesus . . . will punish those who do not know God. . . . They will be punished with everlasting destruction. . . ." (2 Thess. 1:6–9).

Moreover, Travis believes that Hick "underplays man's bias *against* God."[37] This is most evident in Hick's assertion that "God has so made us that the inherent gravitation of our being is towards him." While this may have been true of man before the Fall, we cannot disregard the drastic effects that accompanied the entrance of sin into the world.

Yet Hick is confident that, because of humans' universal "capacity for God," all of the divine Therapist's clients will eventually be healed despite their sin-sickness.[38] On the contrary, the biblical testimony concerning *sinful* human beings is this:

> There is no one righteous, not even one; there is no one who understands, no one who seeks God. All have turned away, they have together become worthless; there is no one who does good, not even one. Their throats are open graves; their tongues practice deceit. The poison of vipers is on their lips. Their mouths are full of cursing and bitterness. Their feet are swift to shed blood; ruin and misery mark their ways, and the way of peace they do not know. There is no fear of God before their eyes. (Rom. 3:10–18)

The most serious of Hick's defections from orthodoxy is his rejection of Christ's incarnation. Because of the demands of his global theology, Hick can no longer accept this biblical teaching.

> Transposed into the theological terms, the problem which has come to the surface in the encounter of Christianity with the other world religions is this: if Jesus was literally God incarnate, and if it is by his death alone that men can be saved, and by their response to him alone that they can appropriate that salvation, then the only doorway to eternal life is Christian faith. It would follow from this that the large majority of the human race so far have not been saved.[39]

Hick regards this conclusion as unthinkable, for it violates his moral criterion: It is incompatible with God's love and justice. Moreover, once Hick jettisons the Incarnation, he also discards other key doctrines (e.g., the Atonement, justification by faith); and so he must, because of the coherence of the Christian faith. Trevor Hart's evaluation of Hick's defections is stern but fair:

> It is quite unnecessary for a person to know about or to believe in Jesus Christ in order to be saved, but strictly

speaking, quite unnecessary also for Christ to have lived or died. . . . A person can be saved apart from Jesus Christ altogether. . . . The cross of Jesus is no longer accorded any objective atoning significance. Rather salvation is to be had, *via* various religious traditions, within the context of a general divine-human relationship in which "if we are truly penitent we can ask for and receive forgiveness and new life" (John Hick, *The Myth of Christian Uniqueness*, 32). The precise role of Jesus or his death in this, for those belonging to the Christian tradition, is reduced to that of an example of self-giving love.[40]

By his own admission John Hick has abandoned the evangelical faith he once professed.[41] In its place, in the words of Nigel Cameron, Hick "has openly taken the path of syncretism as the way to theological truth." The result is a "global theology" in which he has "used the doctrine of universal salvation *post mortem* as a tool for the re-fashioning of the Christian (and with it every other) religion."[42]

The Question of Authority

This brings us to "the crucial question . . . the question of authority. . . . Specifically, it is the question of the competence of the human mind to make the judgements which are required for the eclecticism which Hick evidences in his use of Holy Scripture, and the cognate syncretism by means of which he has begun to construct his 'global theology.'"[43] Simply put, John Hick has rejected biblical Christianity and manufactured another religion.

Let me illustrate: Hick's appeal to authorities other than the Christian Scriptures undergirds his adoption of the view that after death there will be "a series of lives . . . lived in other worlds." On what does Hick base this conclusion? On "the *Tibetan Book of the Dead*, and . . . western mediumistic communications" evaluated on the basis of "reasonable speculation."[44] Richard Bauckham rightly labels this process "highly speculative" and points out that "our ultimate salvation becomes a prospect so distant as to be hardly capable of concerning us at all in this the first of our many lives," a point that Hick himself concedes.[45] How can Hick possibly claim to take Jesus' preaching seriously, when the Redeemer often warns his hearers of the urgency of repenting *now* to escape the coming wrath?

Postmortem Evangelism

It is time to address the issue of postmortem evangelism. We have seen that Hick does not claim biblical support for his view of purgatorial reincarnation leading to universal salvation. Instead, he relies upon the Tibetan Book of the Dead and on material produced by trance mediums.

However, despite the lack of biblical support, the idea of postmortem conversion is gaining in popularity, and not exclusively among universalists. For example, Clark Pinnock, a leading evangelical theologian, finds this logic compelling: God loves and has provided salvation for every human being. God, therefore, must give each the opportunity to believe the gospel.

> The logic behind a postmortem encounter with Christ is simple enough. It rests on the insight that God, since he loves humanity, would not send anyone to hell without first ascertaining what their response would have been to his grace. Since everyone eventually dies and comes face to face with the risen Lord, that would seem to be the obvious time to discover their answer to God's call.[46]

To the suggestion that the unbeliever's encounter with God after death may be unpleasant, Pinnock answers, "God does not cease to be gracious to sinners just because they are no longer living." On this basis he concludes that there will be grace after death for the unevangelized. "Therefore, when humanity [after death] stands before God, they stand before a God of mercy and love."[47]

Pinnock is not espousing universalism, since some may not get a chance after death. "The fate of some may be sealed at death; those, for example, who heard the gospel and declined the offer of salvation." Others may get a chance and not avail themselves of it. "The *oppor-*

tunity would be there for all to repent after death, but not necessarily the *desire.*" Those who lack the desire will be annihilated by God, according to Pinnock.[48]

How are we to evaluate this proposal? Chiefly, by pointing out that it lacks scriptural support. Pinnock himself admits the "scantiness" of "scriptural evidence" for his position. Nevertheless, he appeals to 1 Peter 3:19–20, which speaks of Christ preaching "to the spirits in prison." This is a notoriously difficult passage, which has been variously interpreted.[49] Yet, even apart from the specifics of interpretation of this text, "1 Peter 3 records no positive response to what was preached and therefore provides no basis for conversion after death."[50] And even if we grant for the sake of argument that 1 Peter 3:19–20 teaches that Jesus descended into hell after his death and before his resurrection, and that some responded positively to his preaching and were saved, Pinnock still would not have proved his case. Rather, as Millard Erickson indicates, these verses "would provide evidence for the salvation only of individuals who had died prior to Christ." They say nothing about persons who came after Christ.[51]

Furthermore, to appeal to 1 Peter 3:19–20 in an attempt to prove postmortem evangelism leading to universalism, as is sometimes done, is doomed to failure, because it makes 1 Peter 3 clash with 1 Peter 4. Indeed, as N. T. Wright notes, "The next chapter (1 Peter 4, especially vv. 17–18) rules out the possibility that 'those who do not obey God's gospel' will be saved."[52]

Stephen Travis aptly summarizes: The concept of postmortem conversion "finds no support in the New Testament. . . . There are no reported sayings of Jesus which suggest . . . the possibility of a person's destiny being reversed after death."[53] Rather, Jesus underscores the fact that death seals one's fate, when he says to the Pharisees, "If you do not believe that I am the one I claim to be, you will indeed die in your sins" (John 8:24). Hebrews 9:27 agrees: "Man is destined to die once, and after that to face judgment." Pinnock is far from convincing in his attempt to interpret this facing of judgment in Hebrews 9:27 as an opportunity to receive God's grace.

Furthermore, Pinnock's view of conversion after death is burdened by special problems, as Millard Erickson shows. Pinnock makes a logical mistake when he assumes that "if God loves sinners, he will provide an opportunity in the future for those who have responded positively to the light they have." Since Pinnock never proves this assumption, when he concludes that God does love sinners and will provide them a postmortem opportunity, he is guilty of assuming his conclusion.[54]

In addition, Pinnock's assertion that

> "God . . . would not send anyone to hell without first ascertaining what their response would have been to his grace" implies that God does not know what a person's response would have been. This fits with another of Pinnock's theological tenets, that God is not omniscient. That, however, is a statement that . . . is refuted by Scripture. . . . e.g., Ps. 147:5; Prov. 15:3; Matt. 10:29–30; Rom. 11:33; Heb. 4:13.[55]

These speculative doctrines of postmortem opportunity for salvation must be rejected, for they not only lack biblical authority, but also fly in the face of the teaching of Jesus and his apostles.

Passages Commonly Appealed to by Universalists

It remains for us to examine biblical passages that universalists claim prove their position. These passages can be grouped into three topical categories: God's desire to save all, the work of Christ, and the consummation. We will examine the single most important passage from each of the three groups, judged by frequency of citation in universalist literature.

God's Desire to Save All

Universalists commonly appeal to passages that express God's desire to save all, especially 1 Timothy 2:3–4: "God our Savior . . . wants all men to be saved and to come to a knowledge of the truth." Other texts in this category include 1 Timothy 4:10 and 2 Peter 3:9.

As all other biblical passages, 1 Timothy 2:4 must be interpreted in its literary and historical contexts. Paul has just urged that
prayers be made "for everyone—for kings and all those in authority" in order that believers might enjoy "peaceful and quiet lives"
(vv. 1–2). It is important to realize that in Paul's day, the Roman
emperor and local officials frequently opposed the church. Indeed,
the notorious emperor Nero, who reigned from A.D. 54 to 68, was
on the throne when Paul penned these words. Paul, therefore, in
verse 4 motivates his readers to pray even for ungodly rulers, as
N. T. Wright explains.

> Lest readers should think this is a counsel of folly, advising
> them to pray for people who are hardened and reprobate
> persecutors of the church, vv. 3 and 4 emphasize that God's
> grace knows no human barriers. Universal prayer must be
> made because man cannot tell whom God will save, and
> must realize that human and fleshly categories of who may
> be eligible for grace are just the sort of thing that the gospel
> shatters.[56]

In 1 Timothy 2:4 Paul does not teach that all will be saved in the
end but that it is God's will for the gospel to reach everyone. Moreover, to press this verse into the service of universalism is to do
injustice to the unity of 1 Timothy because "the wider context reveals
a doctrine of final judgment quite irreconcilable with 'universalism:'
compare 1 Timothy 1:6–11; 4:1–2; 5:24; 6:9–10."[57] First Timothy 5:24
bears this out: "The sins of some men are obvious, reaching the place
of judgment ahead of them; the sins of others trail behind them." The
contention that 1 Timothy 2:4 and similar passages prove universalism
is unwarranted.

The Work of Christ

Universalists also argue from passages that allegedly speak of the
unlimited outcome of Christ's saving work. The most frequently cited
Scripture is Romans 5:18: "Consequently, just as the result of one
trespass was condemnation for all men, so also the result of one act of

righteousness was justification that brings life for all men." Additional passages in this category include John 10:16; 12:32; Romans 11:32; Colossians 1:20; and 1 John 2:2.

It is true that the "one act of righteousness" spoken of in Romans 5:18 refers to Jesus' death and resurrection. It is false, however, to claim that this verse supports universalism, as a comparison with the next verse reveals. Romans 5:19 reads, "For just as through the disobedience of the one man the *many* were made sinners, so also through the obedience of the one man the *many* will be made righteous" (emphasis added). The point is that we cannot press the two occurrences of the word "all" in verse 18 ("condemnation for *all* . . . justification that brings life for *all*") any more than we can the two occurrences of the word "many" in verse 19.

If we press either "all" or "many," we make the apostle contradict himself. Readers adopting this approach miss the mark because they try to understand "all" and "many" over against each other—taking "all" as opposed to "many." Instead, "many" and "all" here are relative terms that are contrasted with the "one" trespass of "the one man" Adam and with the "one" act of righteousness of "the one man" Jesus Christ. These contrasts emphasize the great effects of Adam and Christ on the human race. To determine the extent of the effects of Adam's sin or Christ's righteousness we must look at the total context of this passage (and of Scripture).

When we do this, we note that Paul identifies those who will "reign in life" through Christ as "those who receive God's abundant provision of grace and of the gift of righteousness" (v. 17). If we ask what Paul means by "all" in Romans 5:18 in the context of his letter to the Romans, we note, along with N. T. Wright, that "the point Paul has been making all along since 1:5 (see particularly 1:16–17; 2:9–11; 3:21–4:25) is that all men, Jew and Gentile alike, stand on a level before God." Therefore, "within this context, the correct gloss to put on 'all men' in vv. 12, 18 is not 'all men individually,' but 'Jews and Gentiles alike.'"[58]

Furthermore, to argue that Romans 5:18, or any other text in the epistle, demands that all be finally saved, is to disregard Paul's repeated statements to the contrary, for example, in 1:18–20, 32; 2:1–5, 8–9, 12, 27; and 3:5–8. I conclude that the argument for universalism based on the work óf Christ is not convincing.

The Consummation

The most popular argument for universalism is that the New Testament writers, especially Paul, teach the final restoration of all people. In fact, the favorite universalist proof text is 1 Corinthians 15:22, 28: "For as in Adam all die, so in Christ all will be made alive. . . . When he has done this, then the Son himself will be made subject to him who put everything under him, so that God may be all in all." Other Scriptures in this category include Acts 3:21; Romans 8:19–23; Ephesians 1:10; and Philippians 2:9–11.

My strategy here is, again, to argue from the contexts, both near and far, that these verses do not teach universalism. Surely 1 Corinthians 15:22 should be understood in the light of the verse that follows. Verse 23 qualifies the expression "in Christ all will be made alive," with "each in his own turn: Christ, the firstfruits; then, when he comes, those who belong to him." The "all" of verse 22, therefore, is equivalent to "those who belong to him [Christ]." That 1 Corinthians does not teach that all belong to Christ is clear also from 1:18; 5:13; 6:9–10; and 11:32. These texts speak of unbelievers' "perishing" (1:18), being judged by God (5:13), not inheriting "the kingdom of God" (6:9–10), and being "condemned" (11:32).

Last, we deal with 1 Corinthians 15:28, which speaks of God's ultimately being "all in all." In fairness I admit that this and similar passages, such as Ephesians 1:10 and Philippians 2:9–11, if taken by themselves, are compatible with universalism. It is plain, however, from other verses in the biblical books in which these verses appear, that they are not intended to teach that all will be saved. Universalists argue their case from only a portion of the biblical data. But this line of reasoning must be rejected as unsound theological methodology. To know the Bible's teaching we must take the whole Bible into account. Upon close inspection the argument from the consummation passages is no more persuasive than the other two main arguments for universalism.[59]

Conclusion

We carefully examined and repudiated the most influential recent case for universalism—that of John Hick. Next, we weighed the case for postmortem conversion on the scales of Scripture and found it seriously wanting. Finally, we considered alleged biblical proof texts for universalism and found them less than persuasive when interpreted in their contexts. Consequently, in agreement with the evaluation by John Blanchard with which this chapter began, we must reject universalism as contrary to the express teachings of the Word of God. Several implications necessarily follow.

First, although we can sympathize with the desires of universalists that all be saved, we must label universalism a false teaching. In fact, because universalism flies in the face of Scripture and deliberately avoids much of the biblical evidence, it is a sin to hold it. If some readers of this book are entertaining the universalist hope, I plead with them to repent and submit to the truth, albeit painful, of God's Word that not everyone will be saved in the end.

Second, we must beware of the dangers of this false hope. Universalists' claims that their theology does not inhibit Christian missionary efforts ring hollow. J. I. Packer reminds us that Christians' zeal in the eighteenth and nineteenth centuries was fueled by their love for hell-bound sinners.

> Evangelicals know that the power behind the eighteenth century revivals and the great nineteenth century missionary movement was prayer, and that the prayer was made out of hearts agonizing over the prospect of all who leave this world without Christ being lost. Was such prayer misconceived? uninstructed? foolish? wrong-headed? An evangelical who values his heritage must ponder that question, recognizing that if universalism is true, all that missionary passion and praying was founded on a monstrous mistake.[60]

Such evangelical piety was well founded, based as it was on the clear teaching of the Redeemer and his apostles. Because universalism seeks to undermine that foundation, it must be rejected as evil. Although universalism claims to extol the love of God, in reality, as T. F. Torrance reminds us, "No doctrine that cuts the nerve of that urgency in the Gospel can be a doctrine of love, but only an abiding menace to the Gospel and to mankind."[61]

Third, we must replace the false universalism with what N. T. Wright calls a true, "biblical 'universalism.' This is the doctrine, which is in fact totally opposed to the usual 'universalism,' that there is one God and one way of salvation for all, Jesus Christ. . . . This biblical 'universalism' (unlike the other sort) gives the strongest motives for evangelism, namely, the love of God and of men."[62]

As difficult as it is to be biblical realists who believe the teaching of Scripture that not all people will be saved, we have no other choice if we are to be faithful to God, to his Word, and to our fellow human beings. May God strengthen us with his grace and use us to proclaim the Good News, so that many might be saved.

NOTES

1. John Blanchard, *Whatever Happened to Hell?* (Durham, England: Evangelical Press, 1993), 204, 208.
2. John Hick, *God Has Many Names: Britain's New Religious Pluralism* (London: Macmillan, 1980), 4.
3. John Hick, *Evil and the God of Love* (London: Macmillan, 1966), 398–400.
4. Ibid., 377–78.
5. Ibid., 377–78, 385.
6. Ibid., 381–82.
7. Ibid., 382.
8. Ibid., 378–79.
9. Ibid., 379–80.
10. Ibid., 380–81.
11. Ibid., 382–83.
12. John Hick, *Death and Eternal Life* (New York: Harper & Row, 1976), 198–201.
13. Ibid., 181–82.
14. Ibid., 243, 245.
15. Ibid., 244–45.
16. Ibid., 247–48.
17. Ibid., 248–49.
18. Ibid., 249–50.
19. Ibid., 251.
20. Ibid., 251–53.
21. Ibid., 238, 240, 258.

22. Ibid., 455–56. For more details, see 399–424.
23. John Hick, *God and the Universe of Faiths* (London: Macmillan, 1973), 135–36, 138.
24. Hick, *God Has Many Names*, 6.
25. Hick, *God and the Universe of Faiths*, 145. For more extensive treatment see 148–79, and *God Has Many Names*, 59–79.
26. Hick, *God Has Many Names*, 64, 66, 72.
27. John Hick, ed., *The Myth of God Incarnate* (Philadelphia: Westminster Press, 1977).
28. For a fuller critique of Hick's theology see Ronald H. Nash, *Is Jesus the Only Savior?* (Grand Rapids: Zondervan, 1994), 29–100.
29. Nigel M. de S. Cameron, "Universalism and the Logic of Revelation," *Evangelical Review of Theology* 2.4 (October 1987): 326.
30. Hick, *Death and Eternal Life*, 199, 201, 456.
31. Hick, *Evil and the God of Love*, 380.
32. Hick, *Death and Eternal Life*, 244.
33. Ibid., 249–50.
34. Stephen H. Travis, *Christian Hope and the Future* (Downers Grove, Ill.: InterVarsity Press, 1980), 132.
35. Paul Helm, "Universalism and the Threat of Hell," *Trinity Journal* 4 New Series (1983): 40.
36. Cameron, "Universalism and the Logic of Revelation," 328–29.
37. Travis, *Christian Hope and the Future*, 130.
38. Hick, *Death and Eternal Life*, 251–53.
39. Hick, *God Has Many Names*, 73–74.
40. Trevor Hart, "Universalism: Two Distinct Types," *Universalism and the Doctrine of Hell*, ed. Nigel M. de S. Cameron (Grand Rapids: Zondervan, 1992), 13–14.
41. For Hick's statement of his conversion and subsequent "spiritual pilgrimage," see *God Has Many Names*, 1–9.
42. Cameron, "Universalism and the Logic of Revelation," 325, 329.
43. Ibid., 330–31.
44. Hick, *Death and Eternal Life*, 400, 456.
45. Richard J. Bauckham, "Universalism: A Historical Survey," *Themelios* 4.2 (1979), 54. See Hick, *Death and Eternal Life*, 420.
46. Clark H. Pinnock, *A Wideness in God's Mercy: The Finality of Jesus Christ in a World of Religions* (Grand Rapids: Zondervan, 1992), 168–69.
47. Ibid., 170.
48. Ibid., 170–71. For Pinnock's espousing annihilationism see 156–57 and "The Destruction of the Finally Impenitent," *Criswell Theological Review* 4.2 (1990): 243–59.
49. I favor the view of J. Ramsey Michaels, who understands it as speaking of Christ's announcing his sovereignty to evil spirits on his return to heaven (*1 Peter*, Word Biblical Commentary [Waco, Tex.: Word, 1988], 205–13). For a different view see Wayne Grudem, *1 Peter*, Tyndale New Testament Commen-

taries (Grand Rapids: Eerdmans, 1988), 203–39.

50. Larry Dixon, *The Other Side of the Good News: Confronting the Contemporary Challenges to Jesus' Teaching on Hell* (Wheaton, Ill.: Victor Books, 1992), 118.

51. Millard J. Erickson, *The Evangelical Mind and Heart* (Grand Rapids: Baker, 1992), 140.

52. N. T. Wright, "Towards a Biblical View of Universalism," *Themelios* 4.2 (1979): 55.

53. Travis, *Christian Hope and the Future*, 130–31.

54. Erickson, *Evangelical Mind and Heart*, 140.

55. Ibid.

56. Wright, "Towards a Biblical View of Universalism," 57.

57. Ibid.

58. Ibid., 56.

59. For further critique of universalism see Ajith Fernando, *Crucial Questions About Hell* (Wheaton, Ill.: Crossway, 1991), 53–57, 113–22.

60. J. I. Packer, "Evangelicals and the Way of Salvation," *Evangelical Affirmations*, ed. Kenneth S. Kantzer and Carl F. H. Henry (Grand Rapids: Zondervan, 1990), 117.

61. T. F. Torrance, "Universalism or Election?" *Scottish Journal of Theology* 2 (1949): 318.

62. Wright, "Towards a Biblical View of Universalism," 57–58.

9

False Witnesses (2): Annihilationism

Let me say at the outset that I consider the concept of hell as endless torment in body and mind an outrageous doctrine, a theological and moral enormity, a bad doctrine of the tradition which needs to be changed. How can Christians possibly project a deity of such cruelty and vindictiveness whose ways include inflicting everlasting torture upon his creatures, however sinful they may have been? Surely a God who would do such a thing is more nearly like Satan than like God, at least by any ordinary moral standards, and by the gospel itself. . . . Surely the God and Father of our Lord Jesus Christ is no fiend; torturing people without end is not what our God does.[1]

Strong words! Not all annihilationists, however, engage in such heated polemic. Ultimately, it is not the fervor but the rigor of the arguments that matters. In this chapter we will measure the main arguments for annihilationism against the teachings of Scripture.

The four best books espousing annihilationism have been written in this century. Anglican missionary Harold E. Guillebaud completed *The Righteous Judge* shortly before his death in 1941. Basil Atkinson, under-librarian in the University Library at Cambridge, penned *Life and Immortality* in the late 1960s. Seventh-day Adventist professor LeRoy Edwin Froom's massive two-volume work *The Conditionalist Faith of Our Fathers* was published in 1965–66. And in 1982 Edward Fudge, an attorney and Churches of Christ layman, produced *The Fire That Consumes: A Biblical and Historical Study of Final Punishment.*[2]

None of the four books mentioned (which together exceed three thousand pages) offers a succinct summary of the best case for annihilationism. Such a summary is found in John Stott's tentative defense of the doctrine in his nine-page response to liberal theologian David L. Edwards in *Evangelical Essentials.*[3] I will, therefore, use Stott's arguments as an outline, citing the four books to fill out his arguments, and I will add one argument that Stott mentions in passing that features prominently in the annihilationist literature. The arguments are as follows:

- The Argument Based on "the Vocabulary of Destruction"
- The Argument Based on Hell-Fire Imagery
- The Argument Based on God's Justice
- The Argument Based on the "Universalist Passages"
- The Argument Based on Conditional Immortality

The Argument Based on "the Vocabulary of Destruction"

Dr. Stott contends that we should understand the Bible literally when it speaks of the damned as "perishing," or suffering "destruction." He assumes that these words speak of annihilation: "It would seem strange, therefore, if people who are said to suffer destruction are in fact not destroyed."[4]

How are we to evaluate this claim? First, we will examine the passages that Stott maintains teach the extinction of the wicked. Granted, it is possible to construe some of these passages as teaching annihilationism. Jesus' use of the word "destroy" in Matthew 10:28, for example, could be taken this way: "Do not be afraid of those who kill the body but cannot kill the soul. Rather, be afraid of the One who can *destroy* both soul and body in hell." Likewise, Jesus' presentation of stark alternatives in the Sermon on the Mount could be interpreted to support annihilationism: "Enter through the narrow gate. For wide is the gate and broad is the road that leads to *destruction*, and many enter through it. But small is the gate and narrow the road that leads to life, and only a few find it" (Matt. 7:13–14). John 3:16 could also be understood as teaching the final obliteration of the wicked: "For God so loved the world that he gave his one and only Son, that whoever believes in him shall not *perish* but have eternal life."

In fact, many passages that contain "the vocabulary of destruction" could, if taken by themselves, be construed to teach the extermination of the wicked: John 10:28; 17:12; Romans 2:12; 9:22; Philippians 1:28; 3:19; 1 Thessalonians 5:3; Hebrews 10:39; James 4:12; and 2 Peter 3:7, 9. If Scripture gave us no other teaching on the destiny of the wicked than that provided by these and similar passages, annihilationism would be a viable option.

However, these passages are not the only data we have to work with. In fact, even some of the passages Stott cites are difficult to reconcile with annihilationism. Second Thessalonians 1:9 is one example. Paul says that the wicked "will be punished with everlasting destruction and shut out from the presence of the Lord and from the majesty of his power." "Everlasting annihilation" is an unlikely meaning for the words "everlasting destruction."[5]

Moreover, does it make sense for Paul to depict unbelievers' extinction as their being "shut out from the presence of the Lord"? Doesn't their being shut out from his presence imply their existence? Not according to Atkinson: "All will agree that the presence of the Lord is everywhere. To be destroyed from the presence of the Lord can therefore only mean to be nowhere."[6] On the contrary, as Scot McKnight argues: "Paul has in mind an irreversible verdict of eternal nonfellowship with God. A person exists but remains excluded from God's good presence."[7]

The word "destruction" cannot mean what Stott assumes in Revelation 17:8, 11. There "destruction" is prophesied for "the beast." Two chapters later the Beast and False Prophet are "thrown alive into the fiery lake of burning sulfur" (Rev. 19:20). Although Fudge says that "in the case of the beast and false prophet . . . the lake of fire stands for utter, absolute, irreversible annihilation,"[8] they are still there "one thousand years" later (Rev. 20:7, 10). Furthermore, John teaches that the Beast, the False Prophet, and Satan "will be tormented day and night for ever and ever" (Rev. 20:10). The Beast's "destruction," therefore, is not annihilation. It is eternal punishment![9]

Consequently, annihilationists err when they claim that the words "destruction" and "perish" and their synonyms signify the final extinction of the wicked. This claim cannot be established from all of the judgment passages that use these words.

A second way to evaluate Stott's claim that the vocabulary of destruction teaches annihilationism is to consider theological method. Even if one could show that every passage that uses the language of destruction is *compatible* with annihilationism, that still would not prove that it is true. In addition, one would have to show that the other passages that speak of hell are consistent with the extinction of the wicked. And that cannot be done.

The Bible uses five main pictures to speak of hell: darkness and separation, fire, "weeping and gnashing of teeth," punishment, and death and destruction. Only the last fits with annihilationism, and not even every passage in that category fits, as we have seen. We'll postpone study of the fire imagery until our consideration of Stott's second argument. For now, let us examine one passage from each of the remaining three categories.

First, darkness and separation. In Luke 13:25–27 Jesus, "the owner of the house," expels false believers from his presence: "I don't know you. . . . Away from me, all you evildoers!" He continues, "There will be weeping and gnashing of teeth" when they are "thrown out" of God's kingdom. Jesus here presupposes the existence of the wicked; they are alive and suffer great pain of loss. John Wenham, therefore, errs when he insists that separation from God "is another way of describing destruction."[10]

Second, "weeping and gnashing of teeth." Weeping signifies sorrowful crying; the gnashing of teeth, "extreme suffering and remorse."[11] Jesus uses this expression to explain the pictures of darkness (Matt. 8:12; 22:13; 25:30; Luke 13:28), fire (Matt. 13:42, 50), and being cut to pieces (Matt. 24:51). In each of its seven occurrences "weeping and gnashing of teeth" is preceded by the adverb *ekei*, which means "there, in that place,"[12] indicating the suffering of the wicked in hell itself. Weeping and gnashing can be done only by people who exist; it is not possible for those annihilated to cry and grind their teeth. Fudge's claim that this expression speaks of "conscious suffering which precedes final destruction" is unwarranted.[13] In the texts cited above, darkness, fire, and being cut to pieces are pictures not of suffering prior to final punishment, but of final punishment itself.

And third, punishment. Our Lord contrasts the fates of the wicked and the righteous in Matthew 25:46: "Then they [the wicked] will go away to eternal punishment, but the righteous to eternal life." Scot McKnight's comments deserve consideration:

> Because *aionios* ("eternal") modifies both punishment and life in Matthew 25:46, it stands to reason that the same quality and temporal connotations are in view. That is to say, however long the life extends is how long the punishment lasts; the durations are identical. It is grammatically unsuitable to drive a wedge between the two uses of the term *eternal* in Matthew 25:46, suggesting that one refers to endlessness (eternal) and the other to temporal limitation (aeonial). . . . Since it is clear to say that the eternal life is temporally unlimited it follows that eternal punishment is also temporally unlimited.[14]

McKnight's conclusion is fortified by the fact that five verses earlier Jesus says that the wicked will share the same destiny as the Devil, who according to Revelation 20:10 will suffer endlessly in the lake of fire.

Good theological method involves taking into account the whole Bible when constructing a doctrine. Annihilationism can accommodate only a portion of the biblical passages that describe the final destiny of the wicked.[15]

Some may be troubled by the number of passages that I conceded were possibly compatible with annihilationism. It helps to study the way we reach theological conclusions. For example, Jesus' words "the

Father is greater than I" (John 14:28) have been used to deny Christ's deity. Taken by itself, that verse is compatible with such a denial. In fact, some claim that scores of passages that teach Christ's humanity deny his deity. That claim is false, however, since the Bible clearly teaches Christ's deity. Notice that the fact that many passages are *compatible* with a denial of Christ's deity does not disprove his deity. The way to correctly understand Christ's person is to study all of Scripture.

It is the same for the doctrine of hell. The fact that many passages could be interpreted as teaching annihilationism does not prove that doctrine. In order to be true, annihilationism has to account for all of the passages. And at this point it fails.

One loose end remains: What *does* the vocabulary of destruction signify? The honesty of annihilationist Harold Guillebaud is admirable: "It is not denied, that *if* it were clear beyond question from Bible teaching elsewhere that the doom of the lost will be everlasting torment, it would be quite possible to understand 'death', 'destruction' and the like, as meaning a wretched and ruined existence."[16]

The Argument Based on Hell-Fire Imagery

John Stott's second argument involves Scripture's hell-fire imagery. Stott considers it unfortunate that we have been misled by the experience of being burned into associating fire with pain. "But the main function of fire is not to cause pain, but to secure destruction, as all the world's incinerators bear witness."[17] Hot stoves have misled us; incinerators are more trustworthy guides.

Some hell-fire passages can be understood as teaching annihilationism. John the Baptist's warning is one example:

> The ax is already at the root of the trees, and every tree that does not produce good fruit will be cut down and thrown into *the fire*. . . . His winnowing fork is in his hand, and he will clear his threshing floor, gathering his wheat into the barn and *burning up* the chaff *with unquenchable fire*. (Matt. 3:10, 12, emphasis added)

A number of Jesus' sayings could be put in this category. In Matthew 7:19 he says, "Every tree that does not bear good fruit is cut down and thrown into the *fire.*" Elsewhere he says, "If anyone does not remain in me, he is like a branch that is thrown away and withers; such branches are picked up, thrown into the *fire* and *burned*" (John 15:6). Hebrews contains two texts that could be taken in the same way: 10:27 mentions a "raging fire that will consume the enemies of God," and 12:29 notes how "our God is a consuming fire."

These five texts could be interpreted as teaching annihilationism, but *should* they be? We must answer no in view of the abundant scriptural testimony that hell-fire speaks of the pain of the wicked, not their consumption.

Jesus' parable of the weeds sounds like the verses cited above. He says, "Collect the weeds and tie them in bundles to be *burned*" (Matt. 13:30). A picture of the burning of the weeds is built into the parable. Had Jesus wanted to teach annihilationism, here would have been an ideal occasion. His explanation of the parable clearly demonstrates that that is not his intent:

> As the weeds are pulled up and burned in the fire, so it will be at the end of the age. The Son of Man will send out his angels, and they will weed out of his kingdom everything that causes sin and all who do evil. They will throw them into the fiery furnace, where there will be weeping and gnashing of teeth. (Matt. 13:40–42)

When Jesus explains the meaning of the weeds being cast into the furnace, he does not speak of consumption. He warns of suffering. He describes the "fiery furnace" as a place marked by "weeping and gnashing of teeth" in pain (v. 42). Hell-fire here speaks of anguish, not extinction.

That is not to say that this parable is incompatible with annihilationism. An annihilationist could hold that after the crying and gnashing, the damned will cease to exist. Statements like the following, however, are irresponsible: "Penal suffering comes into the application of the parables, for a death by fire is necessarily a very awful death, but it surely is not the main point."[18] On the contrary, Jesus tells us what the main points of his parable are, and here he uses fire to speak of pain.[19]

Historically, the key passage on hell in the Gospels is Jesus' teaching about the sheep and the goats. Jesus, the Son of Man, banishes the accursed to "the eternal fire prepared for the devil and his angels" (Matt. 25:41). Does this "eternal fire" denote pain or extinction? John answers this question: "The devil . . . was thrown into the lake of burning sulfur. . . . [and] will be tormented day and night for ever and ever" (Rev. 20:10). Here fire denotes torment. And this torment, not obliteration, lies ahead for the Devil, his evil angels, and all unrepentant human beings.

The parable of the rich man and Lazarus uses fire imagery in the same way. The rich man died and found himself "in hell where he was in torment." The reason for his plea for mercy is "because I am in agony in this fire" (Luke 16:23–24). Plainly, fire speaks here of the "agony" that one suffers in the "place of torment" (Luke 16:25, 28).

It will not do, as some have tried, to exclude this parable from the discussion on the assumption that it speaks of the intermediate rather than the final state of the wicked.[20] Regardless of its precise focus, we can learn from its use of hell-fire imagery. And that imagery unmistakably equates fire with torment.

The book of Revelation does the same when it says that the wicked "will drink of the wine of God's fury . . . poured full strength into the cup of his wrath." Does this imply the blotting out of the ungodly? Hardly, for John continues, "He will be tormented with burning sulfur" (Rev. 14:10). Here fire ("burning sulfur") is God's instrument to punish the wicked.

Annihilationists claim that verse 11 favors their cause: "And the smoke of their torment rises for ever and ever." John Stott, for example, writes:

> The fire itself is termed "eternal" and "unquenchable", but it would be very odd if what is thrown into it proves indestructible. Our expectation would be the opposite: it would be consumed for ever, not tormented for ever. Hence it is the smoke (evidence that the fire has done its work) which "rises for ever and ever."[21]

On the contrary, our expectation would be that the smoke would die out once the fire had finished its work. How could the smoke from the fire rise forever if its fuel had been consumed? The rest of the verse confirms our interpretation: "There is no rest day or night for those who worship the beast and his image."

Stott is wrong to claim that "it is not the torment itself but its 'smoke' (symbol of the completed burning) which will be 'for ever and ever.'"[22] John says that "there is no rest day or night" for the wicked. When annihilationists assert that John means to say that the wicked have no relief "so long as their suffering lasts," they evade the plain meaning of the text by reading into the text something that is not there.[23] The conclusion is irresistible: The imagery of burning in Revelation 14:10–11 conveys the eternal conscious torment of the ungodly.

So does the next use of fire imagery, the picture of the lost being thrown into the lake of fire. The lake of fire first comes into view in Revelation 19:20, where the "beast" and "false prophet" are thrown alive into it. A "thousand years" later they are still there, when the Devil is thrown in to join them (Rev. 20:7, 10). John explains what this means for all three: "They will be tormented day and night for ever and ever" (Rev. 20:10).

The verses that immediately follow speak of all human beings standing before God at the Last Judgment. People are judged, and the wicked are cast into the lake of fire (Rev. 20:14). The city of God is the final abode of the godly; by contrast, the lake of fire is the place for the ungodly (Rev. 21:8). Does the lake of fire mean unceasing torment for the Devil but annihilation for lost human beings? Hardly, as Beasley-Murray explains: "That it [John's use of the symbol of the lake of fire] does not have the meaning of annihilation is indicated by 20:10. The lake of fire signifies not extinction in opposition to existence, but torturous existence in the society of evil in opposition to life in the society of God."[24]

Annihilationist attempts to argue otherwise are contrived. For example, Guillebaud insists that the lake of fire should be interpreted in light of the second death because of the word order in Revelation 20:14 and 21:8: "The lake of fire is the second death." He then defines the second death as extinction and concludes that the lake of fire means extinction too.[25]

This will not do. We should allow John's description of the lake of fire, given in verse 10, to govern our understanding of it in verse 14. The second death, therefore, is another name for the lake of fire, which John teaches lasts forever. We must conclude that John uses the imagery of the lake of fire to portray damned human beings as forever experiencing the wrath of God, apart from his grace.

We have weighed the argument that hell-fire signifies extermination and found it wanting. Although some hell-fire passages could be interpreted in this way, they should not be, for in the five judgment passages that we examined fire signifies the suffering of pain, not consumption. We conclude, then, contrary to Stott's contention, that the Bible's hell-fire imagery is better illustrated by stoves than by incinerators.

The Argument Based on God's Justice

Dr. Stott's third argument concerns justice. The Bible teaches that "God will judge people 'according to what they have done' (e.g. Rev. 20:12), which implies that the penalty inflicted will be commensurate with the evil done." But because eternal torment is seriously disproportionate to sins committed in time, it clashes with the biblical revelation of divine justice.[26]

At first glance, this argument is appealing. But is it true to God's Word? Measured by biblical standards, few of us take sin seriously. As evidence of this, consider God's judgments against what might be called "little sins."

An impressive list can be drawn up. For example, because Lot's wife looked back at Sodom and Gomorrah, "She became a pillar of salt" (Gen. 19:26)—the death penalty for a glance! Because of irregularities in their priestly service in the tabernacle, Nadab and Abihu "fell dead before the LORD" (Num. 3:4; cf. Lev. 10:1–2)—capital punishment for faulty worship! Because Achan coveted and then stole a robe, silver, and gold, he and his family were stoned and burned (Josh. 7:24–25)—a whole family destroyed for one person's greed! Because Uzzah steadied the ark with his hand, "The LORD's anger burned against Uzzah . . . God struck him down and he died" (2 Sam. 6:6–7)—punishment of death for trying to keep the ark from falling!

Because Ananias and Sapphira lied to the apostles, God struck them dead (Acts 5:1–10)—capital punishment for lying!

Our first response to these examples is that justice was not served; repeatedly, it seems, God was overly severe. God's assessment, however, is far different.

Lot's wife defied God and ignored his warning: "Don't look back, and don't stop anywhere in the plain! Flee to the mountains or you will be swept away!" (Gen. 19:17). Is God unjust to repay disobedience with a previously announced penalty? Not according to Jesus, for he warned, "Remember Lot's wife!" (Luke 17:32).

Leviticus says that Nadab and Abihu acted "contrary to his [God's] command" (Lev. 10:1). God regarded their disobedient priestly service as dishonoring to himself, as is evident from his evaluation of it: "Among those who approach me I will show myself holy; in the sight of all the people I will be honored" (v. 3). Will we question God's right to keep his worship pure?

Achan "acted unfaithfully" (Josh. 7:1), and when confronted, confessed, "I have sinned against the Lord, the God of Israel" (7:20). Do we still want to cry "foul" at God's punishing him?

Uzzah was guilty of what Scripture calls "his irreverent act" (2 Sam. 6:7). God demands to be worshiped in truth. Israel, however, had followed the Philistines' example instead of obeying God's instructions for transporting the ark (cf. 2 Sam. 6:3 with Ex. 25:12–14 and Num. 4:5–6, 15). Shall we criticize God for giving only one person what David and many others deserved?

If we are offended by God's bringing capital punishment on Ananias and Sapphira because they merely lied to the apostles, we miss Luke's point. The husband and wife were ultimately guilty of lying not to men but to God (Acts 5:3–4).

Luke's words serve as a paradigm: "not to men but to God." We have difficulty recognizing God's justice in his punishment of "little sins" because we adopt a human-centered perspective rather than a God-centered one. If people lied to us or disobeyed us, would they deserve death? Of course not. If they do these things against God, do they deserve capital punishment? The Bible's consistent answer is yes. The Bible views sin as an attack on God's character and, therefore, warranting great punishment.

Some readers may agree with me in principle but protest that the examples given illustrate temporal punishment, not eternal. That criticism is fair. I have, however, saved the most scandalous example for last: Because Adam ate the forbidden fruit, he plunged the human race into sin with all of its terrible consequences. Paul writes, with reference to Adam's sin, that

> the many died by the trespass of the one man. . . . The judgment followed one sin and brought condemnation. . . . By the trespass of the one man, death reigned through that one man. . . . The result of one trespass was condemnation for all men. . . . Through the disobedience of the one man the many were made sinners. (Rom. 5:15–19)

Is this penalty proportionate to the crime committed? Notice the penalty. Paul says that Adam's one sin brought death and condemnation. There is no mistaking Paul's meaning in the context of Romans: because of Adam's sin, physical and spiritual death, even eternal condemnation, came to the human race. Damnation of the world for one man's eating a piece of fruit?

Perhaps we have misunderstood the significance of Adam's primal sin. John Calvin thinks so.

> Augustine speaks rightly when he declares that *pride* was the beginning of all evils. For if ambition had not raised man higher than was meet and right, he could have remained in his original state. But we must take a fuller definition. . . . it is already clear that *disobedience* was the beginning of the Fall. . . . Yet it is at the same time to be noted that the first man revolted from God's authority . . . because, contemptuous of truth, he turned aside to falsehood. *Unfaithfulness*, then, was the root of the Fall.[27]

Pride, disobedience, and unfaithfulness: these summarize Adam's sin, if viewed from a God-centered perspective. Adam pridefully wanted to be like his Maker. He disobeyed God's prohibition. And he was unfaithful to his Lord (Gen. 3:1–6). Will we charge him with injustice who warned, "You must not eat from the tree of the knowledge of good and evil, for when you eat of it you will surely die" (Gen. 2:17)? Indeed, will we follow Adam's footsteps and re-volt against our Maker?

If we are to submit to the authority of God's Word, we must accept the fact that God is not unjust for punishing the human race with condemnation for Adam's sin. And not only for Adam's sin, but for our individual sins too, as Paul teaches in Romans.

> The wrath of God is being revealed from heaven against all the godlessness and wickedness of men. . . . Because of your stubbornness and unrepentant heart, you are storing up wrath against yourself for the day of God's wrath, when his righteous judgment will be revealed. . . . "There is no one righteous, not even one. . . . All have turned away, they have together become worthless; there is no one who does good, not even one." . . . All have sinned and fall short of the glory of God. (Rom. 1:18; 2:5; 3:10, 12, 23)

We must learn of divine justice from the Bible itself. It will not do to protest God's revealed judgments on the basis of what seems fair or unfair to us. Instead, we must adjust our thinking, including our view of God's justice, to God's revealed truth.

I respect annihilationist Harold Guillebaud's refusal to argue for annihilationism from a preconceived notion of divine justice.

> For the words of the Lord Jesus Christ with regard to the condemned are so terrible, so final in excluding any idea that mercy may be open to them, that we dare not presume to set limits in advance as to what He might see fit to ordain as their punishment. The character of God is safe in the hands of His Son, who came to reveal Him, and we must trust Him, and receive what He tells us. The question is simply, *What do His words mean?*[28]

In fact, the annihilationists' argument from justice can be turned against their position. Universalists, on the basis of what they deem just and unjust, reject both eternal punishment and *annihilationism* as unworthy of God's love. So J. A. T. Robinson:

> Christ, in Origen's old words, remains on the Cross so long as one sinner remains in hell. That is not speculation: it is a statement grounded in the very necessity of God's nature. In a universe of love there can be no heaven which tolerates a chamber of horrors, no hell for any which does not at the same time make it hell for God.[29]

The annihilationist argument based on justice is a very old one, to which Thomas Aquinas still offers the best response.

> Further, the magnitude of the punishment matches the magnitude of the sin. . . . Now a sin that is against God is infinite; the higher the person against whom it is committed, the graver the sin—it is more criminal to strike a head of state than a private citizen—and God is of infinite greatness. Therefore an infinite punishment is deserved for a sin committed against him.[30]

Aquinas is right. Sin is an attack on the infinitely holy God. He, therefore, justly sets the penalties for sin in this world and the next. He righteously condemns sinners for Adam's sin and for their own. And he plainly teaches that he punishes the wicked forever. We conclude that he is just in so doing.

The Argument Based on the "Universalist Passages"

John Stott's fourth and final argument for annihilationism is based on supposed universalist passages. Stott cannot endorse universalism because the Bible teaches the reality of hell.

> My point here, however, is that the eternal existence of the impenitent in hell would be hard to reconcile with the promises of God's final victory over evil, or with the appar-

ently universalistic texts. . . . These texts . . . lead me to ask
how God can in any meaningful sense be called "everything
to everybody" [1 Cor 15:28] while an unspecified number of
people still continue in rebellion against him and under his
judgment.[31]

Once again, Stott's argument can be turned against him. Universalists' favorite passage is 1 Corinthians 15:24–28.

Then the end will come, when he hands over the kingdom
to God the Father after he has destroyed all dominion,
authority and power. For he must reign until he has put all
his enemies under his feet. . . . When he has done this, then
the Son himself will be made subject to him who put everything under him, so that God may be all in all.

Stott argues that this passage does not teach universalism. On what
basis? He correctly accuses universalists of interpreting this and similar
passages apart from the rest of the Bible's teachings. Yet Stott makes
the same mistake when he cites these passages in support of
annihilationism.

In fact, appealing to "universalist texts" proves neither universalism nor annihilationism. We must study the whole Bible to understand future things. The crucial question is, What does God deem
compatible with his being "all in all"? The Bible's final three chapters
answer: God's ultimate victory does not involve the eradication of evil
beings from his universe.

Revelation 20:11–15 presents the Last Judgment. Here John sees
"the dead, great and small, standing before the throne" of God. John had
just noted that the Devil, Beast, and False Prophet are thrown into the
lake of fire to suffer everlasting torment (Rev. 20:10). Now, God adds to
John's vision: wicked human beings will share the same fate (Rev. 20:14).

Revelation 21:1–8 confirms this conclusion. There, alongside
the new heaven and the new earth, John describes the final destination of the unrepentant: "the fiery lake of burning sulfur" (Rev. 21:8).
Evidently, God does not view unbelievers' being eternally alive in the
lake of fire as incompatible with his being "all in all."

That God's ultimate victory does not include the annihilation of the damned is confirmed by the picture of the New Jerusalem in Revelation 21–22. Blessed are all who live in this city. God will be in their midst to "wipe every tear from their eyes." For them "there will be no more death or mourning or crying or pain" (Rev. 21:3–4). Does John's vision teach the absolute banishment of death and pain? Obviously not, because four verses later the wicked are said to go into the lake of fire (Rev. 21:8).

Furthermore, in chapter 22, he contrasts the joy of those who "may go through the gates into the city" of God with the misery of the godless who are "outside" the city (Rev. 22:14–15). Plainly, the wicked are not annihilated. They are alive but cut off from the happiness of eternal fellowship with God.[32]

If this exposition of Revelation 20–22 is correct, universalists and annihilationists would have to claim that the end depicted in these chapters is not ultimate; there is still more to come after Revelation 22. Later, God will save all the wicked (universalism) or obliterate them (annihilationism). But these scenarios do not square with Revelation 21–22, which presents the ultimate end, the new heaven and new earth (Rev. 21:1–8; 22:12–15).

We must conclude that the traditional view of hell better fits the scriptural vision of the end than does annihilationism. The Bible's concluding chapters will not allow us to understand the "universalist passages" in an absolute sense. God's being "all in all" means that he reigns over the just and the unjust; it does not mean that only the former remain.

We have examined John Stott's four arguments for annihilationism and have not found them compelling. We therefore must respectfully disagree with him when he urges "that the ultimate annihilation of the wicked should at least be accepted as a legitimate, biblically founded alternative to their eternal conscious torment."[33]

The Argument Based on Conditional Immortality

One other argument for annihilationism merits attention. Conditional immortality, sometimes used as another name for annihilationism, is the view that souls are not naturally immortal, but that immortality is a gift given by God only to the righteous, who, as a result, live forever. But the unrighteous, because they lack the gift of immortality, are annihilated and cease to exist. Clark Pinnock regards this issue as crucial.

> This is clearly an important issue in our discussion because belief in the natural immortality of the soul which is so widely held by Christians, although stemming more from Plato than the Bible, really drives the traditional doctrine of hell more than exegesis does. Consider the logic: if souls must live forever because they are naturally immortal, the lake of fire must be their home forever and cannot be their destruction. . . . I am convinced that the hellenistic belief in the immortality of the soul has done more than anything else (specifically more than the Bible) to give credibility to the doctrine of everlasting conscious punishment of the wicked.[34]

This argument has been vastly overrated for four reasons. First, although philosophy has influenced all periods of church history, those who have argued for a traditional view of hell have done so because they believed that this is what the Bible teaches. This is true, for example, of Tertullian, Augustine, Aquinas, Luther, Calvin, Edwards, and Shedd, to name the stalwarts of orthodoxy. It is ludicrous to argue that they held to eternal torment because they were influenced by Platonic philosophy. If we take their own claims seriously, they believed in this terrible doctrine out of fidelity to biblical teaching—sometimes against their own natural inclinations.

Second, their view of immortality was not Platonic but biblical. They did not hold that the souls of humans were inherently immortal, as did Plato. Rather acknowledging that God "alone is immortal," as Paul says (1 Tim. 6:16), they taught that the immortal God grants immortality to all human beings.

Third, we need to define the concept of the immortality of the soul. In fact, to avoid confusion, we might do well to abandon the expression. Some use the words "the immortality of the soul" to refer to the survival of the immaterial part of human nature after death. Though that is a biblical idea,[35] it is better called the survival of the human soul or spirit in the intermediate state. We confuse the intermediate and final states if we refer to the former by the expression "the immortality of the soul."

Most use "the immortality of the soul" to describe our final destiny. That too is misleading since our final state is not a disembodied spiritual life in heaven, but a holistic resurrected one on the new earth. All things considered, it is better to talk about the immortality of people, not of souls. This accords with the language of 1 Corinthians 15, which says of the resurrected righteous, "For the perishable must clothe itself with the imperishable, and the mortal with immortality" (v. 53).

Finally, and most importantly, I do not believe in the traditional view of hell because I accept the immortality of human beings, but the other way around. I believe in the immortality of human beings because the Bible clearly teaches everlasting damnation for the wicked and everlasting life for the righteous.

Conclusion

We have considered the case for annihilationism from the writings of its proponents. We have weighed their arguments on the scales of Scripture and found them wanting. In the process, we have reaffirmed the church's historic doctrine of hell.

Some important applications follow from these conclusions. Since annihilationism contradicts the teaching of the Bible, it must be rejected. Although some evangelical Christians hold this doctrine, I plead with them to renounce it. Because it dishonors God and his truth to believe error, professing Christians need to repent of the sin of accepting this false teaching.

Annihilationism is a most serious error because it leads unrepentant sinners to underestimate their fate. Would not the ungodly be more inclined to live selfishly their whole lives, without thought of God, if they expected after death to face ultimate extinction rather than eternal punishment? The unsaved would probably *like* annihilationism to be true, but it is not. Because we believers love the lost, we must tell them the truth: all who live ungodly lives face eternal conscious torment at the hands of the living God!

This leads to a final application. I fear that if annihilationism is widely accepted by Christians, that will hinder the missionary enterprise. Many people have devoted their lives to bringing the gospel to the unsaved around the globe. Would they continue to do so if they really thought that the worst fate awaiting those who reject Jesus is final extinction? I seriously doubt it. Annihilationists can argue that the obliteration of the wicked is a terrible fate if measured against the bliss of the righteous.[36] But when compared to suffering in hell forever, it is simply not that bad to cease to exist.

I pray that God would spark a revival of the knowledge of the true doctrine of hell in the Christian church. I have no doubt that such a revival would result in gratitude for grace, amendment of life, and ingathering of the lost such as we have not seen in our time. May God grant it!

NOTES

1. Clark H. Pinnock, "The Destruction of the Finally Impenitent," *Criswell Theological Review* 4.2 (1990): 246–47. In response to Pinnock, Millard J. Erickson issues a needed word of caution. "It is one thing to speak emphatically about one's sense of injustice and moral outrage over the idea of God's condemning persons to hell. If, however, one is going to describe sending persons to endless punishment as 'cruelty and vindictiveness,' and a God who would do so as 'more nearly like Satan than God,' and 'a bloodthirsty monster who maintains an everlasting Auschwitz,' he had better be very certain he is correct. For if he is wrong, he is guilty of blasphemy. A wiser course of action would be restraint in one's statements, just in case he might be wrong" (*The Evangelical Mind and Heart* [Grand Rapids: Baker, 1993], 152).
2. Harold E. Guillebaud, *The Righteous Judge* (n.p., 1941); Basil Atkinson, *Life and Immortality* (n.p., n.d.); LeRoy Edwin Froom, *The Conditionalist Faith of Our Fathers*, 2 vols. (Washington, D.C.: Review and Herald, 1965–66); Edward Fudge, *The Fire That Consumes: A Biblical and Historical Study of Final Punishment* (Houston: Providential Press, 1982). The first two books were published privately and are obtainable from the Reverend B. L. Bateson, 26 Summershard, S. Petherton, Somerset, U.K. TA13 5DP.
3. David L. Edwards and John Stott, *Evangelical Essentials: A Liberal-Evangelical Dialogue* (Downers Grove, Ill.: InterVarsity Press, 1988), 312–20.
4. Ibid., 315–16. Cf. Guillebaud, *The Righteous Judge*, 14–19; Atkinson, *Life and*

Immortality, 85–100; Froom, *The Conditionalist Faith of Our Fathers*, 1.105–11, 286–302, 404–14, 486–97; Fudge, *The Fire That Consumes*, 173–78, 243–50, 295–307.

5. Annihilationists claim that *aionios* in this and similar expressions refers to eternal results and not eternal existence (see Guillebaud, *Righteous Judge*, 7–11; Atkinson, *Life and Immortality*, 101; Froom, *Conditionalist Faith*, 1.224, 288–91, 294–95, 441–43; Fudge, *The Fire That Consumes*, 44–50). This claim is arbitrary and unsubstantiated. On the meaning of *aionios*, see W. G. T. Shedd, *The Doctrine of Endless Punishment*, 2d ed. (New York: Scribners, 1887), 82–89; and Scot McKnight, "Eternal Consequences or Eternal Consciousness?" *Through No Fault of Their Own? The Fate of Those Who Have Never Heard*, ed. William V. Crockett and James G. Sigountos (Grand Rapids: Baker, 1991), 147–57.

6. Atkinson, *Life and Immortality*, 101. Further, he would prove too much if his claim were true that "the occurrence of the word [*olethros*, "destruction"] in 1 Thess. 5:3 . . . refers to the same thing as in 2 Thess. 1:9." If 1 Thess. 5:3 refers to annihilation, it is the annihilation taught by Bertrand Russell, not that of the evangelical annihilationists.

7. Scot McKnight, "Eternal Consequences or Eternal Consciousness?" 155–56.

8. Fudge, *The Fire That Consumes*, 304.

9. Atkinson, therefore, errs when he claims, "The use of the word 'drown' in 1 Tim. 6:9 may perhaps be felt on the whole to strengthen our view of perdition, and the two verses (8 and 11) of Rev. 17 make it reasonably certain. They speak of a great political and ecclesiastical power going into perdition, and this can mean nothing but its total destruction and extinction" (*Life and Immortality*, 89).

10. John W. Wenham, "The Case for Conditional Immortality," in *Universalism and the Doctrine of Hell*, ed. Nigel M. de S. Cameron (Grand Rapids: Baker, 1992), 172.

11. Thomas McComiskey, "*brygmos*," *The New International Dictionary of New Testament Theology*, ed. Colin Brown, 3 vols. (Grand Rapids: Zondervan, 1976), 2:421.

12. So W. Bauer, W. F. Arndt, F. W. Gingrich, and F. Danker, *A Greek Lexicon of the New Testament and Other Early Christian Literature*, 2d ed. (Chicago: University of Chicago Press, 1979), 239. Atkinson renders *ekei* in Matt. 24:51 "on that occasion" in an attempt to avoid the idea of hell as a place, but that is arbitrary and unsupported by any lexicon: "Four times in the Gospel of Matthew we are told that on the day of judgment there will be 'weeping and gnashing of teeth' (Matt. 8.12; 22.13; 24.51; 25.30). The first, second and fourth of these passages speak of 'the outer darkness' and continue immediately, '*there* (Greek *ekei*) will be weeping and gnashing of teeth'. Those who believe in the eternal conscious existence of the lost believe that this weeping will be heard for ever in the outer darkness, which they rightly identify with hell. If however we look at the third passage (Matt. 24.51), we shall see that no place is mentioned. 'There' means 'on that occasion.' It is at the throne of judgment,

as the real nature of the wicked is revealed to them in all hideousness, in despair and misery because of what they have lost and missed, as they hear the sentence, perhaps through the temporary suffering, which, as we shall see, precedes their destruction, that the weeping and gnashing of teeth are heard" (*Life and Immortality*, 100). On the contrary, the expression translated "there will be weeping and gnashing of teeth" is exactly the same in the Greek text of the four texts cited above.

13. Fudge, *The Fire That Consumes*, 171–72, 428. Cf. Guillebaud, *Righteous Judge*, 12–14; Atkinson, *Life and Immortality*, 100; Froom, *Conditionalist Faith*, 1.287 n. 1. Kendall S. Harmon refutes this error in "The Case Against Conditionalism: A Response to Edward William Fudge," *Universalism and the Doctrine of Hell*, 210–12.

14. McKnight, "Eternal Consequences or Eternal Consciousness?" 154. Nevertheless, Froom and others claim, "According to the witness of Christ, then, there is eternity of *result* but not of *process*, of punish*ment* but not of punish*ing* of men" (*Conditionalist Faith*, 1.288). This is an example of importing a distinction into the text of Scripture in order to justify theological conclusions.

15. This exposes the fallacy of John W. Wenham's over-reliance on vocabulary counts in "The Case for Conditional Immortality," 169–74.

16. Guillebaud, *Righteous Judge*, 16.

17. Edwards and Stott, *Evangelical Essentials*, 316. Cf. Guillebaud, *Righteous Judge*, 13–14; Atkinson, *Life and Immortality*, 104–12; Froom, *Conditionalist Faith*, 1.264, 291–95, 313–15, 371–72, 405–13; Fudge, *The Fire That Consumes*, 99–106, 110–16, 183–87, 192–202, 285–87, 295–307.

18. Guillebaud, *Righteous Judge*, 14.

19. At the end of the parable of the net our Lord again uses hell-fire to signify anguish (Matt. 13:49–50).

20. Guillebaud, *Righteous Judge*, 12. Atkinson's interpretation is no better: "The flame of *haidees* is the loss of life" (*Life and Immortality*, 50).

21. Edwards and Stott, *Evangelical Essentials*, 316.

22. Ibid., 318.

23. Fudge, *The Fire That Consumes*, 300. Cf. Atkinson, *Life and Immortality*, 109; Guillebaud, *Righteous Judge*, 24.

24. George R. Beasley-Murray, *Revelation*, The New Century Bible Commentary, rev. ed. (Grand Rapids: Eerdmans, 1978), 304.

25. Guillebaud, *Righteous Judge*, 14. Incredibly, Atkinson concludes his discussion of Rev. 20:10, "Thus to be tormented for ever means to be tormented with the *result* of everlasting destruction," which he understands as annihilation (*Life and Immortality*, 112).

26. Edwards and Stott, *Evangelical Essentials*, 318–19. For discussion of wider ramifications of this issue see Carl F. H. Henry, "Is It Fair?" in *Through No Fault of Their Own?* 245–55, and Henri Blocher, "Everlasting Punishment and the Problem of Evil," in *Universalism and the Doctrine of Hell*, 283–312.

27. John Calvin, *Institutes of the Christian Religion*, ed. John T. McNeill, trans. Ford

Lewis Battles, The Library of Christian Classics, vols. 20–21 (Philadelphia: Westminster Press, 1960), 20:245. Emphasis added.

28. Guillebaud, *Righteous Judge*, 47.

29. J. A. T. Robinson, *In the End God* (New York: Harper & Row, 1968), 133.

30. *Summa Theologiae*, Blackfriars (New York: McGraw-Hill, 1974), Ia2ae. 87,4.

31. Edwards and Stott, *Evangelical Essentials*, 319. Cf. Guillebaud, *Righteous Judge*, 5–6; Atkinson, *Life and Immortality*, 112; Froom, *Conditionalist Faith*, 1.23–25, 269, 518–19, 301–2, 413–14, 518–19.

32. Froom's reasons for holding that the end depicted in Rev. 20 and 21 "involves the termination of all sinful and estranged life" (1.301) do not hold up under scrutiny. If the words "fire came down out of heaven and *devoured* them" (Rev. 20:9) refer to annihilationism, it is extinction at death, not extinction following resurrection and judgment, as evangelical annihilationists hold. "The former things are passed away" (Rev. 21:4) refers not to the blotting out of the wicked, but to the end of death, sorrow, crying, and pain for the righteous, as the first half of the verse indicates. Death and hades being cast into the lake of fire does not signify the obliteration of the wicked but the end of the power of the first death over human beings.

33. Edwards and Stott, *Evangelical Essentials*, 320.

34. Pinnock, "The Destruction of the Finally Impenitent," 252. Cf. Edwards and Stott, *Evangelical Essentials*, 316; Guillebaud, *Righteous Judge*, 1–4; Atkinson, *Life and Immortality*, 1–53; Froom, *Conditionalist Faith*, 1.19–23, 31–41, 145–59, 205–6, 212, 233, 262, 265, 305–8, 319–24, 523–28, 2:1257–76; Fudge, *The Fire That Consumes*, 51–76.

35. For the best recent defense see John W. Cooper, *Body, Soul, and Life Everlasting: Biblical Anthropology and the Monism-Dualism Debate* (Grand Rapids: Eerdmans, 1989).

36. So Philip E. Hughes, *The True Image: The Origin and Destiny of Man in Christ* (Grand Rapids: Eerdmans, 1989), 406–7.

10

The Case for Eternal Punishment

Hell—only with deep-seated reluctance can we speak of this terrible prospect, with fear and trembling. Yet we must do so, lest we suppress the awesome witness of Scripture and become accomplices in the condemnation of others to eternal misery (Ezekiel 3:16–21). When people cry out in desperation, "War is hell!"; or, on the other hand, when they compliment a host on serving a "heavenly meal," something in us resonates to such hyperboles. Such overstatements fall short, however, of capturing the intensely urgent meaning which Scripture ascribes to heaven and hell. Their full reality cannot be collapsed into our contemporary life experiences as two historical horizons in conflict. We do indeed experience a foretaste of both eternal life and eternal death already in this present age. But only Christ our Substitute endured the full weight of "the anguish and torment of hell" here on earth (Heidelberg Catechism, Q. & A. 44). And he alone experiences now the full glory of the heavenly state. For the rest of humanity the full reality of hell and heaven awaits the day of judgment. Then the blurred antithesis of the moment will be fully revealed as a fixed contradiction.[1]

There is much to commend in this quotation from Gordon Spykman's contemporary conservative systematic theology. We should speak carefully and fearfully about hell. Christ alone suffered hell in this life. The living await the full reality of their final destinies. Our common uses of the word "hell" fall far short of the biblical meaning. And, most importantly for our present purposes, we must speak of hell, "lest we suppress the awesome witness of Scripture" and fail to show compassion for the lost.

Astonishingly, however, the above quotation is all the writer says about hell in a book of 560 pages! Does one page out of 560 do justice to the topic of hell? Is this not an example of suppressing the witness of Scripture? Does this show compassion for the lost? Unfortunately, the neglect of the doctrine of hell in recent evangelical theology texts is not limited to the above example.[2]

Out of respect for the message of Scripture and compassion for the lost, I devote this chapter to a systematic summary of the doctrine of hell. We will consider the following topics:

- Hell's Place in the Outworking of God's Plan
- Hell's Master
- Hell's Description
- Hell's Duration
- Hell's Degrees of Punishment
- Hell's Occupants

Hell's Place in the Outworking of God's Plan

Hell Is the Final, Not the Intermediate, State

Christian theology distinguishes between the intermediate and final states for the righteous. The final state is believers' existence on the new earth after their resurrection from the dead. The intermediate state is their disembodied existence after death and before resurrection.

Jesus implies the intermediate existence in Luke 23:43 when, on the cross, he promises the dying thief, "I tell you the truth, today you will be with me in paradise." Jesus says the forgiven thief will join him later that day in God's presence. Since their bodies were taken down and buried that same day, there must be an immaterial part of human nature that survives death.

Paul confirms Jesus' teaching when he contrasts being "at home in the body" and "away from the Lord" with being "away from the body and at home with the Lord" (2 Cor. 5:6, 8). He presupposes that human nature is composed of material and immaterial aspects. While believers are living in the body, they are not in Christ's presence in heaven. When believers depart the body, they go to be with the Lord in the intermediate state.[3]

Although the Bible says more about the intermediate state of the righteous than that of the wicked, it implies the latter as well. We see this in the parable of the rich man and Lazarus. We must not press all the details of the parable, as if it were a detailed description of the afterlife.[4] It seems safe, however, to conclude that in Luke 16:19–31 Jesus teaches that after death and before the resurrection believers and unbelievers will experience blessing (v. 25) and woe (vv. 23–25, 28), respectively.

Another passage that suggests the conscious suffering of the wicked in the intermediate state is 2 Peter 2:9: "The Lord knows how to rescue godly men from trials and to hold the unrighteous for the day of judgment, *while continuing their punishment*" (emphasis added).

Hell Follows Christ's Second Coming

Although the Bible whispers about the intermediate state of the wicked, it shouts about their final state. The condemnation of the wicked follows Christ's return: "When the Son of Man comes in his glory . . . he will sit on his throne in heavenly glory" (Matt. 25:31). King Jesus will then separate the nations. Those on his right hand he will welcome into his Father's kingdom, but those on his left he will send into eternal fire (vv. 34, 41). Paul agrees: "When the Lord Jesus is revealed from heaven. . . . He will punish those who do not know God and do not obey the gospel of our Lord Jesus" (2 Thess. 1:7–8).

Hell Follows the Resurrection of the Dead

Although we cannot construct a complete scenario of future events, we can locate more specifically the time of unbelievers' damnation. Jesus proclaims that it will follow the resurrection: "A time is coming when all who are in their graves will . . . come out—those who have done good will rise to live, and those who have done evil will rise to be condemned" (John 5:28–29).

Hell Follows the Last Judgment

Still more precisely, hell follows the Last Judgment. After Jesus returns, he will judge all humanity by separating the people of the world "as a shepherd separates the sheep from the goats." He will invite the sheep into his Father's kingdom, but will evict the goats into hell-fire (Matt. 25:32, 34, 41). John reinforces this truth when he beholds "the dead, great and small, standing before the throne" of God's judgment. At the Last Judgment those whose names are not found in the book of life (i.e., unbelievers) are "thrown into the lake of fire" (Rev. 20:11–15). Plainly, God pronounces sentence upon the wicked prior to casting them into hell.

Conclusion

Hell, then, deals with the final destiny of the wicked. It follows Christ's return, the resurrection of the dead, and the Last Judgment. Thinking about these matters prompts questions such as Who will be the Judge of the earth? and Who is the Master of hell?

Hell's Master

God Is Judge

The executor of the Last Judgment is God himself. Sometimes Scripture presents God the "Father who judges each man's work" as Judge (1 Peter 1:17). At other times, God the Son plays that role: "Moreover, the Father judges no one, but has entrusted all judgment to the Son" (John 5:22).

God Alone Rules over Hell

God not only pronounces sentence, but he also reigns over hell. Unfortunately, some have missed this point. John Gerstner, for example, writes, "Hell is where Satan rules . . . where his complete fury is unleashed."[5] Gerstner doesn't deny that God rules in hell. He says, however, that, under God, Satan also reigns there.

On the contrary, hell is where God alone rules and where his complete fury is unleashed against Satan, his angels, and wicked human beings. That is why Jesus banishes evildoers "into the eternal fire prepared for the devil and his angels" (Matt. 25:41). John leads us to the same conclusion: "The devil . . . was thrown into the lake of burning sulfur. . . . [and] will be tormented day and night for ever and ever" (Rev. 20:10). Rather than being cast in the role of hell's master, Satan is portrayed as one who will suffer eternally alongside wicked angels (20:10) and people (20:15) at the hands of hell's true Master—almighty God.[6]

God's lordship over hell is also expressed by the idea of his throwing people into it. Jesus warns: "Fear him who, after the killing of the body, has power to throw you into hell. Yes, I tell you, fear him" (Luke 12:5). This idea is common in the New Testament. It indicates that the power of God over the wicked extends beyond the grave. God alone rules over hell.

God Is Present in Hell

We need to reconsider the common notion that God is absent from hell. In one sense, he *is* absent from hell. This is why Paul says that unbelievers "will be shut out from the presence of the Lord" (2 Thess. 1:9). God is not present in hell in grace and blessing.

However, since God is everywhere present, he is present in hell. Although he is not there in grace and blessing, he is there in holiness and wrath. We read in Revelation 14:10 that the unsaved will "drink of the wine of God's fury" and "be tormented with burning sulfur in the presence . . . of the Lamb." The word "Lamb" occurs twenty-eight times in the book of Revelation, and every occurrence except one (13:11) is a symbol for Christ. The wicked will suffer eternally in Christ's holy presence![7]

Sobering Implications and Incredibly Good News

Because God alone is Lord of heaven and hell, only he has the right to make the rules for this life—and that is exactly what he has done. God has designed the world so that the decisions of this life have eternal significance.[8] Hence, the Savior warns his hearers, "If you do not believe that I am the one I claim to be, you will indeed die in your sins" (John 8:24).

We misunderstand Jesus' mission, however, if we forget that he also says, "I did not come to judge the world, but to save it" (John 12:47). God openly publishes his priorities.

> For God so loved the world that he gave his one and only Son, that whoever believes in him shall not perish but have eternal life. For God did not send his Son into the world to condemn the world, but to save the world through him. Whoever believes in him is not condemned. (John 3:16–18)

This is incredibly good news! Upon hearing it every sinner ought to come to Jesus, the Savior of the world, who lovingly bids, "Whoever is thirsty, let him come; and whoever wishes, let him take the free gift of the water of life" (Rev. 22:17).

Jesus is a wonderful Savior. He is also a terrible Judge. Think of it: the Savior of the world is also its Judge! He offers the free water of eternal life to everyone who will believe that he is who he claims to be. Everyone who refuses to drink this water, however, "will drink of the wine of God's fury, which has been poured full strength into the cup of his wrath" (Rev. 14:10).

Hell's Description

After Christ's return, the resurrection, and the Last Judgment, God will cast the wicked into hell. How are we to describe hell? As purifying, since eventually all will be saved? As affording an opportunity for faith? As the obliteration of sinners? The New Testament describes hell in none of these ways. Instead, it paints five pictures depicting it as a place of endless misery.

- Darkness and Separation
- Fire
- Crying and Grinding of Teeth
- Punishment
- Death and Destruction

Let us investigate these in turn.

Darkness and Separation

Our Lord uses the image of darkness to speak of hell. For example, after commending the faith of the centurion, Jesus startles his hearers.

> I say to you that many will come from the east and the west, and will take their places at the feast with Abraham, Isaac, and Jacob in the kingdom of heaven. But the subjects of the kingdom will be thrown outside, into the darkness, where there will be weeping and gnashing of teeth. (Matt. 8:12)

Unbelieving Jews will be banished from God's kingdom. Instead of experiencing the joy and fellowship of the messianic feast, they "will be thrown outside into the darkness." This expulsion will involve terrible suffering, because outside "there will be weeping and gnashing of teeth."

Similarly, the parable of the wedding banquet concludes with the king's words concerning the intruder, "Tie him hand and foot, and throw him outside, into the darkness, where there will be weeping and gnashing of teeth" (Matt. 22:13). Once more, banishment from the feast speaks of final banishment from the people of God. Being cast into the darkness signifies forced separation from the light and warmth of the feast. Mention of crying and grinding of teeth leaves no doubt as to the painfulness of this experience.

Jesus' conclusion to the parable of the talents adds to our understanding: "Throw that worthless servant outside, into the darkness, where there will be weeping and gnashing of teeth" (Matt. 25:30). The "wicked, lazy servant" (v. 26) is put out of his master's house because he does not really belong there. Again Jesus associates rejection and darkness with great pain.[9]

The apostles also speak of hell in terms of darkness and separation. Paul does so in 2 Thessalonians 1:9: "They [unbelievers] will be punished with everlasting destruction and shut out from the presence of the Lord and from the majesty of his power." Hell involves eternal separation from the joyous presence of God.

Jude agrees. He assures his readers that ungodly teachers who have infiltrated their church will not escape God's wrath, for they are "wandering stars, for whom blackest darkness has been reserved forever" (v. 13). The heretics are not the spiritual luminaries they claim to be. Instead, they are ignorant ("*wandering* stars"). When they are consigned to "the blackest darkness," their masquerade will be over, and they will suffer eternal separation from God's light.

John ends the Bible with the picture of the New Jerusalem: "Now the dwelling of God is with men, and he will live with them. They will be his people, and God himself will be with them and be their God. He will wipe every tear from their eyes. There will be no more death or mourning or crying or pain." (Rev. 21:3–4). All, therefore, who "go through the gates into the city" will be comforted by God's presence. Not all will do so, however, for "outside are the dogs, those who practice magic arts, the sexually immoral, the murderers, the idolaters and everyone who loves and practices falsehood" (Rev. 22:14–15). If citizenship in the New Jerusalem means belonging to God, then exclusion from the city denotes separation from his love.

To summarize, our Lord and his apostles speak of darkness and separation to communicate the rejection of unbelievers by their Maker and their eternal exclusion from his blessed presence.

Fire

The New Testament also uses fire imagery to depict hell. Jesus warns of the wages of sin: being "thrown into eternal fire. . . . the fire of hell" (Matt. 18:8, 9). This fate is awful because, unlike all fires on earth, hell is "where the fire never goes out. . . . where the fire is not quenched" (Mark 9:48).

What does hell-fire signify? Jesus answers this question in his explanation of the parable of the weeds.

As the weeds are pulled up and burned in the fire, so it will be at the end of the age. The Son of Man will send out his angels, and they will weed out of his kingdom everything that causes sin and all who do evil. They will throw them into the fiery furnace, where there will be weeping and gnashing of teeth. (Matt. 13:40–42)

Although the imagery of the burning of the weeds is built into the parable (in v. 30), Jesus does not use it to teach annihilationism. When he gives the meaning of the weeds being thrown into the furnace, he warns of suffering. To Jesus, the "fiery furnace" is a place typified by "weeping and gnashing of teeth" (v. 42). It is a place of untold anguish.

At the end of the parable of the net our Lord again describes hell as "the fiery furnace, where there will be weeping and gnashing of teeth" (Matt. 13:49–50). Jesus uses fire to symbolize hell, and the fire signifies terrible pain.

After separating the godly from the ungodly, Jesus banishes the latter to "the eternal fire prepared for the devil and his angels" (Matt. 25:41). John instructs us about that fire: "The devil . . . was thrown into the lake of burning sulfur. . . . [and] will be tormented day and night for ever and ever" (Rev. 20:10). Here fire denotes unspeakable torment. This is the common fate that awaits the Devil, his angels, and unbelieving human beings.

The use of fire imagery in the parable of the rich man and Lazarus confirms our conclusion. There the deceased rich man found himself "in hell where he was in torment." He begged for relief because he was in agony in the fire (Luke 16:23–24). Plainly, fire here speaks of the "agony" that one suffers in the "place of torment" (Luke 16:25, 28).

The rest of the New Testament speaks similarly. Jude 7 warns of "those who suffer the punishment of eternal fire." And John teaches that the wicked "will be tormented with burning sulfur. . . . And the smoke of their torment rises for ever and ever. There is no rest day or night" (Rev. 14:10–11). The imagery of burning conveys the eternal torment of the ungodly. So does the picture of the lake of fire. That is where the Devil will be tormented endlessly (Rev. 20:10). Sinners too are cast into this lake (Rev. 20:15); it is said to be their place (Rev. 21:8). Damned human beings, therefore, will suffer forever.

We must conclude that the biblical pictures of fire and burning signify the horrible suffering of the unrighteous in hell. Should we understand the fires of hell as literal flames? The answer is no. As Calvin saw long ago, God did not intend for us to do so.[10] If we take literally the image of hell as fire, it clashes with other images of hell, for example, hell as darkness, or hell as the wicked being cut to pieces (Matt. 24:51). Rather than giving us literal pictures of the fate of the wicked, God uses dreaded pictures from this world to present the terrible reality of hell in the next world. I stand with the majority of contemporary conservative scholars in understanding the biblical imagery of hell metaphorically rather than literally.[11]

Crying and Grinding of Teeth

The image of crying and grinding of teeth adds to our understanding. Seven times we read, "There will be weeping and gnashing of teeth": in Matthew 8:12; 13:42, 50; 22:13; 24:51; 25:30; and Luke 13:28. "Weeping" speaks of crying in sorrow; the "gnashing of teeth" of "extreme suffering and remorse."[12]

In two instances the phrase "weeping and gnashing of teeth" helps explain the meaning of being thrown "into the fiery furnace" (Matt. 13:42, 50). Four times the expression illuminates the ideas of darkness and separation (Matt. 8:12; 22:13; 25:30; Luke 13:28). This image, therefore, ties together the ones we studied previously. Jesus does not leave us to guess about the nature of hell. It will be a place of unspeakable suffering.

Jesus also uses the phrase "weeping and gnashing of teeth" to describe another picture of hell. Concerning the unprepared servant the master says, "He will cut him to pieces and assign him a place with the hypocrites, where there will be weeping and gnashing of teeth" (Matt. 24:51). Both testaments speak of being cut in pieces as severe punishment (Deut. 32:41; Heb. 11:37). The next image confirms that hell is a place of such punishment.

Punishment

Is the terrible suffering of hell just or unjust? We are moved by television images of the unjust suffering of African children bearing the effects of famine. Little walking skeletons with bloated bellies touch our hearts. According to Scripture, however, the suffering of the wicked in hell is just; the enemies of God get what they deserve for rebelling against him.

Jesus contrasts the fates of the wicked and righteous: "Then they [the wicked] will go away to eternal punishment, but the righteous to eternal life" (Matt. 25:46). Eternal punishment, then, is one of our Lord's descriptions of hell.

Jesus imparts the same idea when he says that the Father has granted the Son "authority to judge because he is the Son of Man." He continues, "A time is coming when all who are in their graves will hear his voice and come out—those who have done good will rise to live, and those who have done evil will rise to be condemned" (John 5:27–29). At Jesus' voice the dead will rise. Those who have evidenced their faith by living for God will rise to eternal life. Unbelievers, however, will reap the fruits of their evil lives. They will be raised to condemnation. Jesus is a righteous Judge who will justly condemn the wicked for their iniquity.

Paul echoes Jesus' teaching when he writes to persecuted first-century Christians in Thessalonica.

> God's judgment is right. . . . God is just: He will pay back trouble to those who trouble you and give relief to you who are troubled. . . . when the Lord Jesus is revealed from heaven in blazing fire with his powerful angels. He will punish those who do not know God and do not obey the gospel of our Lord Jesus. They will be punished with everlasting destruction and shut out from the presence of the Lord and from the majesty of his power. (2 Thess. 1:5–9)

Because God is just, his judgment is right. It is right for him to punish those who persecute his people, those who do not obey the gospel. In fact, it would be wrong if he did not punish sinners. He, therefore, will punish his enemies with endless exclusion from the joy of his presence.

Jude regards God's judgment of Sodom and Gomorrah, recorded in Genesis 19:24–25, as an earthly, temporal "example of those who suffer the punishment of eternal fire" (Jude 7). How terrible for the cities of the plain to be destroyed by burning sulfur! How much worse to undergo the penalty of never-ending torment! The wicked will be forced to drink the cup of God's fury. Endlessly they will be tormented with burning sulfur. And they will never have relief from this horrible fate (Rev. 14:10–11).

"Eternal punishment," "condemnation," "everlasting destruction," "eternal fire," and "the cup of God's fury." What horrifying words! How can compassionate people bear to think of hell? Here is a partial answer to this difficult question. We appreciate advanced notice if disaster is going to strike us. If, for example, we are told ahead of time that a hurricane is coming, we can plan accordingly. Similarly, we should be thankful to God that he repeatedly tells us the truth about hell. He is merciful to warn us ahead of time of the consequences of our sins so that we might repent and escape his wrath.

Death and Destruction

The Word of God also uses images of death and destruction to describe the final state of the wicked. Jesus admonishes his hearers, "Do not be afraid of those who kill the body but cannot kill the soul. Rather, be afraid of the One who can destroy both soul and body in hell" (Matt. 10:28). We need not ultimately fear human beings, for the worst they can do is take our lives. Instead, we should fear God, who can bring us to eternal ruin.

Although this passage by itself could be understood as teaching annihilationism, it does not. That is ruled out by many other passages that prove hell to be endless. This destruction, therefore, is the eternal ruin of all that is worthwhile in human existence.

Likewise, Paul's use of the word "perish" in Romans 2:12 ("all who sin apart from the law will also *perish* apart from the law, and all who sin under the law will be judged by the law") speaks not of the extinction of unbelieving Gentiles and Jews but of their utter demise on "the day of God's wrath, when his righteous judgment will be revealed" (v. 5).

Finally, "the second death" in Revelation does not speak of unbelievers' extermination, but of their endless torment. We know this because John equates the second death with "the lake of fire." He introduces the lake of fire when he tells us that "the beast" and "the false prophet" are cast into it (19:20).

Later, John writes, "When the thousand years are over . . . the devil . . . was thrown into the lake of burning sulfur, where the beast and the false prophet had been thrown. They will be tormented day and night for ever and ever" (Rev. 20:7, 10). Plainly, the Beast and the False Prophet were not annihilated when they were cast into the lake of fire but were still there when the Devil was cast in "a thousand years" later. Further, when the evil trio has been flung into hell, John says unequivocally that they will be tormented eternally.

After recounting the Final Judgment, John writes: "The lake of fire is the second death. If anyone's name was not found written in the book of life, he was thrown into the lake of fire" (Rev. 20:14–15). It is irresponsible to conclude from these verses that the second death speaks of the obliteration of the wicked. John, after speaking about the lake of fire in the preceding passages, is here defining the second death in terms of that lake of fire. And, as we have seen, the lake of fire involves endless torment for those cast into it.

Conclusion

We have examined the biblical pictures that depict the final destiny of the wicked. Taken together, these images shock our sensibilities. They present a fate involving utter ruin and loss (death and destruction), the eternal wrath of God (punishment), unspeakable sorrow and pain (crying and grinding of teeth), terrible suffering (fire), and rejection by God and exclusion from his blessed presence (darkness and separation).

Believing readers ought to thank God for sparing them such a horrendous fate. They should pray that he would use them to turn others from the way that leads to hell. Unbelieving readers ought to run to the open arms of Jesus, the Savior of the world, who loves sinners and died to deliver them from the coming wrath.

Hell's Duration

Incredibly, the worst aspect of hell is not its terrifying description summarized in the last section. It is the fact that hell will continue forever. Jesus and his apostles plainly teach the endless duration of hell.

Jesus pronounces woes on those who take no precautions to avoid being "thrown into eternal fire . . . the fire of hell" (Matt. 18:8–9). Although the word translated "eternal" (*aionios*) sometimes means "age-long," it should be rendered "eternal" when speaking of final destinies, because these destinies pertain "to the final age, an age that partakes in God's eternality."[13]

In Mark 9 Jesus confirms that hell never ends. His hearers are in danger of going to hell "where the fire never goes out. . . . where 'their worm does not die, and the fire is not quenched'" (vv. 44, 48). In this life, a fire goes out when its fuel is used up, and a maggot dies when it consumes its prey. Not so in the life to come; there fire and worm never cease. This is figurative language for the endlessness of hell.

In the best-known passage on hell, Jesus twice affirms hell's eternal duration. First, he expels evildoers to "the eternal fire prepared for the devil and his angels" (Matt. 25:41). What our Lord here calls "eternal," his apostle says involves being tormented day and night *"for ever and ever"* (Rev. 20:10). The language could not be clearer; hell is endless.

Second, Jesus places the fates of the wicked and the righteous side by side: "Then they will go away to eternal punishment, but the righteous to eternal life" (Matt. 25:46). The parallelism makes the meaning unmistakable: the punishment of the ungodly and the bliss of the godly both last forever.

Paul concurs with his Lord when he says that unbelievers will experience "everlasting destruction," which involves being "shut out from the presence of the Lord" (2 Thess. 1:9). "Everlasting destruction" is not annihilation, for the wicked must continue to exist to be excluded from the Lord's presence. Rather, "everlasting destruction" is a condition of complete ruin.

Jude follows Jesus' example when he paints pictures of fire and darkness to describe the destiny of the godless. He teaches that hell is endless via both images. The wicked will "suffer the punishment of *eternal* fire" and are "wandering stars for whom blackest darkness has been reserved *forever*" (vv. 7, 13, emphasis added).

The book of Revelation tells of the fates of the just and the unjust. The latter will suffer eternal torment. "And the smoke of their torment rises for ever and ever. There is no rest day or night." (Rev. 14:10–11). The fact that the smoke rises forever indicates that the fire still has fuel. Don't misunderstand; we should not take the image of fire literally, as noted previously. We should interpret it as portraying endless punishment, not extinction.

Notice that when John says that the damned have "no rest day or night" (Rev. 14:11), he implies their ongoing existence. It makes no sense to say that they have no rest if they have ceased to exist. In fact, annihilation, if true, would provide rest for the wicked. The wicked, however, enjoy no relief from the unrelenting wrath of God; their punishment is eternal.

This fact is confirmed by John's use of the images of "the lake of fire" and "the second death." He introduces this latter idea at the end of the letter to the church in Smyrna: "He who overcomes will not be hurt at all by the second death" (Rev. 2:11). Being spared "the second death" parallels other concepts that express gaining final salvation at the end of the letters to the seven churches (in Rev. 2 and 3). John doesn't mention the expression "the second death" again until 20:6, where he teaches that it has no power over believers. John's final two uses of the expression equate it and "the lake of fire" (Rev. 20:14; 21:8).

To identify "the second death," therefore, we must figure out what John means by the symbol "the lake of fire." This is not difficult. He uses this symbol five times. The first time, he says that the Beast and the False Prophet are thrown alive into the lake of fire (Rev. 19:20). Later the Devil is cast in, joining the other two for eternal torment (Rev. 20:10). Finally, lost human beings are thrown into the lake of fire (Rev. 20:14–15).

John discloses the finality and universality of the Final Judgment when he says that the sea and death and hades yielded up the dead that were in them (v. 13). In fact, death and hades themselves "were thrown into the lake of fire" (v. 14). Death and the grave (the intermediate state) thus give way to the lake of fire, the second death (the final state).

Annihilationists err, therefore, when they claim that the second death and the lake of fire signify the extinction of the wicked. On the contrary, John specifically says that the punishment of the lake of fire lasts "day and night for ever and ever" (Rev. 20:10).

The Bible's last two chapters verify that the duration of hell is endless. John records that the destiny of sinners is "the fiery lake of burning sulfur. This is the second death" (Rev. 21:8). The wicked will not cease to exist; they will exist in perpetual separation from God's eternal life ("death") in conscious torment ("fire").

Likewise, although God's people "may go through the gates into the city," the new Jerusalem, "outside are the dogs, those who practice magic arts, the sexually immoral, the murderers, the idolaters, and everyone who loves and practices falsehood" (Rev. 22:15). The wicked are not exterminated; they continue to exist, cut off from the gracious presence of God.

Jesus, Paul, Jude, and John unitedly confess that the duration of hell is endless. If we would be faithful to God's truth, we must do the same.

Hell's Degrees of Punishment

When Christians think about the endlessness of hell, one question frequently comes to mind. Does everyone suffer equally in hell, or are there degrees of punishment? The question is often asked concerning horrendous sinners, Does an unsaved person who never murdered anyone suffer the same punishment as some of the monsters of human history: Hitler, Stalin, Mao, Idi Amin, Pol Pot?

That is a good question, to which the Bible provides at least a general answer. Scripture teaches that although hell is everlasting for all its inhabitants, some suffer worse than others. God's justice demands that there be degrees of punishment. We learn this from Jesus' words denouncing the Galilean cities in which he performed most of his miracles:

> Woe to you, Korazin! Woe to you, Bethsaida! If the miracles that were performed in you had been performed in Tyre and Sidon, they would have repented long ago in sackcloth and ashes. But I tell you, it will be more bearable for Tyre and Sidon on the day of judgment than for you. And you, Capernaum, will you be lifted up to the skies? No, you will

go down to the depths. If the miracles that were performed in you had been performed in Sodom, it would have remained to this day. But I tell you that it will be more bearable for Sodom on the day of judgment than for you. (Matt. 11:21–24)

Plainly, the cities of Israel that witnessed Jesus' miracles and rejected his word will suffer greater punishment than pagan cities that did not experience such great revelation from God. This illustrates one principle of God's judgment: greater light brings with it greater responsibility. A corollary of this principle is that greater light rejected carries greater judgment. That is why the unbelieving residents of Capernaum will endure worse suffering than the people of Sodom.

Jesus also teaches that there are degrees of punishment in his parable contrasting faithful and unfaithful servants in Luke 12:42–48. At the end of this parable Jesus distinguishes punishments of "many blows" and "few blows" based upon the amount of knowledge the unfaithful servants had of their master's will (vv. 47–48). Craig Blomberg, an expert in the study of Jesus' parables, writes, "These verses rank among the clearest in all the Bible in support of degrees of punishment in hell."[14]

The apostle Paul likewise implies that some will endure a worse fate than others when he warns hypocrites that they "are storing up wrath against [themselves] for the day of God's wrath, when his righteous judgment will be revealed" (Rom. 2:5). Paul's mention of the revelation of God's righteous judgment helps us understand the rationale for degrees of punishment in hell. As Anthony Hoekema explains: "Not every lost person will undergo the sufferings of a Judas! God will be perfectly just, and each person will suffer precisely what he deserves."[15]

Although the Bible does not answer every question we might want to ask about degrees of punishment in hell, the main outlines are clear. Because God is just, he will punish the wicked exactly as they deserve; unbelievers will suffer gradations of punishment in hell. An important point to remember, however, is that hell will be terrible for each of its occupants. Nevertheless, it will be more terrible for some and most terrible for others.

Hell's Occupants

The Devil, evil angels, and wicked humans will occupy hell. On Judgment Day Jesus will send the lost "into the eternal fire prepared for the devil and his angels" (Matt. 25:41). Our Lord here teaches that hell was actually prepared for the Devil and his angels, and that "cursed" human beings will share their fate.

God will consign Satan to perpetual torment (Rev. 20:10). The demons will share his fate, and they know it, as their words to Jesus reveal: "What do you want with us, Son of God? . . . Have you come here to torture us before the appointed time?" (Matt. 8:29). Peter says that God has incarcerated evil angels while they await their final condemnation: "God did not spare angels when they sinned, but sent them to hell, putting them into gloomy dungeons to be held for judgment" (2 Peter 2:4). Jude also notes how God has kept these angels "in darkness, bound with everlasting chains for judgment on the great Day" (Jude 6).

The Bible, however, does not focus on the fate of the Devil and demons but is chiefly concerned with human beings. When John writes, "For God so loved the world that he gave his one and only Son" (John 3:16), he speaks of the "world" of human beings. It is they whom Jesus came to save. And it is they who will perish, if they spurn him.

Which people will populate hell? The Bible answers, "The cowardly, the unbelieving, the vile, the murderers, the sexually immoral, those who practice magic arts, the idolaters and all liars" (Rev. 21:8; see also 22:15). Paul tells us another way of identifying the damned. They are "those who do not know God and do not obey the gospel of our Lord Jesus" (2 Thess. 1:8).

Conclusion

In this topical summary of the doctrine of hell we have seen that, according to Holy Scripture, hell represents the final stage in the outworking of God's plan for the wicked. It follows Christ's return, the resurrection of the dead, and the Last Judgment.

The Judge and Ruler over hell is God himself. He is present in hell, not in blessing, but in wrath. Hell entails eternal punishment, utter loss, rejection by God, terrible suffering, and unspeakable sorrow and pain. The duration of hell is endless. Although there are degrees of punishment, hell is terrible for all the damned. Its occupants are the Devil, evil angels, and unsaved human beings.

How are we to respond to these things? Thinking about hell is overwhelming. I know, for I have devoted considerable time to this topic in order to write this book. Recently during a time of group prayer, a friend prayed that God would protect me. Afterward he explained that he had known another professor who had written a book on hell. I will not soon forget his next words, "And he had a breakdown." I immediately identified with my unknown colleague. To think of human beings—not to mention friends and loved ones— suffering God's wrath forever is almost too much to bear. It is hard to cope with the emotional weight that meditating on hell lays on our shoulders.

I thank God that, although I will never be the same since undertaking this project, I have not become depressed. Why? For at least two reasons.

First, studying hell increases my appreciation for the Savior's sufferings. When tempted to be overcome by thoughts of hell, I turn my thoughts to the cross, and my distress turns to gratitude. Think of it—the Son of God bore the terrors of hell to save us sinners! His love is incomprehensible. When I shift my focus to Christ's saving work, I am overwhelmed by his grace. In fact, I now realize that until we stare hell in the face, we take Christ's love for granted.

Second, I am learning that the burden of hell can be put to good use. Before I undertook this study, my desire for comfort often outweighed my concern for lost people. However, after shouldering some of the emotional burden of hell, I find that the scales tip in the opposite direction. My desire that people be spared such a fate has produced in me a greater boldness to tell them the Good News.

As a result I am praying about my part in fulfilling the Great Commission. At present I think I can best serve as a seminary professor, helping to train men and women to take the gospel to the ends of the earth. But I am praying that God might lead one or more of our four sons into missionary service. And although I previously decided to limit my service on the boards of organizations out of fear of spreading myself too thin, I recently began serving on a mission board, hoping to further the spread of the gospel. In addition, my wife and I are planning to serve as short-term missionaries in Uganda this summer.

NOTES

1. Gordon J. Spykman, *Reformational Theology: A New Paradigm for Doing Dogmatics* (Grand Rapids: Eerdmans, 1992), 557.

2. H. Ray Dunning (*Grace, Faith, and Holiness: A Wesleyan Systematic Theology* [Kansas City, Mo.: Beacon Hill, 1988]) has one page out of 628. Otto Weber (*Foundations of Dogmatics*, trans. Darrell L. Gruder, 2 vols. [Grand Rapids: Eerdmans, 1981, 1983]) has two pages out of 1316. Thomas N. Finger (*Christian Theology: An Eschatological Approach,* 2 vols. [Nashville: Thomas Nelson, 1985]), in spite of deliberately attempting to remedy the lack of attention given to eschatology, has only four pages out of 874.

3. Phil. 1:21–24 expresses the same truth. An outstanding resource for this subject is John W. Cooper's *Body, Soul, and Life Everlasting: Biblical Anthropology and the Monism-Dualism Debate* (Grand Rapids: Eerdmans, 1989).

4. Craig L. Blomberg, *Interpreting the Parables* (Downers Grove, Ill.: InterVarsity Press, 1990), 206–7.

5. John H. Gerstner, *Repent or Perish: With a Special Reference to the Conservative Attack on Hell* (Ligonier, Pa.: Soli Deo Gloria, 1990), 189–90. I suspect that Gerstner has allowed his love for the theology of Jonathan Edwards to mislead him on this point.

6. See also Matt. 5:29; 18:8–9; Mark 9:45–47; Rev. 20:15.

7. Indeed, they will endure "the wrath of the Lamb" (Rev. 6:16).

8. This theme is powerfully communicated by Harry Blamires in *Knowing the Truth about Heaven and Hell: Our Choices and Where They Lead Us* (Ann Arbor, Mich.: Servant, 1988).

9. Though there is no mention of darkness, the picture is similar in Luke 13:27–28.

10. See the quotation from Calvin cited on p. 112.

11. See the impressive list compiled by William V. Crockett in *Four Views on Hell* (Grand Rapids: Zondervan, 1992), 44 n. 6.

12. *The New International Dictionary of New Testament Theology*, ed. Colin Brown. 3 vols. (Grand Rapids: Zondervan, 1976) 2:421.

13. Scot McKnight, "Eternal Consequences or Eternal Consciousness?" in *Through No Fault of Their Own?* ed. William V. Crockett and James G. Sigountos (Grand Rapids: Baker, 1991), 154.

14. Craig L. Blomberg, *Interpreting the Parables* (Downers Grove, Ill.: InterVarsity Press, 1990), 192.

15. Anthony A. Hoekema, *The Bible and the Future* (Grand Rapids: Eerdmans, 1979), 273; see also p. 260.

11

Other Pieces of the Puzzle

I am suggesting that the Bible is like a jigsaw puzzle that provides five thousand pieces along with the assurance that these pieces all belong to the same puzzle, even though . . . pieces . . . are missing. Most of the pieces that are provided, the instructions insist, fit together rather nicely. . . . the assurance that all of the pieces do belong to one puzzle is helpful, for that makes it possible to develop the systematic theology, even though the systematic theology is not going to be completed until we receive more pieces from the One who made it.[1]

All analogies have their limitations, including this puzzle analogy. Nevertheless, it conveys important truths. It is humbling to admit that we lack pieces to the puzzle: the Bible doesn't tell us everything we might want to know. We must, for example, confess ignorance concerning certain details of the doctrine of hell.

The key truth that the puzzle analogy teaches is that the puzzle pieces we have do fit together. Because the Bible is given by God, its doctrines cohere. Therefore, as we explore other biblical teachings, we will see how they support or complement the doctrine of hell. In this chapter we will consider hell in relation to the following doctrines:

- God
- Sin
- Punishment
- Christ's Saving Work
- Heaven

God

Although the Bible contains many important themes, including those related to human salvation, its crowning theme is God himself. It is important, therefore, for us to understand the doctrine of hell in light of the doctrine of God. It is common knowledge that the book of Revelation speaks often of the judgments of God. It is less commonly recognized that Revelation has much to say about the character of God in connection with his judgments.

God's Majesty

Contemporary Christianity generally lacks an awareness of the majesty of God. Only the Scriptures can remedy this problem. The book of Revelation repeatedly sings of God's magnificence. In chapter 1, John is overwhelmed by a revelation of the grandeur of the Son of God.

> I turned around to see the voice that was speaking to me. And when I turned I saw . . . someone 'like a son of man'. . . . His head and hair were white like wool, as white as snow, and his eyes were like blazing fire. His feet were like bronze glowing in a furnace, and his voice was like the sound of rushing waters. . . . His face was like the sun shining in all its brilliance. (Rev. 1:12–16)

What was John's response to this awesome revelation? "When I saw him, I fell at his feet as though dead" (v. 17).

At times John combines God's wrath and majesty:

> Then one of the four living creatures gave to the seven angels seven golden bowls filled with the wrath of God, who lives for ever and ever. And the temple was filled with smoke from the glory of God and from his power, and no one could enter the temple until the seven plagues of the seven angels were completed. (Rev. 15:7–8)

The revelation of God's wrath was the occasion for the display of his glory and power. So much so that, like Moses long ago (see Ex. 40:34–35), no one could enter the dwelling place of God.

The splendor of God shines brightly in the final vision of the book of Revelation, that of the city of God on the new earth: "I did not see a temple in the city, because the Lord God Almighty and the Lamb are its temple. The city does not need the sun or the moon to shine on it, for the glory of God gives it light, and the Lamb is its lamp" (Rev. 21:22–23).

Not only does God's magnificence shine in the final fate of the godly, but it also shines in that of the ungodly, as indicated by the color of his judgment throne: "Then I saw a great white throne and him who was seated on it. Earth and sky fled from his presence, and there was no place for them. And I saw the dead, great and small, standing before the throne" (Rev. 20:11–12). The words "earth and sky" direct our thoughts to God's creation of the universe. The universe itself cannot abide God's presence; it flees from the splendor of him who sits on the throne. Surely God's majesty is great in blessing and woe!

God's Holiness and Righteousness

God's holiness is his absolute moral purity. His righteousness is "the holiness of God applied to his relationships to other beings."[2] The book of Revelation is replete with the praises of God. One theme of praise concerns God's holiness. Of the angels we read: "Day and night they never stop saying: 'Holy, holy, holy is the Lord God Almighty, who was, and is, and is to come'" (Rev. 4:8). Here (echoing the language of Isa. 6:3) holiness is perpetually ascribed to the powerful and eternal One.

God's holiness and righteousness combined are also the subject of praise. After the third angel pours the bowl of God's wrath on the rivers and springs of water, "the angel in charge of the waters" breaks into praise: "You are just in these judgments, you who are and who were, the Holy One, because you have so judged; for they have shed the blood of your saints and prophets, and you have given them blood to drink as they deserve" (Rev. 16:5–6). God the Holy One is worthy of praise because of the justice (righteousness) of his judgments in vindicating the deaths of his servants.

God's Wrath

We must distinguish God's wrath—his holiness asserting itself against all that is unholy—from sinful human wrath. Revelation 14:10 warns idolaters that they "will drink of the wine of God's fury, which has been poured full strength into the cup of his wrath." Drinking from this cup involves everlasting torment from which there is no relief (v. 11).

Although it cuts across the grain of modern thinking, the Bible teaches that thanksgiving is due God for his wrath. After the announcement, "The kingdom of the world has become the kingdom of our Lord and of his Christ, and he will reign for ever and ever," we read of the worship of God in heaven.

> We give thanks to you, Lord God Almighty, the One who is and who was, because you have taken your great power and have begun to reign. The nations were angry; and your wrath has come. The time has come for judging the dead, and for rewarding your servants . . . and for destroying those who destroy the earth. (Rev. 11:17–18)

Praise is also directed to God for his holy hatred of sin. In Revelation 15:1 John says that he saw "seven angels with the seven last plagues—last, because with them God's wrath is completed." The redeemed in heaven sing praise to God.

> Great and marvelous are your deeds, Lord God Almighty. Just and true are your ways, King of the ages. Who will not

fear you, O Lord, and bring glory to your name? For you alone are holy. All nations will come and worship before you, for your righteous acts have been revealed. (vv. 3–4)

The "great and marvelous" deeds and "righteous acts" for which God is praised include the outpouring of his wrath, as verses 1 and 7 indicate.

God's Grace

Having considered God's majesty, holiness, righteousness, and wrath, it is time to ponder his grace. Revelation begins with an ascription of praise to Christ for his redeeming love: "To him who loves us and has freed us from our sins by his blood . . . to him be glory and power for ever and ever! Amen" (Rev. 1:5–6).

Throughout, Revelation celebrates God's grace. Christ the Lamb is praised for his redeeming blood (Rev. 5:9–12; 14:1–4). The Father and Son are extolled for salvation and blessing (Rev. 7:9–17). The redeemed almost burst with joy as they await the consummation of their relationship with God's Son (Rev. 19:6–8).

Revelation also reveals the final manifestation of God's grace: his ministering to his people on the new earth (Rev. 21:1–4). The book ends with a gracious invitation: "Come! Whoever is thirsty, let him come; and whoever wishes let him take the free gift of the water of life" (Rev. 22:17). Even its final words bespeak Christ's love: "The grace of the Lord Jesus be with God's people" (Rev. 22:21).

Conclusion

Studying God's qualities helps us to view hell from an important perspective, that of God himself. God is majestic beyond all our imagining. He, therefore, deserves the eternal praise of every one of his creatures. Many human beings, however, refuse to bow before him as Lord, and because God is holy and righteous he must punish their rebellion. Revelation, therefore, declares the wrath of almighty God against unrepentant sinners.

To all who heed his warnings and accept his offer of grace, he shows himself loving. For those who refuse to repent even at the judgments of God (see Rev. 9:20–21; 16:9, 11), nothing awaits but the cup of God's wrath (Rev. 14:10).

Lest we think that somehow God is defeated by his enemies, Revelation assures us that, because God is infinitely majestic, his glory is the supreme good in the universe. God will manifest his glory in the eternal salvation of his people and in the eternal damnation of his foes.

Our Response

We should expect unbelievers to have difficulty accepting the Bible's teaching on God and hell. But if Christians are honest, they too will admit to a certain uneasiness over these conclusions concerning the fate of the wicked.

Actually, it is not surprising that believers have this difficulty, because today even pastors are uncertain about God's wrath, as the following incident reveals. Two ministers were discussing God's destruction of Sodom and Gomorrah. The first cringed at the awfulness of the judgment, but accepted it out of obedience to God's Word. The second objected, "Well, if that's the way God really is, then I'm not going to believe in him." After reflection his colleague remarked, "Here we have the quintessential act of rebellion. We make ourselves the final judge, and in that capacity rule all evidence to the contrary inadmissible."[3]

That is exactly what unbelieving modern men and women have done. They are so used to viewing reality from a human-centered perspective that they naturally look at God, heaven, and hell in the same way. Christians too are influenced by the tendency to make human beings the measure of all things, and this helps to explain their uneasiness over certain elements of God's truth.

The antidote to this confused thinking is repentance. We must repent if we have (even unconsciously) removed God from his rightful place in our thinking. And we must deliberately and consistently crown him as Lord of our whole lives, including our minds. Nothing less will enable us "to glorify God and to enjoy him forever."[4]

Sin

Having considered hell in relation to the character of God, we turn our attention to the doctrine of sin. Although sin can be defined in various ways, in the most profound sense sin is offense against God's holiness. We see this offense in the historical narrative of Joseph.

Although Joseph was sold by the Ishmaelites to the Egyptian Potiphar, God was with Joseph and he rose to a place of prominence in Potiphar's household (Gen. 39:1–6). Unfortunately, however, Potiphar's wife was attracted to the handsome Joseph and tried to seduce him (vv. 6–7). Joseph's response is remarkable on two counts: it demonstrates his faithfulness to Potiphar in spite of his unfaithful wife, and it shows Joseph's faithfulness to God. His fidelity to Potiphar and to God is summed up in his response to the temptress.

> "With me in charge," he told her, "my master does not concern himself with anything in the house; everything he owns he has entrusted to my care. . . . My master has withheld nothing from me except you, because you are his wife. How then could I do such a wicked thing and sin against God?" (Gen. 39:8–9)

Joseph followed through on his good intentions too, for "though she spoke to Joseph day after day, he refused to go to bed with her or even be with her" (v. 10). Here was a person who resisted one of the keenest human temptations because he refused to sin against God.

Unlike Joseph, David gave in to this temptation. But like Joseph, David understood that all sin is ultimately an affront to the character of God. That is why after committing adultery and murder David prayed:

> Have mercy on me, O God, according to your unfailing love; according to your great compassion blot out my transgressions. Wash away all my iniquity and cleanse me from my sin. For I know my transgressions, and my sin is always before me. Against you, you only, have I sinned and done what is evil in your sight. (Ps. 51:1–4)

David had committed adultery with Uriah's wife Bathsheba and had then conspired to have Uriah put to death in order to conceal what he had done. How, then, could he claim that he had sinned against God alone? David was not denying that he had sinned against human beings; this is evident from verse 14, where he asks God for deliverance from bloodguilt. David recognized that all sin ultimately is an attack on God's holiness.

Paul agrees with this analysis of sin, "The sinful mind is hostile to God. It does not submit to God's law, nor can it do so" (Rom. 8:7). Underlying Paul's statements is the fact that the law is a revelation of God's holy character. The apostle, therefore, associates failure to obey God's law with animosity toward God. Once again we see that sin is opposition to God himself.

Conclusion

Joseph, David, and Paul teach us that sin must be defined with reference to God. Is this the way we view sin, especially our own? Do we hate it because it offends our holy God? Or do the words of Anselm ring true for most of us, "You have not as yet estimated the great burden of sin"?[5] If we catch a glimpse of the holiness of God, and consequently of the ugliness of sin in his sight, we will have less trouble with the Bible's teachings on hell.

Earlier in this chapter we noted that because God is holy, he must punish sin. The question before us now is How does God punish sin?

Punishment

We can distinguish at least three types of punishment: preventative, remedial, and retributive. Preventative punishment is penalty meted out to someone to deter others from transgressing. An example is a teacher's sending the ringleaders of a classroom disruption to the principal's office; the effects on the rest of the class are usually dramatic.

Remedial punishment is penalty inflicted to bring about improvement in the persons punished. An example is a teacher's keeping students after class to finish an overdue assignment. The punishment is intended to make the students think twice before coming to class unprepared again.

Retributive punishment is penalty given according to desert. An example is a student's being imprisoned and therefore suspended from school for shooting a fellow student. This example, however, illustrates that it is not always possible to separate the various types of punishment. There is reason to hope that the suspension and imprisonment will have a beneficial effect on others (preventative punishment) and that the imprisonment will deter the student from repeating his crime (remedial punishment). The student's punishment is retributive inasmuch as he *deserves* to be in prison for what he did.

All three types of punishment are biblical. Preventative punishment is seen in Paul's guideline concerning church officers who fall into serious sin, "Those who sin are to be rebuked publicly, so that the others may take warning" (1 Tim. 5:20).

Remedial punishment is observable in Hebrews 12, where readers are exhorted to "endure hardship as discipline; God is treating you as sons" (v. 7). What is the Father's goal in this? "God disciplines us for our good, that we may share in his holiness. No discipline seems pleasant at the time, but painful. Later on, however, it produces a harvest of righteousness and peace for those who have been trained by it" (Heb. 12:10–11).

The principle of retributive punishment undergirds the instructions God gave Noah after the Flood. "Whoever sheds the blood of man, by man shall his blood be shed; for in the image of God has God made man" (Gen. 9:6). Although capital punishment may have a deterrent effect, its primary purpose is to repay the offender for taking a human life.

Which of these three kinds of punishment results in hell? Specifically, when Jesus spoke of "eternal punishment" (Matt. 25:46), did he have in mind preventative, remedial, or retributive punishment, or a combination of these?

The *preaching* of hell certainly involves preventative punishment. When we warn people of God's wrath, our desire is that they might repent and believe, so as to be spared the pains of hell. Hell, however, does not involve remedial punishment. The idea of hell as a school from which the wicked eventually graduate, as Origen and

John Hick have taught, is contrary to the Bible's teachings and, therefore, must be rejected as false. Finally, hell itself must be seen as retributive punishment. Jesus teaches this when he speaks of "those who have done evil" being resurrected on the Last Day "to be condemned" (John 5:29). Paul does the same when he encourages persecuted believers with the knowledge that

> God's judgment is right. . . . God is just: He will pay back trouble to those who trouble you. . . . This will happen when the Lord Jesus is revealed from heaven in blazing fire with his powerful angels. He will punish those who do not know God and do not obey the gospel of our Lord Jesus. They will be punished with everlasting destruction. (2 Thess. 1:5–9)

God will bring relief to his persecuted people and punish those who have persecuted them. This punishment is retributive: God "will pay back" the wicked with eternal ruin.

Furthermore, Jude cites the wicked citizens of Sodom and Gomorrah "as an example of those who suffer the punishment of eternal fire" (Jude 7). The burning sulfur that God rained down on these ancient cities prefigures hell-fire. Although the example of Sodom and Gomorrah may be preventative punishment for all who heed it, time has run out for the former inhabitants of those cities. They will receive retributive punishment for their "so grievous" sin (Gen. 18:20).

John also views the punishment of hell as recompense. He warns idolaters that they "will drink of the wine of God's fury, which has been poured full strength into the cup of his wrath" (Rev. 14:10). This involves eternal torment without relief (vv. 10–11). Plainly, God will inflict retributive punishment on unbelievers.

To summarize, there are three kinds of punishment (preventative, remedial, and retributive), all three of which are biblical. The punishment of hell is preventative for those who hear of it and repent in time. For those who die in their sins, however, the punishment of hell is only retributive.

Over the centuries faithful Christians have been moved to action out of fear for others' damnation. One pastor shares his burden with his listeners. "I lay last night by the hour on my bed awake, tossing with a burden on my heart, and I tell you that the only burden I had was your soul. I cannot endure it, man, that you should be cast into the 'lake that burneth with fire and brimstone' (Rev. 21:8)."[6] May we follow his example of godly concern for souls.

Christ's Saving Work

> When men talk of a little hell, it is because they think they have only a little sin, and they believe in a little Savior. But when you get a great sense of sin, you want a great Savior, and feel that if you do not have him, you will fall into a great destruction, and suffer a great punishment at the hands of the great God.[7]

These words of Charles Haddon Spurgeon, the renowned nine-teenth-century British Baptist preacher, underscore the connection between sin, hell, and the work of Christ.

The traditional understanding of the retributive punishment of hell involves two elements: separation from God (*poena damni*, the punishment of the damned) and the positive infliction of torments in body and soul (*poena sensus*, the punishment of sense). The former is subtraction of desired blessing, the latter addition of undesired punishment.

Jesus combines these two when he says to the lost (in Matt. 25:41), "Depart from me, you who are cursed [the punishment of the damned, subtraction] into the eternal fire prepared for the devil and his angels [the punishment of sense, addition]." At the cross Jesus suffered the retributive punishment of hell for sinners. He endured both the subtraction of the Father's love and the addition of God's wrath.

Jesus Suffered Separation from the Father

Scripture teaches that the Son of God endured separation from the Father's love when he died on the cross. We learn this from the terrible words of Matthew 27:45–46: "From the sixth hour until the ninth hour darkness came over all the land. About the ninth hour Jesus cried out in a loud voice, *'Eloi, Eloi, lama sabachthani?'*—which means, 'My God, my God, why have you forsaken me?'"

As our Lord hangs on the cross, he raises his voice to directly address God the Father. Matthew translates Jesus' Aramaic words for his readers: "My God, my God, why have you forsaken me?" These words, quoted from Psalm 22:1, are among the most shocking in Scripture. Especially important is the word "forsaken." It means to "abandon, desert," and is used here "of being forsaken by God."[8]

Imagine, God the Son abandoned by God the Father! The Father deserting his Son! Such abandonment becomes even harder to comprehend when we contrast it with the general attitude of the Father toward the Son. At both Jesus' baptism and his transfiguration the Father utters these same words from heaven: "This is my Son, whom I love; with him I am well pleased" (Matt. 3:17; 17:5). Jesus also testifies repeatedly of the Father's love for him: "The Father loves the Son and has placed everything in his hands" (John 3:35), "The reason my Father loves me is that I lay down my life" (John 10:17), and "As the Father has loved me, so have I loved you" (John 15:9).

So the general attitude of God the Father toward God the Son is not hard to discover: the Father dearly loves his Son! In fact, the Father has loved the Son from all eternity, according to Jesus' prayer in John 17:24: "Father, I want those you have given me to be with me where I am, and to see my glory, the glory you have given me because you loved me before the creation of the world."

Viewed in the light of the Father's everlasting love for him, Jesus' cry of abandonment in Matthew 27:46 is almost impossible to understand. The eternal relations between Father and Son were temporarily interrupted! The preceding verse hints at this when it tells us that darkness covered the land of Israel from noon until 3 P.M.; a profound judgment was taking place.

At the cross, then, we catch a glimpse of the enormity of our sins' offense to God. Here we learn about hell as Jesus, God's beloved Son, takes the retributive punishment that we deserved, even separation from God, to deliver us. Here we look deeply into the mystery of the love of a holy and righteous God for sinners.

Elizabeth Browning put these truths into poignant poetic form:

Yea, once Immanuel's orphaned cry his universe hath shaken.
It went up single, echoless, "My God, I am forsaken!"
It went up from the Holy's lips amid his lost creation,
That, of the lost, no son should use those words of
    desolation.

True, no son should, but thank God that *his* Son did, for the result is our salvation.

Jesus Suffered the Wrath of God

Scripture also teaches that on Calvary's cross Jesus endured God's wrath. He suffered the positive infliction of torments in body and soul that the church fathers called the punishment of sense (*poena sensus*). We learn this from studying Jesus' prayers in Gethsemane. There the Savior was deeply grieved: "My soul is overwhelmed with sorrow to the point of death" (Matt. 26:38). How do we account for such sorrow? And why did he repeatedly ask the Father, "If it is possible, may this *cup* be taken from me?" (Matt. 26:39, 42, 44). What cup was this? Why did the prospect of drinking it inflict such trauma on his holy soul?

To answer these questions we must investigate the Old Testament background of the cup to which Jesus referred. Psalm 75 speaks of the God who judges uprightly and upbraids the arrogant for their boasting (vv. 2, 4–5). Contrary to the pretensions of human beings, "It is God who judges: He brings one down, he exalts another" (v. 7). Verse 8 is important: "In the hand of the LORD is a cup full of foaming wine mixed with spices; he pours it out, and all the wicked of the earth drink it down to its very dregs." The Lord is pictured as a host serving a cup of powerful wine. He pours it out and the people of the earth have no choice but to drink it. Who are the drinkers who drain this cup? "All the wicked of the earth." The wicked drink to the bottom the cup of God's judgment.

In Jeremiah 25:15–29 we learn more about "this cup filled with the wine of my [God's] wrath" (v. 15). The prophet is commanded by

God to take it and make the evil nations drink it. The resultant drunken stupor depicts the judgment of God against them. As powerful wine causes people to stagger and fall, so the sword that God sends will cause them to fall, never to rise again (vv. 16, 27). And if they refuse to drink, God will force them! (v. 28).

This is the cup from which our holy Savior recoiled. A cup for "all the wicked of the earth" (Ps. 75:8), this cup, full of the wine of God's wrath (Jer. 25:15), should never have touched Jesus' sinless hands. That is why he was "overwhelmed with sorrow to the point of death" (Matt. 26:38) and prayed three times for the Father to take it away.[9]

On the cross the Son of God drank to the dregs the cup of God's wrath for sinners like you and me. He endured the pains of hell, positive infliction of torments in body and soul. And he did so willingly! Listen to his resolve after Gethsemane when Peter begins to fight to prevent Jesus' arrest: "Put your sword away! Shall I not drink the cup the Father has given to me?" (John 18:11).

A Choice with Eternal Consequences

The cross sheds light on the fate of the wicked, because on the cross the sinless Son of God suffered that fate. He bore the retributive punishment of hell in being separated from the Father's love (subtraction) and in enduring God's wrath (addition).

What happens if someone refuses to trust Jesus as Lord and Savior, if a person rejects his death and resurrection as the only way to God? The Bible answers frankly: "He too will drink of the wine of God's fury, which has been poured full strength into the cup of his wrath. He will be tormented with burning sulfur. . . . And the smoke of their torment rises for ever and ever. There is no rest day or night" (Rev. 14:10–11).

So we have a choice: Either we will trust Jesus to have taken the wrath of God for us, or we will drink the cup of God's wrath ourselves. Dear unsaved person, run to the cross! Turn from your sins and by faith embrace Jesus, who alone can rescue you from the wrath to come. Trust him to have taken the punishment of hell for you so that you will not have to endure it yourself.

Heaven

Disregarding the doctrine of eternal damnation tends to make us doubt eternal salvation. When I mentioned at a pastors' prayer meeting in Switzerland that I was scheduled to give a lecture on universalism, the doctrine that all will eventually be saved, one pastor's wife said, "Here, officially we believe that everyone will be saved; practically, we do not believe that anyone will be saved."[10]

These words by Harold O. J. Brown, an American seminary professor, underscore the link between belief in hell and belief in heaven. Doubting hell raises questions about the reality of heaven. Likewise, studying hell helps us understand heaven.

Though Revelation 21–22 proclaims the final fate of the wicked—existence in the lake of fire (21:8) and exclusion from the city of God (22:15)—these chapters trumpet more loudly the final destiny of the redeemed. Let us examine John's pictures of heaven.

The City of God

After announcing the arrival of a new heaven and a new earth, John saw "the new Jerusalem, coming down out of heaven from God, prepared as a bride beautifully dressed for her husband" (Rev. 21:2). What does this vision mean? John himself tells us: "Now the dwelling of God is with men, and he will live with them. They will be his people, and God himself will be with them and be their God" (v. 3). God is present with his people as never before.

Here is the fulfillment of the covenantal promises, going all the way back to God's pledge to Abraham, "I will establish my covenant as an everlasting covenant between me and you and your descendants after you for the generations to come, to be your God and the God of your descendants after you" (Gen. 17:7).

Here is the consummation of the revelations of God's presence in the tabernacle, in the temple, and in the incarnation of his Son: God will forever be with his own. That is why John uses the image of marriage, the closest of human relationships, to portray the intimacy between God and his loved ones.

Here also is the antithesis of separation as a picture of hell. Separation conveys rejection by God and exclusion from his joyous presence. The city of God descending from heaven to dwell on earth and the bride adorned for her husband communicate God's *blessed* presence with his people; he will be their eternal source of joy.

Joy

The very next verse of Revelation speaks of this joy: God "will wipe every tear from their eyes. There will be no more death or mourning or crying or pain, for the old order of things has passed away" (Rev. 21:4). God's presence—notice that God himself will wipe away every tear—will eternally comfort his people.

The redeemed, therefore, will never again be saddened by the loss of a loved one, never again endure heartache or despair, never again suffer at the hands of sinners. For all eternity God will be their delight! Because heaven is the opposite of hell, this joy contrasts vividly with the anguish of the wicked as conveyed by the images of hell as fire and as "weeping and gnashing of teeth."

Light

The last two chapters of the Bible blaze with the light of the glory of God: "The city does not need the sun or the moon to shine on it, for the glory of God gives it light, and the Lamb is its lamp" (Rev. 21:23). John portrays the majesty of God the Father and God the Son as providing illumination for the New Jerusalem.

Because of this illumination, "There will be no more night. They will not need the light of a lamp or the light of the sun, for the Lord God will give them light" (Rev. 22:5). Both of these texts picture God himself shining in the midst of his people. And both draw upon Isaiah 60:19: "The sun will no more be your light by day, nor will the brightness of the moon shine on you, for the LORD will be your everlasting light, and your God will be your glory." John thereby affirms "the unsurpassed splendor which radiates from the presence of

God and the Lamb."[11] His point is that the glory of the Father and Son manifested in the city of God will far exceed the brightness of the heavenly luminaries.[12]

Again John presents heaven as the antithesis of hell. Instead of despairing over banishment into eternal darkness, believers will bask in the warmth of eternal light.

The Family of God

A gracious invitation from God follows John's description of the glories of the new heaven and new earth: "To him who is thirsty I will give to drink without cost from the spring of the water of life" (Rev. 21:6). Next comes a promise to the one who accepts the invitation and perseveres: "He who overcomes will inherit all this, and I will be his God and he will be my son" (v. 7). This is a promise of sonship to believers. God will be father to the man or woman who demonstrates faith in Christ by persevering to the end.

God will thus welcome believers as his sons and daughters, and heirs! God's people will inherit the riches of the new heaven and new earth. The next verse, however, provides a stark contrast to the theme of sonship: "But the cowardly, the unbelieving, the vile, the murderers, the sexually immoral, those who practice magic arts, the idolaters and all liars—their place will be in the fiery lake of burning sulfur" (v. 8). What alternatives! Having a place in the family of God or in the lake of fire!

Eternal Life

John offers another theme of heaven—eternal life. Revelation 21 and 22 overflow with life: "the spring of the water of life" (21:6), "the free gift of the water of life" (22:17), "the Lamb's book of life" (21:27), "the river of the water of life" (22:1), and "the tree of life" (22:2, 14, 19). John's message rings loudly and clearly: the redeemed will enjoy the life of God forever.

This does not imply an obliteration of the Creator-creature distinction; God alone will always be God, and his redeemed finite creatures will know him forever. This picture of heaven must be viewed against the second death, the final and everlasting separation from the joyous presence of God.

Conclusion

By studying other related doctrines, we have been able to gather more pieces to the puzzle about hell. It is time to look at the resultant picture. The all-majestic God deserves everlasting praise. However, because many human beings do not give him his due, and because he is holy and righteous, he punishes them for their irreverence. He is gracious and offers eternal life to all who will own him as Lord and Savior. But those who spurn his offer of grace will endure his wrath forever.

Sin is best defined in relation to God's perfect character; at root it is an attack against his holiness. It must therefore be punished. Although three kinds of punishment are spoken of in Scripture—preventative, remedial, and retributive—only the first and last pertain to hell. Warnings of hell are preventative for all who heed them, but those who reject God's warnings will endure his retributive punishment forever.

On the cross Christ endured that retributive punishment, separation from God's love and the infliction of divine wrath. Consequently, God confronts us with a momentous decision: either we trust Christ to have taken the punishment of hell for us or we take that punishment ourselves.

Revelation 21 and 22 present heaven as the opposite of hell. Hell is separation from the gracious presence of God; heaven, living in that presence. Hell involves terrible pain; heaven, unceasing joy. Hell means the darkness of banishment from God's glory; heaven, basking in its light. Hell consists of everlasting rejection by God; heaven, being his son or daughter forever. Hell entails the second death; heaven, eternal life.

It is impossible for the redeemed to express adequately their gratitude for the grace of God in giving his Son to redeem them from hell so that they might enjoy heaven forever. Nevertheless, hymnist Venantius offered the following attempt:

"Welcome, happy morning!" Age to age shall say:
Hell today is vanquished; Heav'n is won today.
Lo! the Dead is living, God forevermore!
Him, their true Creator, All his works adore.

Maker and Redeemer, Life and health of all,
Thou, from heav'n beholding Human nature's fall,
Of the Father's Godhead True and only Son,
Manhood to deliver, Manhood didst put on.

Thou, of life the Author, Death didst undergo,
Tread the path of darkness, Saving strength to show;
Come then, True and Faithful, Now fulfil thy word,
'Tis thine own third morning; Rise, O buried Lord.

Loose the souls long-prisoned, Bound with Satan's chain;
Thine that now are fallen Raise to life again;
Show thy face in brightness, Bid the nations see;
Bring again our daylight; Day returns with thee.

[Refrain]
"Welcome, happy morning!" Age to age shall say:
Hell today is vanquished, Heav'n is won today.[13]

NOTES

1. D. A. Carson, "Unity and Diversity in the New Testament: The Possibility of Systematic Theology," in *Scripture and Truth*, eds. D. A. Carson and John D. Woodbridge (Grand Rapids: Zondervan, 1983), 81–82.
2. Millard J. Erickson, *Christian Theology* (Grand Rapids: Baker, 1983), 286.
3. William Eisenhower, "Sleepers in the Hands of an Angry God," *Christianity Today*, 20 March 1987, 26.
4. The Westminster Shorter Catechism, Answer to Question 1.
5. Anselm, *Cur Deus Homo*, trans. S. N. Deane, 2d ed. (LaSalle, Ill.: Open Court, 1962), 228.
6. Tom Carter, *Spurgeon at His Best* (Grand Rapids: Baker, 1988), 36.
7. Ibid., 99.
8. W. Bauer, W. F. Arndt, F. W. Gingrich, and F. Danker, *A Greek Lexicon of the New Testament and Other Early Christian Literature*, 2d ed. (Chicago: University of Chicago Press, 1979), 215.

9. Moreover, this is what Heb. 5:7 talks about: "During the days of Jesus' life on earth, he offered up prayers and petitions with loud cries and tears to the one who could save him from death, and he was heard because of his reverent submission." The Father answered the Son's prayer by raising him from the dead, not by removing the cross.

10. Harold O. J. Brown, "Will the Lost Suffer Forever?" *Criswell Theological Review* 4.2 (1990): 265.

11. George Eldon Ladd, *A Commentary on the Revelation of John* (Grand Rapids: Eerdmans, 1972), 284.

12. G. R. Beasley-Murray, *The Book of Revelation*, rev. ed. (Grand Rapids: Eerdmans, 1978), 327.

13. Venantius H. C. Fortunatus (c. 530–609).

12

What Difference Does It All Make?

On 22 October 1939, C. S. Lewis undertook a difficult assignment. By invitation he preached to a great crowd of Oxford undergraduates distressed by World War II. Because Lewis was an ex-soldier, a professor, and a Christian, he was thought to be just the person for the job. He began predictably enough.

> A university is a society for the pursuit of learning. As students you will be expected to make yourselves . . . into philosophers, scientists, scholars, critics, or historians. And at first sight this seems to be an odd thing to do during a great war. What is the use of beginning a task which we have so little chance of finishing? Or, even if we ourselves should happen not to be interrupted by death or military service, why should we—indeed how can we—continue to take an interest in these placid occupations when the lives of our friends and the liberties of Europe are in the balance? Is it not like fiddling while Rome burns?

But he soon shifted gears and took his audience by surprise.

Now it seems to me that we shall not be able to answer these questions until we have put them by the side of certain other questions which every Christian ought to have asked himself in peacetime. I spoke just now of fiddling while Rome burns. But to a Christian the true tragedy of Nero must be not that he fiddled while the city was on fire but that he fiddled on the brink of hell. You must forgive me for the crude monosyllable. I know that many wiser and better Christians than I in these days do not like to mention heaven and hell even in a pulpit. I know, too, that nearly all the references to this subject in the New Testament come from a single source. But then the source is Our Lord Himself. . . . These overwhelming doctrines. . . . are not really removable from the teaching of Christ or of His Church. If we do not believe them, our presence in this church is great tomfoolery. If we do, we must sometime overcome our spiritual prudery and mention them.

At this point Lewis had his audience exactly where he wanted them, and so he drove home his point.

The moment we do so we can see that every Christian who comes to a university must at all times face a question compared with which the questions raised by the war are relatively unimportant. He must ask himself how it is right, or even psychologically possible, for creatures who are every moment advancing either to Heaven or to Hell to spend any fraction of the little time allowed them in this world on such comparative trivialities as literature or art, mathematics, or biology. If human culture can stand up to that, it can stand up to anything. To admit that we can retain our interest in learning under the shadow of these eternal issues but not under the shadow of a European war would be to admit that our ears are closed to the voice of reason and very wide open to the voice of our nerves and our mass emotions.[1]

Although the rest of Lewis's essay is brilliant, at present we are concerned with his introduction. Lewis is right in arguing that we become confused if we adopt the wrong outlook on life. Indeed, it is easy to become world-centered or people-centered, rather than God-centered. And because of our tendency toward idolatry, God graciously has given us his Word to teach us to put him in the center of everything, including our thinking.

This chapter concerns how we may incorporate the reality of hell into our view of life and the world. I propose two ways of attaining this goal: first, by exploring three nagging questions pertaining to the hereafter; then, by bringing the doctrine of hell to bear on both sinners and saints.

In the past two years I have spoken more on hell than in the previous fifteen years of my ministry combined. Frequently I am asked three questions: What about purgatory? What is the fate of those who have never heard? What happens to babies who die? I want to address each of these honest queries.

What About Purgatory?

Many misunderstand the Roman Catholic doctrine of purgatory. It does not afford the chance for salvation after death. Instead, it enables Catholics to purge sins not atoned for in this life. To quote a Catholic textbook: "The souls of the just which, in the moment of death, are burdened with venial sins, or temporal punishment due to sins, enter Purgatory. The cleansing fire (*purgatorium*) is a place and state of temporal penal purification."[2]

A few definitions of uniquely Catholic terms will help. Roman Catholic teaching distinguishes "venial" from "mortal" sins. "Venial sin differs from mortal sin in the punishment due to it; it merits a temporal rather than an eternal penalty."[3] Catholic doctrine also differentiates between eternal and temporal punishments due sin.[4]

According to Catholic teaching, therefore, purgatory is a place where the venial sins of the faithful are cleansed after death. Indeed, "the cleansing fire" purifies their souls until they are ready for heaven.[5]

Purgatory, then, is not a final destination since all who go to purgatory eventually reach heaven.

Catholic theology has paid little attention to the assurance of salvation. Unfortunately, however, on a practical level, the doctrine of purgatory has helped fill this void. In fact, many Catholics have consoled themselves with the belief that after death they would go to purgatory and eventually reach heaven.

Today, however, despite scholars' efforts to refine the concept of purgatory,[6] many Catholics have abandoned belief in it. Nevertheless, their church still holds to this doctrine, as the documents of Vatican II show.[7] Consequently, many Catholics have a problem. They want to remain faithful to the church while rejecting its official teaching on purgatory.

This problem is compounded by asking what the Bible has to say about purgatory. For although at one time Roman Catholic scholars claimed biblical support for the doctrine, they generally no longer do. Catholic theologian Zachary Hayes admits, "Roman Catholic ex-egetes and theologians at the present time would be inclined to say that although there is no clear textual basis in Scripture for the later doctrine of purgatory, neither is there anything that is clearly contrary to that doctrine."[8]

Two comments are in order. First, finding nothing in the Bible against a view is not an adequate basis for making it an article of faith. Second, I will take issue in a moment with Hayes's claim that Scripture does not contradict the doctrine of purgatory. But first, let us consider the texts Catholics have used in support of purgatory: Matthew 12:32; 1 Corinthians 3:15; and from the apocrypha, 2 Maccabees 12:42–46.

In Matthew 12:32 Jesus warns that anyone who blasphemes "will not be forgiven, either in this age or in the age to come." He does not say that some sins will be forgiven after death, as some have wrongly implied from his words. Rather, he emphatically declares that he who commits this sin will never find forgiveness. Today Roman Catholic biblical scholars admit that this text has "little if anything to do with purgatory."[9]

Another text Catholics use to argue for purgatory is 1 Corinthians 3:15: "If it is burned up, he will suffer loss; he himself will be saved, but only as one escaping through the flames." In fact, however, "the Day" mentioned in verse 13 refers not to the time of death, but to the return of Christ and the Last Judgment that follows. Furthermore, it is the "man's work" that is tested and, if it fails the test, burned. There is nothing here about sins being purged after death or of people moving from purgatory to heaven. Hayes actually concedes that "the text provides no significant basis for the doctrine of purgatory."[10]

Second Maccabees 12:42–46, from the apocrypha, is also cited as evidence for purgatory. We reject this appeal, however, for the Jews, the custodians of the Old Testament, never accepted the apocryphal books as a part of Scripture, and neither do we.

It is no wonder, then, that the majority of Roman Catholic scholars base their belief in purgatory on church tradition. Catholic theology holds to the dual authority of Scripture and tradition, and primary support for the doctrine of purgatory is found in the writings of the church fathers. That evidence, however, is not overwhelming either. In fact, although earlier writers taught the concept of purgatory, it was not until 1274 that it became the official teaching of the Roman Church.[11]

At issue here is the matter of religious authority. As Christians we do not put human tradition on the same plane as the Bible. We evaluate all human teaching on the basis of God's Word. Together with Luther and Calvin we must reject the doctrine of purgatory because, worse than being absent from Scripture, it contradicts the explicit teaching of Scripture.

The Reformers correctly viewed purgatory as an insult to Christ's saving work. On the basis of Scripture they held that all believers "have been made holy through the sacrifice of the body of Jesus Christ once for all" (Heb. 10:10).[12] It is by his suffering on the cross, not our suffering after death, that sins are purged: "Jesus also suffered . . . to make the people holy through his own blood" (Heb. 13:12).

The Reformers also noted how Scripture does not allow for a "third place." Jesus and his apostles consistently speak of only *two* destinies for humans: heaven and hell (Matt. 25:46; John 5:28–29; Rom. 2:6–10; Rev. 21:7–8; 22:14–15).

If there is no purgatory, then what happens to the sins with which believers are still tainted when they die? The Bible says that when we enter Christ's presence, he will immediately and entirely purify us by his grace, as Paul teaches: "May God himself, the God of peace, sanctify you through and through. May your whole spirit, soul, and body be kept blameless at the coming of our Lord Jesus Christ. The one who calls you is faithful and he will do it" (1 Thess. 5:23–24).

　　Where does this leave contemporary Roman Catholics on the question of purgatory? Frankly, they are left on shaky ground. Many are studying the Bible and are questioning the doctrine of purgatory, although they are understandably reluctant to reject the church's teachings. Nevertheless, I respectfully appeal to them to follow the teachings of Scripture wherever they lead. Specifically, I urge them to abandon the false hope offered by purgatory, because God's Word allows no such opportunity to expiate sins after death. Instead, it promises forgiveness to all who trust Jesus as Lord and Savior in this life. Moreover, it assures believers that "neither death nor life . . . nor anything else in all creation will be able to separate us from the love of God that is in Christ Jesus our Lord" (Rom. 8:38–39).

What Is the Fate of Those Who Have Never Heard?

A second persistent question is What is the eternal destiny of persons who never hear the gospel in their lifetime?

The Church's Traditional Answer

According to Jesus and the apostles the message of salvation is exclusive. The Redeemer condemns the Samaritans' religion: "You Samaritans worship what you do not know; we worship what we do know, for salvation is from the Jews" (John 4:22). Moreover, his frank words are partially responsible for many Samaritans confessing, "We . . . know that this man really is the Savior of the world" (v. 42). Later, Jesus affirms, "I am the way. . . . No one comes to the Father except through me" (John 14:6).

　　When the Jewish leaders call the apostle Peter on the carpet for healing in Jesus' name, he refuses to be intimidated by their opposition to the gospel. Instead, he boldly proclaims, "Salvation is found in no one else, for there is no other name under heaven given to men by which we must be saved" (Acts 4:12).

The apostle Paul teaches that only those who confess that Jesus is Lord and believe that God raised him from the dead will be saved (Rom. 10:9).[13] According to Paul, the Lord Jesus is the object of saving faith. Indeed, he despairs about those who have not heard the gospel of Christ: "How, then, can they call on the one they have not believed in? And how can they believe in the one of whom they have not heard? And how can they hear without someone preaching to them? And how can they preach unless they are sent?" (Rom. 10:14–15).

With statements like these from Jesus, Peter, and Paul, it should not surprise us that the traditional message of the Christian church has been exclusivism.[14]

Pluralism

The twentieth century has witnessed two major challenges to exclusivism: pluralism and inclusivism. Both refuse to accept the idea that people who do not hear the gospel are condemned. Pluralism states that all religions are legitimate ways of worshiping God. In chapter 8 we rejected John Hick's "global theology," which is a type of pluralism. Although evangelical Christians are not tempted by the religious vision of pluralism, some find inclusivism attractive.

Inclusivism

Inclusivism holds that although Christianity is the true religion and Jesus the only way to salvation, more people are saved through Christ than the church traditionally has thought. Accordingly, God forgives followers of the world's religions on the basis of their response to the revelation they have. If those who have never heard the gospel respond in faith, God will save them on the basis of Christ's saving work. "In other words, people can receive the gift of salvation without knowing the giver or the precise nature of the gift."[15]

Clark Pinnock's Inclusivism. Clark Pinnock is an evangelical theologian whose reflection on the fate of those who have never heard has led him to espouse inclusivism.[16] He gives two reasons. The first is "God's boundless generosity." Pinnock is convinced that because of God's grace most of the human race is going to be saved, and he adduces biblical support for this conviction. John anticipates this racial salvation, Pinnock believes, when he tells of "a great multitude that no one could count . . . standing before the throne and in front of the Lamb" (Rev. 7:9). Pinnock insists that "this must include a substantial number of the unevangelized."[17]

Pinnock bases this "optimism of salvation" on Jesus' words "People will come from the east and west and north and south, and will take their places at the feast in the kingdom of God" (Luke 13:29) and on similar passages.[18] Pinnock argues that interpreters have often misunderstood John's saying that those who put Jesus to death will weep because of him at his second coming (Rev. 1:7). In fact, they will not weep "in shock and dismay at their fate . . . but for what they did to Jesus by nailing him to the cross." According to Pinnock, John implies that they will realize that Jesus is the Messiah.[19] Moreover, he rejects the common view that Revelation is a pessimistic book. Indeed, John looks forward to even "the nations that Satan had deceived coming into the new Jerusalem with the glory and honor of their cultures (Rev. 21:26)."[20]

Pinnock's second reason for promoting inclusivism is what he calls "the faith principle." He explains:

> According to the Bible people are saved by faith, not by the content of their theology. Since God has not left anyone without witness, people are judged on the basis of the light they have received and how they have responded to that light. Faith in God is what saves, not possessing certain minimum information. One does not have to be conscious of the work of Christ done on one's behalf in order to benefit from that work.[21]

Pinnock has six arguments from Scripture for the faith principle. First, Hebrews 11:6 announces it: "Without faith it is impossible to please God, because anyone who comes to him must believe that he exists and that he rewards those who earnestly seek him." The Old Testament champions of faith who are mentioned in Hebrews 11 did not have the knowledge of New Testament revelation. Therefore, they were saved by faith, not primarily by knowledge.[22]

Second, Pinnock cites the record of "the holy pagans" of biblical history. People such as Abel, Noah, Enoch, Job, and Jethro "were saved by faith without any knowledge of the revelation vouchsafed to Israel or the church."[23]

Third, the Old Testament Jews are another class of people redeemed apart from belief in Jesus.

Fourth, argues Pinnock, Jesus' words "Whatever you did for one of the least of these brothers of mine, you did for me" (Matt. 25:40) prove that "Serving the poor embodies what the love of God himself is, and it is accepted as the equivalent of faith."[24]

Fifth, Cornelius was already saved from God's wrath before he believed Peter's message (Acts 10). If this is true, why did he still need to hear the gospel? "He needed to become a Christian to receive messianic salvation, including assurance and the Holy Spirit, but not to be saved from hell."[25]

Pinnock's sixth argument involves the case of babies who die in infancy, "a practically uncontested example of unevangelized people being saved." Pinnock suggests that they mature after death so that they can make a decision for God.

An Evaluation of Pinnock's Argument. It is true that God is a God of "boundless generosity," who will save "a tremendously large number of people." However, the conclusion that Pinnock draws from this—that God will save people apart from the gospel—is unwarranted. His alleged biblical proofs for inclusivism are especially unconvincing. Pinnock fails to support his conclusions from Scripture. For example, how does he *know* that the great multitude mentioned in Revelation 7:9 "must include a substantial number of the unevangelized"? He assumes his conclusion without proving it.

Similarly, Pinnock fails to prove inclusivism from Jesus' statement in Luke 13:29 that people will come from the four points of the compass to share in the messianic feast. Jesus means that Gentiles throughout the world will be saved, but he says nothing about the unevangelized. This text offers no support for the claim that people can be saved apart from faith in Christ.[26] Nor does Revelation 1:7. How does Pinnock know that the tears shed at Jesus' second coming are tears of repentance? There is nothing in the context to suggest this. Again Pinnock begs the question.[27]

Pinnock rightly describes Revelation as an optimistic book. It is optimistic concerning the glory and triumph of the sovereign God of creation and redemption. Nevertheless, it is pessimistic concerning people being saved apart from the gospel. In fact, it specifically includes "idolaters" among the damned in the lake of fire, and among those excluded from the new Jerusalem (Rev. 21:8; 22:15).[28]

Pinnock's claim that "the nations that Satan had deceived" will come "into the new Jerusalem with the glory and honor of their cultures" (Rev. 21:26) is misleading. In Revelation 20:10 John speaks of the Devil's deceiving "them," and in the preceding verse he gives the antecedent to the pronoun "them." They are the people who joined the Devil's army to fight against God. God does not bring these people into the new Jerusalem. Rather, "Fire came down from heaven and devoured them" (Rev. 20:9)!

Thus, Pinnock's alleged scriptural basis for inclusivism is too weak to support the doctrine. The most he can claim is that his view is not incompatible with certain passages, but this hardly constitutes a convincing argument. Perhaps that is why he resorts to name-calling and pejorative language when discussing his opponents' views.[29] That is unfortunate, for it only detracts from his case.

Let us also examine each of the six arguments for Pinnock's "faith principle." First, he claims that Hebrews 11:6 sets forth the faith principle when it says, "Without faith it is impossible to please God." Pinnock's interpretation, however, betrays a misunderstanding, for although the Old Testament saints lacked New Testament revelation, they were not without Old Testament revelation. That is, they do not qualify as examples of people who lived apart from the redemptive revelation of God.

Furthermore, Pinnock sets up a false dichotomy between faith and knowledge when he says, "What God was looking for in Abraham was faith, not a certain quotient of knowledge."[30] Of course, God required faith of Abraham, but that faith was based on God's revelation to Abraham. Unlike his ancestors, who worshiped "other gods"

(Josh. 24:2), Abraham worshiped "God Almighty" (Gen. 17:1), who entered into a covenant with Abraham, promising to be his God (17:7), and who revealed himself to Abraham as his "shield" and "very great reward" (15:1). This is not faith devoid of content. God conveyed information to Abraham that was the foundation for his faith. This is a far cry from people among the world's religions exercising "the faith principle."

Pinnock's second argument, based on the Bible's record of "the holy pagans," fares no better, for God gave special revelation to Abel's parents (Gen. 2:16–17; 3:16–19), to Noah (Gen. 6:13–21), and to Job (Job 38:1–40:2). They, therefore, do not qualify as "pagans," if by that term one means people divorced from the Word of God.

The Bible's few verses concerning Enoch and Jethro do not prove that they "were saved by faith without any knowledge of the revelation vouchsafed to Israel or the church."[31] It is safer to say that we don't know how they were saved. In any case, it is unwise to argue for the salvation of multitudes of the unevangelized on the basis of this scant biblical testimony.

Concerning his third argument, it is surprising that Pinnock regards the Old Testament Jews as such clear proof of the faith principle. God's revelation of himself through the prophets sharply contrasts with the general revelation in creation, conscience, and history that God gives to all people.[32]

Pinnock's fourth argument equates Jesus' words "Whatever you did for one of the least of these brothers of mine, you did for me" (Matt. 25:40) with serving the poor, so that such service is accepted as "the equivalent of faith."[33] But Pinnock errs when he takes "brothers" here as a reference to the poor. Jesus says, "Whoever does the will of my Father in heaven is my brother" (Matt. 12:48–49; cf. 28:10).

Moreover, Jesus does not teach that people will be saved *because of* their deeds, for example, aiding the poor. Rather, he says that believers, who are saved by faith in him, demonstrate their faith by performing deeds of mercy for his children.

The fifth argument Pinnock advances for the faith principle is the salvation of Cornelius, whom Pinnock calls the New Testament's "pagan saint par excellence."[34] There are problems with Pinnock's treatment of Acts 10. Cornelius is not someone completely cut off from God's special revelation; Acts 10:22 tells us that he was known and "respected by all the Jewish people." Furthermore, when Peter brings the gospel to Cornelius, he says, "You know the message God sent to the people of Israel, telling the good news of peace through Jesus Christ, who is Lord of all" (Acts 10:36). This implies that Cornelius had already heard of Jesus. Finally, Pinnock's claim that although Cornelius received assurance and the Holy Spirit by believing the gospel, he was earlier saved from God's wrath "appears to be an ad hoc distinction introduced to bolster the theory," notes Millard Erickson.[35]

In Pinnock's sixth argument, concerning the case of babies who die in infancy, he assumes that babies who die grow up and are given the opportunity to believe by virtue of a postmortem encounter with Christ. Since Pinnock's whole scenario is so speculative, I do not consider this a good argument for inclusivism. This is Pinnock's way of introducing the concept of postmortem evangelism, an idea we rejected in chapter 8. I will say more on this topic in the next section.

Thus, each point of Pinnock's case for inclusivism is weak. In fact, studying it has only strengthened my conviction that the church's historic view is correct: People need to hear the Good News of Jesus to be saved. Paul's teaching that, because of human perversity, the general revelation of God in creation serves only to leave sinners "without excuse" (Rom. 1:20) makes me skeptical that people may be saved apart from a knowledge of the gospel.[36] Moreover, Paul's description of what sinners do with "the law . . . written on their hearts" (Rom. 2:15) does nothing to relieve my skepticism. They either plunge headlong into depravity, taking as many others with them as possible (Rom. 1:32), or they engage in damnable hypocrisy (Rom. 2:1–5).[37] I am constrained, therefore, to affix the same label to the hope offered by inclusivism as I did to that offered by universalism—*false* hope.

Nevertheless, I bow before God's sovereignty and am willing to entertain an openness for God to work in ways beyond our understanding. Still, I agree with J. I. Packer that "we have no warrant from Scripture to expect that God will act [savingly] in any single case where the Gospel is not yet known." Packer correctly contends that "living by the Bible means assuming that no one will be saved apart from faith in Christ, and acting accordingly."[38]

What Happens to Babies Who Die?

Here we arrive at the third question that I frequently encountered while working on this book: What is the fate of those who die in infancy? I confess that I do not have much wisdom concerning this issue.

Two biblical passages are often cited as proof of infant salvation. The first is David's words after the death of his son born of Bathsheba: "Now that he is dead, why should I fast? Can I bring him back again? I will go to him, but he will not return to me" (2 Sam. 12:23). John Sanders, however, urges this caution: "Modern interpreters are prone to read into David's words our understanding of heaven, hell and the afterlife and fail to understand the development of doctrines in the Bible."[39]

I agree that David did not possess as clear a hope of eternal life as New Testament saints. But Old Testament saints did have a hope for life after death with God, as I indicated in chapter 2, where I cited Job 19:26, Psalm 73:23–24, Isaiah 26:19, and Daniel 12:2. Still, David's statement is hardly proof that all children who die are saved. At best, it hints that the children of believers go to bliss, but it does not speak of the children of the unsaved.

The other commonly cited text for infant salvation is Jesus' rebuking his disciples, "Let the little children come to me, and do not hinder them, for the kingdom of God belongs to such as these. . . . anyone who will not receive the kingdom of God like a little child will never enter it" (Mark 10:14–15).

Two opposite conclusions have been reached from this passage. Robert P. Lightner concludes that Jesus here promises eternal life to all who die in infancy.[40] John Sanders is not so sure: "It is not clear what Jesus meant by 'the kingdom of God belongs to such as these.' Did he mean that heaven is filled with little children, or did he mean that all must become like little children to enter the kingdom? The context favors the latter."[41]

I am inclined to steer a middle course between the conclusions of Lightner and Sanders. I agree with Sanders that Jesus here primarily uses childlike trust as a description of the humility of faith needed to enter the kingdom. He is not chiefly teaching infant salvation. Yet doesn't he imply it when he likens true faith to that of the little ones? I believe so. Lightner errs, however, when he extends this principle to all babies, for Jesus, like David, is operating in the context of the covenant that God made with Abraham. Jesus is blessing Jewish babies, who are within the covenant family, not those of pagans, who do not possess God's covenant promises.

I would not dogmatically teach that the infants of unsaved people are damned, but neither would I confidently assert that they are saved. I believe that Holy Scripture says enough for us to give hope to believers when their infants die but that it simply doesn't speak to the fate of the deceased babies of unbelievers. In cases like this I follow the counsel of John Calvin, who advised restraint.

> Scripture is the school of the Holy Spirit, in which, as nothing is omitted that is both necessary and useful to know, so nothing is taught but what is expedient to know. . . . Let us, I say, permit the Christian man to open his mind and ears to every utterance of God directed to him, provided it be with such restraint that when the Lord closes his holy lips, he also shall at once close the way to inquiry. The best limit of sobriety for us will be not only to follow God's lead always in learning but, when he sets an end to teaching, to stop trying to be wise.[42]

The Doctrine of Hell Applied to Sinners

According to a 1990 Gallup survey, although 78 percent of Americans thought they had an "excellent or good chance of going to heaven," only 4 percent thought they had the same chance "of going to hell."[43] These statistics should not surprise us since it is terrible to contemplate going to hell! Nonetheless, one of my goals in writing this book is to raise the statistics in the second category. I want people who do not know the Lord to fear God's wrath. In fact, anyone who cares for the lost will attempt to warn them of hell.

Let me illustrate by contrasting two pastors. The first one admits, "My congregation would be stunned to hear a sermon on hell." His parishioners are "upper-middle-class, well-educated critical thinkers" who view God as "compassionate and loving, not someone who's going to push them into eternal damnation."[44] Tragically this pastor has not helped his church members view God as Jesus and the apostles did: as loving *and* just, gracious *and* holy. That is tragic because, in keeping God's truth about hell from the people in his care, he is lullabying them to hell. Furthermore, using Jesus' words in Matthew 18:6–7 as a measuring stick by which to evaluate ministries, I shudder for this pastor.

> If anyone causes one of these little ones who believe in me to sin, it would be better for him to have a large millstone hung around his neck and to be drowned in the depths of the sea. Woe to the world because of the things that cause people to sin! Such things must come, but woe to the man through whom they come!

Now, compare the first preacher with a second one. The second pastor expresses surprise that believers are as uncomfortable with the idea of hell as are unbelievers.

> What is surprising is that Christians are equally uneasy with God's wrath. It is hardly mentioned in our churches and our literature, and that fact ought to concern us. God's wrath is a central piece in the biblical jigsaw puzzle; if we have made the other pieces fit without it, doesn't that suggest we have forced them into a pattern God never intended?[45]

This pastor laments our neglect of the doctrine of hell. Moreover, in view of the unity of biblical doctrine, he fears that our faith may erode in other areas too. "Once we have given up wrath, can sin, judgment, or the Cross be far behind? Without the one, the others lose their meaning. Wrath measures sin, produces judgment, and necessitates the Cross."[46]

How can Christians halt this slide away from the truth? By realizing that we need a drastic change in perspective, as the second preacher illustrates by recalling a childhood experience.

I remember going to Idaho one summer to visit my cousins. One Saturday we went to a public swimming pool, which featured what had to be the world's highest diving platform. "Come on," they said. I looked up. It didn't seem too high. So I stood in line, climbed the ladder, walked out to the edge—and nearly died! It was too far down! Very humiliated, I climbed back down, having learned a very important theological truth: How it looks from below only matters if you are planning on staying below.[47]

Our problem is that we have foolishly taken to ourselves the prerogative of making judgments about the afterlife. We have cast ourselves in the role of God and decided to outlaw hell. The second pastor summarizes the problem, "In our sin, we have rejected God, and thus forfeited our ultimate reference point."[48]

In fact, we should not *expect* people to arrive at the truth concerning God, salvation, or hell apart from God's Word. The sinful mind naturally rejects God's truth, as Paul explains: "Their thinking became futile and their foolish hearts were darkened. Although they claimed to be wise, they became fools. . . . Furthermore, since they did not think it worthwhile to retain the knowledge of God, he gave them over to a depraved mind" (Rom. 1:21–22, 28).

Indeed, as sinners we are unqualified to make accurate judgments concerning life after death. We are totally dependent on God to reveal eternal matters to us. And that is exactly what he has done in his Word. Specifically, as we learned in chapters 3 and 4, it is Jesus Christ, the divine-human Redeemer, who is the author of the doctrine of hell.

Dear unsaved readers, as a pardoned sinner I appeal to you who still need to be pardoned. Heed the warning of the Savior of the world, "Unless you repent you too will perish" (Luke 13:3, 5). Acknowledge your rebellion against God, turn from your sins, and trust Jesus as your Lord and Savior. Only Jesus is qualified to save. Indeed, he is God the Son who became a human being so that he could suffer the penalty of hell for sinners. I, therefore, urge you to throw away any hope of meriting heaven. Instead, place all of your confidence for salvation in Jesus' death and resurrection. When you do, you will be able to sing with all the redeemed:

Jesus, my great High Priest,
Offered his blood and died;
My guilty conscience seeks
No sacrifice beside.
His pow'rful blood did once atone,
And now it pleads before the Throne.

To this dear Surety's hand
Will I commit my cause;
He answers and fulfils
His Father's broken laws.
Behold my soul at freedom set;
My Surety paid the dreadful debt.

My Advocate appears
For my defense on high;
The Father bows his ears
And lays his thunder by.
Not all that hell or sin can say
Shall turn his heart, his love away.

Should all the hosts of death
And pow'rs of hell unknown
Put their most dreadful forms
Of rage and mischief on,
I shall be safe, for Christ displays
His conqu'ring pow'r and guardian grace.[49]

The Doctrine of Hell Applied to Saints

Evangelicals do not dismiss the doctrine of hell as outmoded, as did the seminary professor who deemed it "part of an understanding of the cosmos that just doesn't exist anymore."[50] Because evangelicals' faith is tied to Scripture, they cannot simply discard the biblical teaching on hell, so instead they ignore it. Indeed, Martin Marty's comment in 1985 on American religious trends is still true of conservative churches today: "Hell has disappeared and no one noticed."[51]

This avoidance of the doctrine of hell by Bible-believing Christians is undeniable. Few sermons mention eternal destinies, and even fewer are devoted to the topics of heaven and hell. One prominent evangelical leader admitted a few years ago that he had not "preached a sermon on hell in more than three decades."[52]

In 1985 a professor wrote a systematic theology to remedy the lack of attention given to the doctrine of last things. He moved topics such as Christ's return and heaven and hell from their customary position at the end of theology texts to the beginning of his. Furthermore, his publisher generously allowed his two volumes to run to 874 pages. We, therefore, would expect a reversal of the trend of recent evangelical theology books to neglect the fate of the wicked. Sadly, such was not the case, for he devoted less than four pages to the topic of hell.[53]

The doctrine of hell has not fared any better in personal evangelism. Few Christians speak of the destiny of the lost when they share the gospel with unsaved people. Moreover, although churches use numerous books to train members in evangelism, it is difficult to find even one such book that tells sinners the truth about their eternal destiny apart from Christ.

In the face of evangelical churches' neglect of the doctrine of hell, a question plagues us: *Why* do preachers, teachers, and lay people shy away from telling people the truth about hell? Is it because Christian churches historically have failed to affirm eternal punishment? This clearly is not the reason, as the following examples demonstrate.

The Athanasian Creed, an early statement of faith, proclaims: "At his [Jesus'] coming all men shall rise with their bodies and. . . . those who have done evil will go into everlasting fire."[54] The Roman Catholic Church officially believes in the traditional doctrine of hell, as is evidenced by this statement of the Fourth Lateran Council in 1215: "Those (the rejected) will receive a perpetual punishment with the devil."[55]

The Lutheran Church's Augsburg Confession (1530) affirms, "It is also taught among us that our Lord Jesus Christ will return on the last day for judgment and will raise up all the dead . . . to condemn ungodly men and the devil to hell and eternal punishment."[56] Presbyterians likewise historically have believed in hell, as the Westminster

Confession of Faith bears witness: "The wicked . . . shall be cast into eternal torments, and be punished with everlasting destruction from the presence of the Lord, and from the glory of His power."[57]

Baptists also have declared in writing their commitment to the orthodox doctrine. We see this in the Southern Baptist Convention's "The Baptist Faith and Message" of 1963: "Christ will judge all men in righteousness. The unrighteous will be consigned to hell, the place of everlasting punishment."[58]

We cannot blame Christians' reluctance to speak about hell on their churches' failure to take a stand on the doctrine. To the contrary, these churches have testified to their belief in eternal punishment. So, our problem remains, and, in fact, is compounded. How can we account for Christians' neglect of the doctrine of hell, in spite of their churches' official affirmations? I offer at least two answers to this question.

First, church leaders bear some responsibility. When pastors preach on certain themes, they put them in their people's minds. Conversely, when preachers ignore a subject, it tends to slip away from their parishioners. Christians' disregard for the doctrine of hell, therefore, is attributable in part to their pastors' failure to preach the whole counsel of God. As preachers realize their fault, they need to repent and by God's grace be more faithful to their charge to "preach the Word" (2 Tim. 4:2). Seminary professors too deserve part of the blame since they train pastors for the churches. Yesterday's seminary professors are part of the reason why today's pastors rarely speak of hell. My prayer is that God might awaken today's professors to accept their responsibility to equip tomorrow's pastors with the knowledge of the realities of heaven and hell.

Second, we cannot lay all the blame at the feet of church leaders; every believer is also responsible for avoiding the topic of hell. Why do we avoid it? Because we value our personal comfort more than the salvation of fellow human beings. Shame on us! Unwilling to suffer for Christ, we push the idea of hell to the back of our minds. To the extent that we are personally guilty we need to confess it to God and ask his forgiveness. First John 1:9 is one of the most important verses for Christians: "If we confess our sins, he is faithful and just and will forgive us our sins and purify us from all unrighteousness."

Good things will come from acknowledging to God that we have not taken hell seriously enough. First, God will be glorified by our repentance. Second, he may grant us the spiritual revival that so many have prayed about for so long. As William Eisenhower notes, "Spiritual awakenings have always emphasized God's jealous rage." In fact, "A revival without wrath would be pointless—like a sewing machine without a needle. It would not penetrate into the fabric of our lives, which is to say it would not revive."[59]

A third benefit will come from admitting that we have neglected the doctrine of hell: more unsaved people will hear God's truth concerning their fate, and by God's grace, will turn to Christ for salvation. The question is whether we are burdened at the thought of people hurtling toward hell.

> On 12 December 1984 dense fog shrouded M25 near Godstone, in Surrey, a few miles south of London. The hazard warning lights were on, but were ignored by most drivers. At 6.15 a.m. a lorry carrying huge rolls of paper was involved in an accident, and within minutes the carriageway was engulfed in carnage. Dozens of cars were wrecked. Ten people were killed. A police patrol car was soon on the scene, and two policemen ran back up the motorway to stop oncoming traffic. They waved their arms and shouted as loud as they could, but most drivers took no notice and raced on towards the disaster that awaited them. The policemen then picked up traffic cones and flung them at the cars' windscreens in a desperate attempt to warn drivers of their danger; one told how tears streamed down his face as car after car went by and he waited for the sickening sound of impact as they hit the growing mass of wreckage farther down the road.[60]

How does our urgency to warn the lost of the danger of hell compare to the policemen's efforts to spare the motorists from accident and possible death? May God stir us to be faithful to him and to our fellow human beings who need to know him who died to redeem sinners from hell. To God alone be the glory!

NOTES

1. C. S. Lewis, "Learning in War-Time," in *The Weight of Glory and Other Addresses* (New York: Macmillan, 1949), 20–21.

2. Ludwig Ott, *Fundamentals of Catholic Dogma*, 4th ed. (Rockford, Ill.: Tan Books and Publishers, 1960), 482.

3. The *New Catholic Encyclopedia*, s.v. "Sin (Theology of)," by I. McGuiness.

4. After the guilt of sin and its eternal punishment have been forgiven, temporal punishment remains. This temporal punishment can be atoned for by the sacrament of penance, which involves a priest's declaring the penitent forgiven and prescribing deeds of penance for the person to perform. See Ott, *Fundamentals of Catholic Dogma*, 434.

5. "For the individual souls the purifying fire endures until they are free from all guilt and punishment. Immediately on the conclusion of the purification they will be assumed into the bliss of heaven" (Ibid., 485).

6. For example, Zachary Hayes, "The Purgatorial View," in *Four Views on Hell*, ed. William Crockett (Grand Rapids: Zondervan, 1992), 91–118.

7. "The doctrine of purgatory clearly demonstrates that even when the guilt of sin has been taken away, punishment for it or the consequences of it may remain to be expiated or cleansed. They often are. In fact, in purgatory the souls of those who died in the charity of God and truly repentant, but who had not made satisfaction with adequate penance for their sins and omissions are cleansed after death with punishments designed to purge away their debt" (Austin P. Flannery, ed. *Documents of Vatican II* [Grand Rapids: Eerdmans, 1975], 64).

8. Hayes, "The Purgatorial View," 107.

9. Ibid., 105.

10. Ibid., 106.

11. This occurred at the Second Council of Lyons. See Jacques Le Goff, *The Birth of Purgatory*, trans. A. Goldhammer (Chicago: University of Chicago Press, 1984), 237.

12. See also Heb. 7:27; 9:12, 26; 10:14.

13. Paul applies the Old Testament promise "Everyone who calls on the name of the Lord will be saved" (Rom. 10:13; from Joel 2:32) to the name of Jesus.

14. Millard Erickson helpfully summarizes the "orthodox consensus" in six points: "1. All humans are sinners, by nature and by choice; they are therefore guilty and under divine condemnation. 2. Salvation is only through Christ and his atoning work. 3. In order to obtain the salvation achieved by Christ, one must believe in him; therefore Christians and the church have a responsibility to tell unbelievers the good news about him. 4. The adherents of other faiths, no matter how sincere their belief or how intense their religious activity, are spiritually lost apart from Christ. 5. Physical death brings to an end the opportunity to exercise saving faith and accept Jesus Christ. The decisions made in this life are irrevocably fixed at death. 6. At the great final judgement

all humans will be separated on the basis of their relationship to Christ during this life. Those who have believed in him will spend eternity in heaven, where they will experience everlasting joy and reward in God's presence. Those who have not accepted Christ will experience hell, a place of unending suffering and separation from God" (*The Evangelical Mind and Heart* [Grand Rapids: Baker, 1993], 130–31).

15. John Sanders, *No Other Name: An Investigation into the Destiny of the Unevangelized* (Grand Rapids: Eerdmans, 1992), 215. This is the view that he adopts (282–83). Contemporary Roman Catholicism shows tendencies in this direction, as Millard Erickson notes: "Vatican II . . . distinguished degrees of membership in the church, including non-Catholic Christians, who are 'linked' to the church, and non-Christian religious persons, who are 'related' to the church. Witness also Karl Rahner's concept of 'anonymous Christians'" (*The Evangelical Mind and Heart*, 131).

16. Clark H. Pinnock, *A Wideness in God's Mercy: The Finality of Jesus Christ in a World of Religions* (Grand Rapids: Zondervan, 1992), 149–50; "Toward an Evangelical Theology of Religions," *Journal of the Evangelical Theological Society* 33.3 (1990): 359–68.

17. Pinnock, *A Wideness in God's Mercy*, 153.

18. Pinnock claims that "the men of Nineveh will be part of the resurrection, and . . . the queen of Sheba will be there along with the blessed" (Matt. 12:41–42) (Ibid.).

19. Pinnock sees this intimated in other passages as well, such as Rev. 3:9: "I will make those who are of the synagogue of Satan, who claim to be Jews though they are not, but are liars—I will make them come and fall down at your feet and acknowledge that I have loved you" (Ibid., 153–54).

20. Ibid., 154.

21. Ibid., 157–58.

22. Ibid., 160.

23. Ibid., 161–62.

24. Ibid., 163–65.

25. Ibid., 165–66.

26. Pinnock's use of the Ninevites and the queen of Sheba (Matt. 12:41–42) as examples of "pagan saints" actually works against his position rather than for it. The Ninevites did not repent on the basis of "the faith principle" operative in Assyrian religion. Instead, "they repented at the preaching of the [Israelite] prophet Jonah" (Matt. 12:41)! They were thus "evangelized" by the special revelation sent by the true and living God. And the queen of Sheba hardly qualifies as a good example of someone being saved apart from biblical religion. For, if she repented, she did so because "she came from the ends of the earth to listen to Solomon's wisdom" (Matt. 12:42). Solomon, remember, was endowed with prudence by God in answer to prayer (1 Kings 3:9, 12; 4:29–31) and subsequently became renowned for his proverbial wisdom (1 Kings 4:32; Prov. 1:1).

27. Pinnock's proofs from Rev. 3 are no better. Christ indeed promises to make "the synagogue of Satan" come and fall down at the feet of the church in Philadelphia and acknowledge that he loves the saints in that city (Rev. 3:9). But Jesus means that he will punish the false Jews by humiliating them before the true believers. He says nothing about forgiving those he labels "liars." On the contrary John later tells us that the place of "all liars" will be in the fiery lake of burning sulfur (Rev. 21:8). In addition, liars are excluded from the city of God (Rev. 22:15). How can anyone read inclusivism into the scenario of Revelation 3:9, when John indicates that these people are hypocrites: they "claim to be Jews though they are not"?

28. I admit that "John says that the people were so terrified by God's judgments that they 'gave glory to the God of heaven'" (Rev. 11:13). John says nothing, however, about these people believing in God or repenting. This is a precarious foundation upon which to build a theology of inclusivism.

29. For criticism of this tendency in Pinnock, see Erickson, *Evangelical Mind and Heart*, 148–50.

30. Pinnock, *A Wideness in God's Mercy*, 160.

31. Ibid., 161.

32. Indeed, as Millard Erickson points out, "The difference in the potential efficacy of these two sources of the knowledge of God leads us to be skeptical that large numbers of the second group will be saved" (*Evangelical Mind and Heart*, 138).

33. Pinnock, *A Wideness in God's Mercy*, 163–65.

34. Ibid., 165.

35. Erickson, *Evangelical Mind and Heart*, 137.

36. See the helpful study by Aída Besançon Spencer, "Finding God in Creation," in *Through No Fault of Their Own? The Fate of Those Who Have Never Heard*, ed. William V. Crockett and James G. Sigountos (Grand Rapids: Baker, 1991), 125–35.

37. For profitable discussion, see Douglas Moo, "Romans 2: Saved Apart from the Gospel?" in *Through No Fault of Their Own?* 137–45.

38. J. I. Packer, "Evangelicals and the Way of Salvation," *Evangelical Affirmations*, ed. Kenneth S. Kantzer and Carl F. H. Henry (Grand Rapids: Zondervan, 1990), 123.

39. Sanders, *No Other Name*, 289.

40. Robert P. Lightner, *Heaven for Those Who Can't Believe* (Schaumburg, Ill.: Regular Baptist Press, 1977), 39–41.

41. Sanders, *No Other Name*, 290.

42. John Calvin, *Institutes of the Christian Religion*, ed. John T. McNeil, trans. Ford Lewis Battles, The Library of Christian Classics, vols. 20–21 (Philadelphia: Westminster Press, 1960), 21:924.

43. "Hell's Sober Comeback," *U.S. News & World Report*, 25 March 1991, 57.

44. "Revisiting the Abyss," *U.S. News & World Report*, 25 March 1991, 60.

45. William D. Eisenhower, "Sleepers in the Hands of an Angry God," *Christianity Today*, 20 March 1987, 26.

46. Ibid.
47. Ibid., 26–27.
48. Ibid., 27.
49. Isaac Watts, "Jesus, My Great High Priest" (1709).
50. "Revisiting the Abyss," 60.
51. "Hell's Sober Comeback," 56.
52. Ibid.
53. Thomas N. Finger, *Christian Theology: An Eschatological Approach*, 2 vols. (Nashville: Nelson, 1985), 1:158–61.
54. Theodore G. Tappert, ed. *The Book of Concord: The Confessions of the Evangelical Lutheran Church* (Philadelphia: Fortress, 1959), 21.
55. Ott, *Fundamentals of Catholic Dogma*, 481.
56. Tappert, *Book of Concord*, 38–39.
57. *The Westminster Standards* (Philadelphia: Great Commission Publications, n.d.). Reformed churches likewise affirm the doctrine of hell; see the Second Helvetic Confession, chap. 26, and the Dordrecht Confession, art. 18.
58. *Encyclopedia of Southern Baptists,* 3 vols. (Nashville: Broadman, 1971), 3:1592. An older symbol, respected by many Baptists, is The Philadelphia Confession of Faith of 1742, which was modelled after The Second London Confession of 1689. Its chap. 32, sec. 2 is almost identical to the section of the Westminster Confession of Faith quoted above.
59. Eisenhower, "Sleepers in the Hands of an Angry God," 27.
60. John Blanchard, *Whatever Happened to Hell?* (Durham, England: Evangelical Press, 1993), 297.

Index of Scripture

Page numbers in bold type indicate major discussions of the respective Scriptures.

Index of Names

Page numbers in bold type indicate major discussions of the respective names.

Index of Topics

Page numbers in bold type indicate major discussions
of the respective topics.